Power and Negotiation

The International Institute for Applied Systems Analysis

is an interdisciplinary, nongovernmental research institution founded in 1972 by leading scientific organizations in 12 countries. Situated near Vienna, in the center of Europe, IIASA has been for more than two decades producing valuable scientific research on economic, technological, and environmental issues.

IIASA was one of the first international institutes to systematically study global issues of environment, technology, and development. IIASA's Governing Council states that the Institute's goal is: *to conduct international and interdisciplinary scientific studies to provide timely and relevant information and options, addressing critical issues of global environmental, economic, and social change, for the benefit of the public, the scientific community, and national and international institutions*. Research is organized around three central themes:

- Environment and Natural Resources;
- Energy and Technology;
- Population and Society.

The Institute now has national member organizations in the following countries:

Austria
The Austrian Academy of Sciences

Bulgaria*
The Bulgarian Committee for IIASA

Finland
The Finnish Committee for IIASA

Germany**
The Association for the Advancement of IIASA

Hungary
The Hungarian Committee for Applied Systems Analysis

Japan
The Japan Committee for IIASA

Kazakhstan*
The Ministry of Science –
The Academy of Sciences

Netherlands
The Netherlands Organization for Scientific Research (NWO)

Norway
The Research Council of Norway

Poland
The Polish Academy of Sciences

Russian Federation
The Russian Academy of Sciences

Slovak Republic*
The Slovak Committee for IIASA

Sweden
The Swedish Council for Planning and Coordination of Research (FRN)

Ukraine*
The Ukrainian Academy of Sciences

United States of America
The US Committee for IIASA

*Associate member
**Affiliate

Power and Negotiation

*Edited by I. William Zartman and
the late Jeffrey Z. Rubin*

Published in conjunction with the
International Institute for Applied Systems Analysis

Ann Arbor

THE UNIVERSITY OF MICHIGAN PRESS

Copyright © by the University of Michigan 2000
All rights reserved
Published in the United States of America by
The University of Michigan Press
Manufactured in the United States of America
♾ Printed on acid-free paper

2003   2002   2001   2000   4   3   2   1

A CIP catalog record for this book is available from the British Library.

Library of Congress Cataloging-in-Publication Data

Power and negotiation / edited by I. William Zartman and Jeffrey Z.
   Rubin.
        p.   cm.
   Includes bibliographical references and index.
   ISBN 0-472-11079-9 (cloth : alk. paper)
   1. Diplomatic negotiations in international disputes. 2. Balance
of power. I. Zartman, I. William. II. Rubin, Jeffrey Z.
JZ6045.P69 2000
327.1'7—dc21   99-43531
                                                        CIP

Dedication

This project evolved from my conversations with Jeff Rubin over matters of crosscutting interest – Jeff's curiosity over propositions generated two decades ago in experimental literature in social psychology but little tested in the real world and my longstanding interest in working from the tautologies of political science's central concept of power. The question of negotiations under asymmetry began to intrigue my colleague, and I had already completed two books on applications of the problem. The project was adopted by the Program on the Processes of International Negotiation (PIN) of the International Institute for Applied Systems Analysis (IIASA) and a conference of authors was held in the summer of 1992.

Bridging disciplinary concerns and crafting appropriate case studies proved a major challenge. In addition, in the midst of this work, my colleague was taken from us, in 1995, in a lamentable hiking accident, leaving a large gap in the PIN group and its projects. Yet the paradox of the subject and attraction of some counter-intuitive findings continued to beckon, calling for additional work and luring inquiry into broader paths ranging from international political economy to evolutionary game theory. Two years later the work was finished, to the point at least of informing further debate and nourishing further studies. That is the sort of result Jeff would have liked, and it is to him, ever searching for new intellectual apple carts to upset, that this product – which he helped begin – is dedicated.

Contents

Preface

This study is the seventh to be produced by the Program on the Processes of International Negotiation (PIN) at the International Institute for Applied Systems Analysis (IIASA) in Laxenburg, Austria. The PIN Program was established in 1986 following the recommendation of a steering committee of IIASA's Council in 1981 and a decision by the Council in 1984. It owes much to IIASA's first director, Howard Raiffa of Harvard University. Its first product was *Processes of International Negotiations* (Westview, 1989), edited by Frances Mautner-Markhof. The Program was fully constituted in 1988 by Robert Pry, the IIASA director, and Bertram I. Spector was engaged as its director.

The work of the project has been organized by an international steering committee of six scholars: Guy Olivier Faure, a French sociologist from the Sorbonne; Victor A. Kremenyuk, a Russian political scientist from the Russian Academy of Sciences; Winfried Lang, an Austrian diplomat and jurist from the University of Vienna; Jeffrey Z. Rubin, an American social psychologist from Tufts University; Gunnar Sjöstedt, a Swedish political economist from the Swedish Foreign Policy Institute; and I. William Zartman, an American political scientist from Johns Hopkins University. Rudolf Avenhaus, a German game theorist from the Munich Defense University, later joined the project. Three times each year, this international committee has met to work on the study of international negotiations in its many forms; the gatherings, lasting for up to a week, have been exciting, collegial exercises in international negotiation.

The keystone work of the Program is *International Negotiation: Analysis, Approaches, Issues* (Jossey-Bass, 1991), edited by Kremenyuk. It has been followed by *International Environmental Negotiation* (Sage, 1993), edited by Sjöstedt; *Culture and Negotiation* (Sage, 1993), edited by Faure and Rubin; *International Multilateral Negotiations* (Jossey-Bass, 1994), edited by Zartman; *Negotiating International Regimes: Lessons Learned from UNCED* (Graham and Trotman, 1994), edited by Spector, Sjöstedt, and Zartman; *International Economic Negotiation: Models versus Reality* (Edward Elgar, 2000), edited by Kremenyuk and Sjöstedt; and *Preventive Negotiation: Avoiding Conflict Escalation* (Rowman & Littlefield, 2000), edited by Zartman. Other works are in progress, including *Professional Cultures in International Negotiations*, edited by Lang and Sjöstedt; *Informal Negotiations*, edited by Faure; and *Nuclear Negotiations*, edited by Avenhaus, Kremenyuk, and Sjöstedt. Each work has been the product of collaboration among a large group of international scholars, meeting and working together.

Acknowledgments

In this effort, I express the feelings of both myself and my late colleague in acknowledging with appreciation the helpful participation of the steering committee members and the flexible and responsive collaboration of the chapter authors. We appreciate too the comments of John Odell and Kalypso Nikolaides and other readers. We are grateful for the initial support of IIASA for the Program and for this particular project. In addition, we would like to thank the Swedish National Research Foundation and the William and Flora Hewlett Foundation for their generous and timely assistance. Basic help for all our activities and careful attention to this work in particular has come from Ulrike Neudeck, Program administrative assistant. Our thanks would not be complete without a word of appreciation to Gordon MacDonald, the current IIASA director, for the renewed authorization to base our activities in Maria Theresia's hunting lodge in Laxenburg, an appropriately inspiring setting from which to scrutinize power and negotiation.

I. William Zartman
Laxenburg, Austria, and Washington, DC

Contributors

Elizabeth DeBoer-Ashworth is an Associate of the Centre for Governance and Public Management at the University of Limerick, Ireland. She also lecturers on International Relations Theory in the Department of Government and Society at the same institution. Her doctorate, *The Global Political Economy, and Post-1989 Change: The Place of the Central European Transition* is to be published in Macmillan's International Political Economy series. She has worked as a research consultant to private industry in London as well as having held a trade policy analyst position in Canada. Her research specialization includes economic integration, countries in transition and international studies from both a public management and an economic development point of view.

Xibo Fan is a scholar of Polimetrics. He created the mathematical definition for the concept of "national interest" in his Ph.D. dissertation titled *Polimetrics: A Formal Model for State Capability and National Interest, and Its Application in Generating Pay-off Functions for Games Among Nations*. He received his B.S. degree from Tsinghua University, China, in 1984, and his M.S. from the computer department of the University of Science and Technology of Beijing in 1987. He then studied international relations and international economics at the Johns Hopkins University School of Advanced International Studies (SAIS) and received a Ph.D. degree in 1999. Dr. Fan is currently a consultant to the World Bank.

Guy Olivier Faure is associate professor of sociology at the Sorbonne University, Paris, where he teaches international negotiation. His major research interests are in business negotiations, especially with China and Asian countries, focusing on strategies and cultural issues. He also is concerned with developing interdisciplinary approaches, and engages in consulting and training activities. Among his most recent publications are chapters in several of the PIN studies, as well as in the following edited volumes: *Processes of International Negotiations, Evolutionary Systems Design: Policy-Making under Complexity*, and *Conflits et Négociations dans le Commerce International: L'Uruguay Round*. Together with the late Jeffrey Z. Rubin, he edited *Culture and Negotiation*, the third volume in the PIN series.

Dipak Gyawali is Pragya (Academician) of the Royal Nepal Academy of Science and Technology, member of the International Research Committee of the Regional Center for Strategic Studies (RCSS) in Colombo and Co-Editor of WATER NEPAL, a biannual journal published from Kathmandu. His research interests lie in the interdisciplinary interface between resource base and society, and he has participated in the past in water negotiations with India and Bangladesh while in service with Nepal Government's Ministry of Water Resources.

William M. Habeeb is an international consultant based in Washington, DC. He is the author of *Power and Tactics in International Negotiation*, co-author of *The Panama Canal Negotiations and co-editor of Polity and Society in Contemporary North Africa*. He has conducted seminars in negotiation theory and practice for the United Nations and for a number of government ministries in newly independent states. He is past Chairman of the Forum for US–Soviet Dialogue and of the Society for International Development's Middle East Roundtable. Dr. Habeeb received his Ph.D. from the Johns Hopkins University Nitze School of Advanced International Studies.

Timo Kivimäki is a Senior Fellow at the Nordic Institute of Asian Studies (NIAS) in Copenhagen. He joined NIAS in July 1999, after serving three years as an Acting Professor of International Relations, in charge of the international relations program at the University of Helsinki. Timo Kivimäki leads an international group of experts who work on the interrelationship between conflicts and economic development; research has been carried out for the Department of Political Affairs of the Finnish Foreign Ministry, the United Nations University's World Institute for Development Economics Research (WIDER), the United Nations Institute for Disarmament

Research (UNIDIR), the Swedish International Development Co-operation Agency (SIDA) and Nokia. Timo Kivimäki has published widely on domestic and interstate conflicts in various parts of the world. His current research interests include international diplomacy and political bargaining between Southeast Asian Nations, the United States, and the EU, the phenomenon of "long interstate peace of ASEAN," and the conflicts of Indonesia.

Patrick Klaousen received his Doctor of Law from the University of Toulouse, France, in 1989. His doctoral thesis dealt with the evolution of the juridical system of Andorra's trade exchanges, in view of the extension of the EEC to Spain and Portugal. Dr. Klaousen is a senior lecturer at the University of Rennes, France, and his fields of research are European law and international law.

Jean-Emmanuel Pondi is Director of the International Relations Institute of Cameroun (IRIC), and author of a number of works on African international relations, including *L'OUA: Rétrospective et Perspectives Africaines and Le Secrétaire-Général de l'OUA dans le Système International*. He has been a visiting scholar at Cambridge University and The Johns Hopkins University. His doctorate is from Pennsylvania State University.

The late Jeffrey Z. Rubin was professor of social psychology at Tufts University, and a founding member of the IIASA PIN Steering Committee. He was also a founding member of the Harvard Program on Negotiation (PON) and of the Negotiation Journal. He is author of important works in social psychology and negotiations, including Social Conflict and The Social Psychology of Bargaining and Negotiation, and editor of others, including The Dynamics of Third Party Intervention. For the PIN Program, he was co-editor of Culture and Negotiation. His doctorate was from Columbia University.

Jeswald W. Salacuse is Henry J. Braker Professor of Law at the Fletcher School of Law and Diplomacy, Tufts University. He served as Dean of the Fletcher School for over eight years and is the author of more than ten books on negotiation, law, and international development. His recent books include *The Wise Advisor*, *Making Global Deals*, *The Art of Advice*, and *International Business Planning: Law and Taxation* (with W.P. Streng).

Gunnar Sjöstedt is senior research fellow at the Swedish Institute of International Affairs and also associate professor of political science at the University of Stockholm. His research work is concerned with processes of international cooperation and consultations in which negotiations represent an important element. He has studied the OECD as a communication system and the external role of the European community, as well as the transformation of the international trade regime incorporated in GATT and its external relations. He is the editor of *International Environmental Negotiations* and the co-editor of *Negotiating International Regimes*, the second and fourth books, respectively, in the PIN series.

Saadia Touval teaches at the Paul H. Nitze School of Advanced International Studies, Johns Hopkins University, in Washington. He is former Professor of Political Science and Dean of the Faculty of Social Sciences at Tel Aviv University. He has been Visiting Professor at Brown, Cornell, and Harvard Universities, and is author of *The Peace Brokers*, *The Boundary Politics of Africa*, and a forthcoming book on the breakup of Yugoslavia.

Gilbert R. Winham is professor of political science at Dalhousie University in Halifax, Nova Scotia, Canada. His interests include international negotiation and diplomatic practice, and he specializes in international commercial policy and trade negotiations. He has extensive experience in training government officers in negotiation methods through simulation exercises. His recent books include *International Trade and the Tokyo Round Negotiation*, *Trading with Canada: The Canada–US Free Trade Agreement*, and *The Halifax G-7 Summit: Issues on the Table* (with Sylvia Ostry). Professor Winham has served on numerous NAFTA dispute settlement panels, and is also included on the roster of panelists accredited to the World Trade Organization.

I. William Zartman is Jacob Blaustein Professor of Conflict Resolution and International Organization at the Nitze School of Advanced International Studies of Johns Hopkins University. He is the author of *The Practical Negotiator*, *The 50% Solution*, and *Ripe for Resolution*, editor of *The Negotiation Process* and *Positive Sum*, among other books, and the editor of *Preventive Negotiation*, the most recent book in the PIN series. He is organizer of the Washington Interest in Negotiations (WIN) Group and was distinguished fellow at the US Institute of Peace.

Part I

Introduction

Chapter 1

The Study of Power and the Practice of Negotiation

I. William Zartman and Jeffrey Z. Rubin

An age-old puzzle in negotiation is the structuralists' paradox: how can weaker parties negotiate with stronger parties and still get something?[1] Or more specifically: how do known (or perceived) weaklings negotiate at all with known (or perceived) heavies and emerge satisfied with the results? Expecting to lose, a weaker party would want to avoid negotiation with a stronger party at all costs; a stronger party would have no need to negotiate since it could simply take what it wants. Even when linked together in a relationship, the two unequals should seek the greatest independence of action rather than submit to the other's restraints. Yet weak parties not only take on stronger ones in negotiation, they often emerge with sizable – even better than expected – results. How so? And what do we mean by weaker and stronger (i.e., power) anyhow?

If this were not enough of a paradox, another part of the literature on power distribution talks of the "tendency for the 'exploitation' of the small" (Olson 1965:35), and the almost characteristic ability of the Lilliputians to tie up Gullivers in any negotiated encounter. This aspect is often explained by the fact that stronger parties tend to be purveyors of public goods for small parasites and weaker parties tend to care more about small items beyond large parties' concerns (Waltz 1979:194, 208). Yet these explanations may be ultimately contradictory, and may also point to a reverse paradox: Why do stronger states negotiate with weaker states over things that are unimportant to them, if they are going to be taken in the process?

These questions would be old and answered if popular discussions did not leave them surrounded by misleading commonplaces and folk wisdom and if the various disciplinary attempts to provide answers were not incomplete or contradictory. Instead, popular wisdom still holds that apparently powerful parties do better in negotiation and that parties need to start from positions of equality for both of them to do well in negotiation. Furthermore, social psychology, international politics, evolutionary game theory, and public choice theories provide opposite and unreconciled pieces of advice on how to analyze and practice negotiation or to consider power. It is these gaps and gambles that this study seeks to overcome, by building on the knowledge already achieved.

This introductory discussion, along with the following case studies and the book's concluding analysis, attempts to advance our understanding of the concept of power beyond its present state. In doing so, the study evaluates the relationship of power to international negotiation where, in the extreme, there are two very different schools of thought. One argues that power asymmetries are evened by the negotiation process. The very act of negotiating has the real effect of leveling the playing field, producing at least rough symmetry. Initial differences in power dissolve in the recognition that each side in a negotiation needs the other's assent and is blocked by the other's veto. Negotiations mediate a prior power distribution.

The opposing school of thought argues that differences in power *do* make a difference in the way negotiations proceed and the outcomes that result. More powerful parties are better able to control the negotiation process and obtain results to their liking; negotiations only confirm a given power distribution. However, a further debate divides those who believe that power matters. The dominant school – which includes the contributors to this work (Deutsch 1973; Kritek 1994:35; Luterbacher 1999; Mitchell 1995:36, 39, 53; Morgan 1994:141; Raiffa 1982; Ross 1993: ch. 5; Rubin and Brown 1975; Snyder and Diesing 1977:18; Young 1967; Zartman and Berman 1982; see also Deutsch and Singer 1964) – has long maintained that power symmetry is the condition most propitious for mutually satisfying negotiations and efficient attainment of optimal results; if asymmetry favors the more powerful, it indisposes the less powerful and delays joint agreement. The opposing argument – that it is asymmetry that produces faster, better agreement – has rarely been made, as the reasoning behind it is not intuitively obvious. This premise is examined here, with some surprising results. Beyond evaluating the extent to which power differences make a difference in the international negotiation process and outcome, this book provides a close look at the various ways in which power is exercised before, during, and at the conclusion of negotiations.

Other works have examined power asymmetry and come to prescriptive conclusions, particularly for the weak (Aggarwal and Allan 1983; Deutsch 1973; Fox 1959; Habeeb 1988; Kritek 1994; Rothstein 1977; Singer 1972; Telhami 1990; Wriggins 1987; Zartman 1971, 1987). This study carries these works forward by placing strategies within specific and new conceptualizations of power, in addition to shedding new light on the symmetry assumption. Through a more explicit analysis, or disaggregation, of the power concept, this study examines the implications of both symmetry and asymmetry to inform the negotiation process itself and to ground sounder understandings of the ways of conducting it.

The recent literature on regimes and interdependence does not address these issues. The reason for this is not due to any inherent weakness, but rather that it is not attempting to address them (see especially Keohane and Nye 1989). Regime literature is more interested in emphasizing the importance of nonmilitary resources and relations in an understanding of international politics, a point with which the present inquiry concurs and on which it builds. Despite evocations of "power" and claims about the importance of "bargaining theory," neither is employed by studies of interdependence in a process analysis that the concepts and questions require. Interdependence involves linkages and asymmetries, but more must be done than simply repeating that fact and rewording the notions of tradeoffs to understand how weak and strong states deal with one another in negotiations, what effect perceived asymmetry has on both strong and weak states' behavior, and how power can be conceptualized to be useful in the analysis of negotiatory interactions and processes. These questions are left unanswered in interdependence studies, as in other disciplinary approaches, and addressed here in an effort to complement earlier analysis and to push forward an understanding of power and negotiation.

1.1   The Sciences of Power

The beginning of the problem lies with the notion of power itself: What is it that enables one party to gain something from the other in negotiation? More specifically: What are the interconnections among the various concepts of power – power as determined by the resources one controls, the relationships one has, the perceptions one holds (Hart 1976) – and what are the effects of power variously conceived on negotiated outcomes? Power comes in so many forms, subsumed under so many definitions, that it must be separated into component parts before the whole can be properly understood. To begin addressing these conundrums, we turn first to the concept of power, then its role in negotiation, and finally the specifics of power asymmetry.

Power is the basic concept of both physics and political science and a key element in other sciences as well. To the physicist, power has a precise definition (Hewitt 1985:81–86; Rothman 1963:37–50). To the political scientist, it is vague and ultimately tautological, and its use in political analysis poses epistemological difficulties of definition and operationalization (Bell et al. 1969). At the same time, it is hard to go very deep into an analysis of negotiation without invoking the concept and thereby posing the need for clear, workable understandings and definitions.

Examination of the natural science definition of power reveals some of the conceptual problems found in the social sciences. In physics, power is defined simply as work divided by the time taken to accomplish it; time has a standard measurement, and work is conventionally, if less popularly, defined by the components of its result, force, and distance. Force is what is required to move an object, the weight and speed of the acceleration being measured in specific, standard terms. Energy is what enables an object to do work; it comes in different forms and can be transformed from one form to another, but it exists as a fixed quantity and (in Newtonian physics at least) can be neither created nor destroyed.

Although there are interconnections among the concepts of force, energy, and power, specific measures of each have been developed and definitions established using these measures. It should be noted that force, energy, and power are conceived and measured in terms of their results or output; force can be expressed either as applied forces working in various directions on an object or as net (resultant) force, the sum of these compounded and/or opposed forces. This aspect, known as the conclusionary nature of a concept, does not appear to trouble physical scientists, although it bothers social scientists.

Since the early 1930s, seizing on a conceptualization used a century earlier by von Clausewitz (1832/1968:101), social scientists have had at their disposal a good working definition of power as *the ability of one party to move another in an intended direction.* Originally formulated by Tawney (1931/1952:159), it was adopted by a number of disciplines in the 1950s – decision theorists such as Herbert Simon (1953), political scientists such as Robert Dahl (1957), and social psychologists such as John Thibaut and Harold Kelley (1959) – who were seeking a definition to identify power with its effects and to move or separate it from its identification with its sources provided in earlier definitions (e.g., Morgenthau 1948). It is obvious that "move" refers here not to physical displacement but to changes in positions in thought and action.

This definition contains a number of important elements. First, it focuses on social power, the relation between parties abstracted from other causes of movement. Second, by extension, it implies the notion of applied and net power, recognizing that although the parties may apply pressure or power on each other, net power in the relation is registered by the resultant movement. Third, by further extension, power is conceptualized conclusionarily by its results, that is, the movement of the target. It cannot be measured by output because there is as yet no standard concept – let alone measurement – of effort or "force" (in the physics sense). Indeed, even movement is not standardized, since there is no single measure of "weight" or "speed" in social science.

It is this third implication that creates conceptual problems. For example, if one party (the agent) prevails over another (the target), does that mean that the target has no power? The concept as stated is unable to distinguish between an agent that prevails against no resistance (power) and one that prevails by a hair with tremendous effort. Or if it can make that distinction, as between net and applied power, it has no one criterion by which to evaluate – let alone measure – the competing applications. It tells who wins but does not tell the score! Or again, if the target decides to give in, for its own moral or tactical reasons (such as to buy a counter-concession from the agent), does that mean that the agent has power, whereas it has none if the target is willing or able to hold that same amount of effort in check?

Or even more problematically, consider the assertion of Crozier (1964:55):

> If the two parties are completely free and the exchange is equal,
> neither party would be said to be in a position of power vis-à-vis
> the other. But if the terms of trade are definitely biased in favor of
> one or the other and if that inequality corresponds to the respective
> situation of the two parties and not to chance or to error, then one
> can speak of a power relation.

This view would exclude consideration of situations where parties
have the power to hold each other in check or to obtain equal value from
each other, that is, in relations where the parties or the outcomes are symmetrical. In sum, the definition is weakened by an inability to handle
notions of competing power(s), resistance as well as pressure as power,
and applied power as distinct from net power.[2]

The fact that the moving parts in this interaction are social beings
rather than inanimate objects adds new twists as well. The relation becomes no longer a simple one of force and counterforce, but of volition
or intention as well. Movement produced in an intended direction defines power, but movement somewhere else is evasion or blunder. Similarly, movement that was unintended by the target shows agent power,
but movement intended anyhow annuls it. In the end, the target is largely
in control of the definition of the agent's power when power is defined as
results. The target can deny, refuse, or co-opt the power as well as resist
it – options that are not available in the relations of objects in the physical
sciences. Rocks resist but don't push back; people can do both.

More troublesome yet, this social science definition has serious tautological difficulties, in that the operative element of the defining phrase
is the very term being defined (Hobbes 1651/1964:55; Maoz 1989:240;
Zartman 1974:394–397). Power is defined as the ability to move another, but power and ability are synonyms, and power becomes the power
to move another.[3] Rather than serving as a definition that helps researchers to analyze and explain, the clause returns to its social setting
and becomes merely a qualifier, specifying social power rather than all
sources of movement. In other words, to look for power is merely – but
importantly – to pose the causal question: What is it that enables one
party to move another in an intended direction (Dahl 1976:29–30, 37–39;
Simon 1953:5; Zartman 1974:396–397)?

To avoid this problem and to provide a usable definition of the concept, power here is defined as *an action by one party intending to produce
movement by another*. Thus, power is defined neither as a source nor as
a result but, in between the two, as a purposeful action, leaving the analysts' hands free to study the relationship of power with both its sources

and its results. This definition includes the elements in the Tawney concept, while taking care of many of the deficiencies noted above. It is closer to (but more succinct and less conclusionary than) W.M. Habeeb's definition of power as "the way in which actor A uses its resources in a process with actor B so as to bring about changes that cause preferred outcomes" (Habeeb 1988:15; cf. Bull 1995:12). Focusing on a particular type of move opens the way to useful subcategorizations and causal distinctions.

Thus, the search for power in any social situation returns the analyst to the initial objective of the quest, to explain how outcomes are caused. This reformulation at least allows a more useful statement of the analytical question and the introduction of contingencies or intervening variables to refine analysis: What kinds of action in a social encounter enable an agent, under what conditions, to cause the target to move in the direction the agent intends? This becomes the fundamental question in the analysis of the specific social encounters known as negotiation.[4]

1.2 Behind the Causal Question

The traditional answer in political science to the causal question has been *power as force*. This answer is the basis of the "realist" school in international politics (Dahl 1976:47–48; von Clausewitz 1832/1968; Waltz 1954). It is also an answer that is ideological, reductionist, inaccurate, and narrowing, and has done much to weaken a sound, thorough discussion of power. The equation of power with force (in the social, not natural, science sense) is so pervasive that any discussion of power is "forced" to first clear the air by pointing out that there is much more to power than violence and constraint. As a result, the water is further muddied by the need to relate power to other notions such as persuasion, influence, leverage, and pressure, when they are more usefully employed as synonyms.

Conceiving of power as force alone is ideological because it becomes a justification for violence and a devaluation of nonviolent means of causation. It is reductionist because it equates cause with its ultimate expression alone.[5] It is inaccurate since it denies the power of other causes. And it is narrowing in that it divides political science from its own subject, since force as power is of no help in analyzing intrastate as opposed to interstate politics. Force is indeed an element of power, a causal factor of importance, but it stands with others in producing the same effect.

Another standard way of answering the causal power question is to relate it to resources, leading to the "neorealist" view of power as *a possession* (Knorr 1975; Organski 1968); for recent attempts to quantify power, see Stoll and Ward (1989). The answer is logical and specific, since it gives a precise and direct answer to the search for the sources of the agent's ability to cause the target to move. It also lends itself to comparative analysis, since both sides can have power through the resources they control, and the more powerful can easily be calculated in these terms. Unfortunately, resources come in many shapes and sizes, destroying the ability to aggregate them in a single measure. Resources also come shapelessly, in such items as leadership or moral sources of power, which cannot be measured at all (except tautologically, by their effects).

The greater problem is that size alone is not ability; indeed, the two may be inversely related, as noted in the structuralists' paradox. In fact, if size were power, parties could calculate ahead of time and decide (like dogs or baboons) to avoid certain social encounters, notably negotiation, because they could figure out who would lose (Hammerstein and Parker 1982; Maynard Smith 1982). Yet the small and weak often do very well in negotiation, and the explanation of why is one of the tasks of this book. Discussion of this problem, however, has produced the concept of aggregate power or position power – referring to the total resources held by an agent – contrasted with relevant power or issue power – which refers to those resources that can be directed toward a particular conflict or concern in the exercise that produces movement (Habeeb 1988; Lockhart 1979). It is the latter that must be considered in answering the analytical or causal question.

The issue behind power as a possession is that it fails to take into account control of the resources through will and skill. It takes more than brushes and paints to paint a picture, a point that seems curiously lost on the neorealists. The search for answers to the causal question then turns to mediating concepts relating the particular uses of resources and other elements to movement in the target – that is, to the "exercise" that is the basic term of the definition.

1.3   Extended Concepts of Power

A variant conceptualization, stemming from a rational choice approach, considers power as *the value added to a particular outcome* (Schelling 1960; Zartman 1974). One agent exercises power in its relations with another when its actions can negatively or positively alter the value of a particular action's outcome for the target. This approach retains the bilateral relational notion of power, and provides a common dimension in which to compare and aggregate different exercises of power. A stronger party is one that can add (or subtract) more value to (or from) the other's outcome.

One way of categorizing the actions that produce movement is as pressure (negative), inducement (positive), and resistance (negative or positive response). Thus, contingent moves can be divided into threats and warnings (negative) and promises and predictions (positive), depending on whether the source of the move is the agent or an external force (Duffy et al. 1998; Schelling 1960; Tedeschi 1970; Zartman 1987). In Habeeb's definition (1988:21 et seq.), the "way" resources are used to bring about changes and cause preferred outcomes relates to three variables: alternatives, commitment, and control. Raven and Kruglanski (1970), as well as Raven and Rubin (1983), write in the same vein of informational, referent, expert, legitimate, reward, and coercive power.

Conceptualizations such as these have the strength of breaking down the exercise of power (a single concept, not two) into a number of alternatives, closer to the notion of different types of energy used in the physical sciences. They have the weakness of not constituting different points along a single dimension, so that it becomes impossible to identify missing forms or to establish whether or not the components comprise a universe. The fact that the components do not lend themselves to quantification is probably less important than the fact that they differ among themselves in nature, that fruit is defined as apples plus oranges rather than as different forms of a single characteristic (such as flesh-covered seeds, for example). Using decision analytic techniques, concepts and measures of value can be developed for use in a modification of Schelling's (1960:47–51) diagram (*Figure 1.1*) as a simple portrayal of improved and weakened outcomes. In the figure, if A has the ability to reduce the value – or the perception of the value – of option r for B (from r to r') and to increase the value of option s for B (from s to s'), then A has the power to obtain a more favorable outcome for itself. Thus, comparative effects of power can be measured. Such attempts illustrate

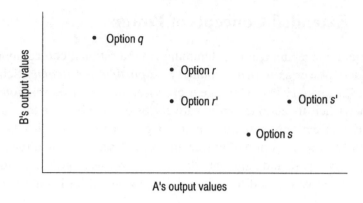

Figure 1.1. Diagram of improved and weakened output.

the reality of power and causality on social encounters, seeking to translate the essence of the phenomenon into definitions and concepts. Such ideas must be tested, refined, and expanded through use in case analysis so that inductive insights can be played back into deductive thinking.

1.4 Power and Negotiation

Negotiation is joint decision making under conditions of conflict and uncertainty, in which divergent positions are combined into a single outcome. Each of two or more sides attempts to obtain what it wants through the exchange of information, typically in the form of offers and counteroffers. As conflict theorists have observed, negotiation is only one of a family of approaches to the settlement of conflict; the others are domination, capitulation, inaction, withdrawal, and the intervention of third parties (Rubin et al. 1994). As decision theorists have noted, negotiation constitutes one of three modes of social decision making; the other two are adjudication and coalition formation (Zartman 1974). A vast literature on negotiation has emerged in recent decades, and this volume builds on this substantial foundation to look more closely at the meaning of power in international negotiation.

Refinements in the conceptualization of power, as discussed above, are necessary if the concept is to be useful in the analysis of negotiation as a social encounter. Power as force and power as a possession provide little insight and slim basis for an analysis of negotiation. Instead they set up the structuralists' paradox – that the most powerful party in terms of force or resources does not always win at negotiation. But when power is separated from both its source and its effect and conceptualized as an exercise using resources and adding value, it is hard to define the most powerful party as the one that wins, other than in tautological or conclusionary terms. Since winning is rejected as a component of many definitions of negotiation – as a win–win rather than a win–lose proposition, or as an encounter in which both parties are better off or they would not agree – the tautological definition is misleading as well as inadequate. Indeed, any definition that separates power from its sources, even the definition adopted here, of power as an action, does not permit a judgment of the most powerful party until the contest is over. It still leaves unanswered the specific question of this inquiry. Does unequal power (as an estimate or as resources) produce dissimilar behavior (as actions) yielding unequal results?

How, then, can one talk of asymmetry, one of the central concepts of international relations and international negotiations? To answer, one must focus on a different aspect of the concept, emphasized by Singer (1972:77–79; Hart 1976; cf. Hammerstein 1981:194–202; Hammerstein and Parker 1982:648–650) and Doran (1995:46) in regard to this very problem – on power as *a perceived relation*. Part of any social interaction is a matter of perception; this is a problem that natural scientists need not worry about – when one object acts upon another, neither has any perception to distract it. Perception mediates objective reality, although of course reality imposes certain limits on the implications of perception; if one party perceives itself to be better armed, richer, or more skilled – that is, at least potentially more powerful – than the other, when in fact it is not, that party may act on the basis of its perception but will most likely fail, tripped up by reality. Much of power is a matter of perception, which may help the party produce its intended results or may stymie it. Of course, perception is not immutable either: The target may have the ability to change the agent's perception. Therefore, the perceived symmetry or asymmetry of a relationship is related to elements such as force and resources, as well as to the reputation and prospects of a party to produce past and future movements on the part of its targets. As such, it becomes the basis of an action that constitutes power.

Investigating asymmetry in perceptions of power rather than seeking an objective reality has several advantages. It approaches power as the parties do, through their own eyes, instead of relying upon some ostensibly scientific standard that they might not use. It registers the element that governs behavior – the parties' perception of their own power, the other's power, and the relative standing of self and other – whether these are "objectively correct" or not. And it obviates all problems of tautology, with the causative element focused on motivating perceptions. It is to perceptions of power, therefore, that this inquiry turns, combining Tawney's definition of power with the new definition proposed here: *the perceived capacity of one side to produce an intended effect on another through a move that may involve the use of resources.*

A slight return to the previous discussion is necessary, however, to anchor perceived power in reality. Although it is perceptions that matter in determining one party's behavior toward a perceived target, those perceptions are not unrelated to objective reality, as noted. Thus, a party perceived to be stronger is so viewed because of attributes it holds that can be or have been converted into effects. In international negotiations, this relation between attributes and perceptions often returns the consideration of power to resources, although past successes may be another source of the perception. Obviously, neither of these two indicators can be equated to success in upcoming negotiations; this much is already known about the structuralists' paradox. But structural or resource inequalities and reputational or outcome inequalities remain the two major bases of perceptions and are often directly equated with power status.

1.5   Negotiations and Asymmetry

The question about the effect of perceived asymmetry on negotiation is examined in this work in an unusual manner, by bridging two worlds of data. Rarely are the findings of experiments from the laboratories of social psychology combined with results of events from the arenas of international politics (but see Druckman 1977; Zartman et al. 1996). Here experimental data are used to generate propositions, which will then be tested in the "real world" using historical cases. There are differences between the two worlds. Experiments aim at controlling everything except the variables specified in the hypotheses. But they also involve players who are part of the situation only as naked humans, with no other background, position, or role to clothe their actions and motivations.[6] Historic events contain no controls; they can only be selected for apparent similarities. But they contain real people in real situations, constituting the ultimate events one seeks to explain and understand. It is therefore appropriate to play the two series of data against each other, to obtain the deepest comprehension of asymmetry in negotiation.

Experimental findings from laboratory research in psychology were summarized in a 1975 review about 1,000 experimental studies of negotiation, more than 60 of them devoted to perceptions of power (Rubin and Brown 1975), and then used to develop hypotheses about negotiations under asymmetry. A far smaller number of studies have been conducted since then, as social psychology has turned to other topics to investigate. Much of the recent work has focused on coalition games – the condition under which coalitions are likely to form and the particular ways in which outcomes are divided or exchanged among coalition partners; little of the coalition research has focused on power asymmetry per se, nor is this research relevant to bilateral negotiation. These hypotheses provide both a summary of experimental finding and a set of propositions to focus the analysis of the case studies in this volume.

1.5.1 Perceptions of equal power among negotiators tend to result in more effective negotiation than unequal power.[7]

The basis for this hypothesis goes back as far as the Melian Dialogue between Athens and Sparta as recorded by Thucydides. In 30 recent experiments, power equality was manipulated either through status variations (as when undergraduates were told that they were playing against another undergraduate instead of a graduate student or a professor) or, more often, through variations in reward structure provided to participants. For example, Komorita and Barnes (1969), using a research paradigm in which there is a single buyer and a single seller of merchandise (hence, a bilateral monopoly), varied the cost of making an offer from $2 to both buyer and seller, or $0 for both, to $2 for buyer and $0 for seller, or $0 for buyer and $2 for seller. Power was equal – high and low, respectively – in the first two cases and unequal in the second pair. The authors found that pairs with equal power reached agreement more often, required fewer trials to do so, and made larger concession than those with unequal power. Pairs in the low equal power condition ($2 and $2) functioned more effectively overall – like the no "gate" pairs in the Acme-Bolt trucking experiments of Deutsch and Krauss (1960, 1962) and the no "lock" pairs in the chicken research of Deutsch and Lewicki (1970).[8] Lawler et al. (1988) studied the effects of coercive tactics in an equal versus unequal power relationship and found that both low- and high-power actors in unequal relationships used more "damage tactics" than those in equal power relationships. Of the 30 studies, 22 provide unequivocal support for the hypothesis, 5 report no difference as a function of power equality, and 3 report findings in the opposite direction.

Findings in the opposite direction tend to point out that true equality is hard to find, particularly when several measures are involved, and the closer parties come to equality without reaching it, the more difficult negotiations become. Thus, appearances of equality become important, as noted again in proposition 3 in Section 1.5.3.

1.5.2 Under conditions of perceived power inequality among negotiators, the party with high power tends to behave exploitatively, whereas the less powerful party tends to behave submissively – unless certain special conditions prevail.

As support for the first proposition makes clear, unequal distribution of power generally results in less effective negotiation, overall, than does equal distribution. Unequal power, moreover, appears to affect the behavior of the more powerful and the less powerful parties differently: Negotiators with high relative power tend to behave manipulatively and exploitatively, whereas those with perceived lower power tend to behave submissively.

This finding is supported by 28 of the 32 experimental studies reviewed, with the remaining four studies reporting either no differences or more cooperative (less exploitative) behavior for the high-power negotiators compared with the low-power negotiators. Thirteen of the experiments reporting support for this hypothesis utilized the Prisoner's Dilemma game or some variant of it, four used the Ace-Bolt trucking game, six used a bilateral monopoly paradigm, and the remaining studies used some other experimental vehicle.

Michener et al. (1975), in a bilateral monopoly paradigm, found that subjects in a strong power position did not reciprocate concessions made by their counterpart whereas weaker subjects did. Murnigham (1985) found that when retribution is possible, and when the individuals involved can identify one another, there are severe limits on the exercise of power. Similarly, Kim and Smith (1993) report that high-power parties are less likely to seek revenge in an escalating conflict when their behavior is visible to an observing audience; the same audience offers protective cover to the less powerful member seeking revenge. In other words, relatively low-power negotiators will seek to redress their grievances only if they think they can get away with it – by having the protection of anonymity, by joining forces with other weak negotiators, or by operating under the protective course of an observing audience. Finally, Komorita and Nagao (1983) found that the more powerful partner in a five-party coalition game demanded and received a greater share of the payoff than the less powerful, and Dwyer and Walker (1981) found that dependent negotiations used fewer threats and complied more readily than high-power counterparts.

The special conditions mentioned above refer to organizations or ideologies, the weapons of the weak (Michels 1962) that allow a sufficient number of "disenfranchised" parties to work together to form a winning coalition. Ideology too can be the vehicle of an attitudinal coalition and lead to assertiveness, rather than submissiveness, even (or maybe especially) if the coalition of the weak is not winning. Under these circumstances, coalitions are likely to form to offset the initial power disadvantage and to transform submission into resistance. Another special condition is identified in the concept of interpersonal orientation discussed in proposition 6 in Section 1.5.6. The question arises in either case whether coalitions – tactical or ideological – are special conditions that allow alternatives to submissiveness or whether they are the results of prior insubmissiveness, invalidating the proposition. The latter is the more likely, leading to a search for a prior variable to indicate which weak party will act submissively and which will seek out weapons of the weak to act insubmissively.

1.5.3 The smaller the perceived difference in negotiators' power, the more effective their negotiations are likely to be.

Given the support for the first two hypotheses, it follows that the greater the gap between the parties' perception of their power, the less effectively they are likely to function as a unit. Or, as a corollary of the first hypothesis, the closer the parties are to power equality, the more effectively they should function. Nine studies varied the degree of power differential, and seven of these found support for the hypothesis. As an illustration of the kind of research conducted, Aranoff and Tedeschi (1968) had pairs of participants play a 200-run Prisoner's Dilemma game in which one player, chosen at random, was awarded an initial advantage of 0, 25, 50, 100, or 500 points; as the size of the initial advantage increased, the frequency of mutual cooperation decreased.

However, a number of experiments indicated a contrary finding; when parties were nearly equal, negotiations were the most difficult. The researchers noted that negotiations tended to derail when power escalates and parties challenge their near-symmetry rather than accepting their asymmetry (Pruitt and Carnevale 1993:131–132).

1.5.4 The smaller the total amount of power in the system, the more effectively negotiators are likely to function.

Of the 17 studies reviewed, in which the amount of power was varied, 11 lend support to this fourth hypothesis concerning the effects of power. Consistently, researchers using the Acme-Bolt trucking game, as well as its several variants, have found that mean joint and individual outcomes are most favorable when neither player has a "gate" (a device meant to be used as a threat or as a signal of one's intentions), least favorable when both players have gates, and neutral when only one player has a gate. Similar results have been obtained in modified Prisoner's Dilemma games, where either or both participants and a simulated other have the power to punish another's noncompliance.

1.5.5 If the parties perceive themselves to be of equal power and the negotiators share a cooperative motivational orientation, the more effectively they are likely to function; if the parties perceive themselves to be of equal power and they share a competitive motivational orientation, the less effectively they are likely to function.

This proposition modifies proposition 1 in Section 1.5.1 by introducing an intervening variable, that of motivational orientation (MO): the cooperativeness or competitiveness of the parties' attitude toward each other (Deutsch 1960, 1973). Only two studies deliberately set out to explore the interaction of MO and power perceptions. Both lend support to the hypothesis, although caution should be taken in generalizing them to other contexts, given the size of the sample. Nonetheless, the hypothesis is interesting for this power project. When negotiators share a cooperative MO and perceive themselves to be of equal power, conditions are most favorable for the resolution of a conflict of interest. Each party has an interest in the other's welfare as well as its own. The negotiators' search for a fair and equitable allocation of payoffs is buttressed by the perception of equal (or roughly comparable) power. In contrast, when negotiators have a shared cooperative MO but a perception of unequal power, they are presented with a potentially soluble but nevertheless more complex coordination problem: They now must find some way to take into account the differential resources that they bring to the table. When negotiators share a competitive MO, each is trying to beat the other and is looking for some basis on which to leverage a competitive advantage. When power is unequal, outcomes will tend to be overdetermined, with the more powerful being relatively successful in its attempts to take advantage of the weaker, which has little choice but to behave relatively submissively (unless a winning coalition or an invigorating ideology can be found).

Finally, when negotiators are competitive in MO and equal in power, all hell breaks loose! As Rubin and Brown (1975:246) put it:

> The same equality of power which facilitated the resolution of conflict when the parties shared a cooperative MO will now lead to a ferociously intense struggle over intangible issues. If both are equally powerful (or equally weak), why should one give in to the competitive, exploitative behavior that the other is likely to display?

Transferring this insight to the international level, when states in conflict tend to be competitive, equal power may be expected to be the least productive condition for negotiation.

1.5.6 When the parties perceive themselves to be equal in power and high in interpersonal orientation, they negotiate more effectively than if they perceive themselves to be unequal in power.

1.5.7 When parties are perceived to be equal in power and high in interpersonal orientation, they negotiate more effectively if they share a cooperative motivational orientation, and less effectively if they share a competitive motivational orientation.

These propositions introduce a different intervening variable into proposition 1 – interpersonal orientation (IO), the degree of interest among the conflicting parties in interpersonal information. IO reinforces the effects or perceived power asymmetry or symmetry. High IO negotiators are in the position to be unusually interested in, and reactive to, social cues, whereas their low IO counterparts rely instead on nonsocial cues. Studies that have examined IO have varied the amount of interpersonal information available to negotiators (e.g., information about the other's perceived similarity or dissimilarity to oneself) and history and expectations of prior and future relationships, among other things.

Little experimental research has been conducted to evaluate these hypotheses. Still, their relevance for power asymmetry make them worth exploring. When power is roughly equal, negotiators exist in a "democratic" relationship of sorts; there is no a priori basis for one side to attempt to dominate the others. Negotiators are likely to be concerned about the fair division or exchange of resources – and in the presence of interpersonally salient information (high IO conditions), problems of coordination and distribution should be a bit easier to solve. In contrast, when high IO conditions obtain an unequal power situation, one side attempts to take advantage of its greater strength to impose a settlement on the other. The presence of a high IO is likely only to enhance the salience of this power inequality. Instead of leading the weaker side simply to submit passively, this information may heighten concerns with intangible issues (such as losing face at the hands of an exploitative other) and may lead to greater resistance. In summary, equal power tendencies to divide or exchange outcomes fairly and equally are enhanced by the presence of interpersonally relevant information; but unequal power tendencies for the weaker to submit are offset by the accentuated importance of intangible concerns (as in the case of ideology).

1.6   Cases of Power and Negotiation

The following case studies constitute historical research to test these experimentally derived hypotheses to evaluate the effects of perceptions of one's own power and the other's power on the negotiation process and its outcome. It is clear that in the above discussions, it is the *perception* of power – or more precisely, the reality of power mediated by perception – that is involved in questions of symmetry and asymmetry, rather than raw measures of force or resources. Three types of situations are used to test notions of asymmetrical or symmetrical perceptions.

In one, if parties to international negotiations vary their behavior in relation to their *own* perceived power, independent of the other's perceived power, then members of high- versus low-power negotiating pairs should behave differently from each other, but members of equal high power pairs should behave the same. In this view, parties who see themselves as strong should behave the same, no matter what the perceived power of the opponent. Thus, the behavior of both parties in HH negotiations (high self-perception of power for both parties) should resemble the behavior of the first party in HL (one party's high self-perception of power and the other's low self-perception of power), but both of these types should be different from LL or LH negotiations, where in turn both parties should resemble each other.

In another situation, if international negotiators vary their behavior in relation to the *other's* perceived power, independent of their own, then HL situations should produce the same behavior on the part of the first party as LL situations, and HH situations should produce the same as LH situations, the difference lying between the two pairs. In this view, parties act tactically, with their behavior dictated by the perceived power of the opponent, independent of their own perceived power position.

In a third type of situation, power effects in international negotiation would be understood in terms of the *relation* between the two perceptions of power. In this case, behavior would be different in each of the three situations, with HH producing different behavior from LL, which differs in turn from HL and LH, which differ from each other. The parties' behavior would be shaped both by each party's perception of its power position and by each party's perception of its opponent's power in comparison with its own, with both powerful and powerless parties acting differently toward their peers and toward each other.

Nine cases of negotiations follow in which these propositions are tested and the interactions of the parties are analyzed using the concepts of power discussed above. Most cases are examples of HL or LH power relations, depending on which member of the pair comes first. The US–Canada free trade exchange of 1985–1987, the US–Indonesian aid negotiations of the early 1950s, the US–Egyptian aid and reform discussions of the 1980s and early 1990s, the Andorra–European Community exchange on free trade between 1979 and 1987, the Nepal–India discussions on water resources between the 1960s and the 1990s, the Arab–Israeli negotiations over peace and territory in 1949, 1974, and 1977–1979, and the North–South discussions at the United Nations Conference on Environment and Development (UNCED) in 1990–1992 represent negotiations between a strong and a weak(er) party. These asymmetrical encounters can be compared among themselves and also to the more nearly symmetrical cases, two of which are included: The Mali–Burkinabê negotiations in 1986 over disputed territory constitute a LL case, whereas the US–Chinese negotiations to end the Korean War in 1952–1954 constitute an HH case. A disproportionately large number of asymmetrical cases has deliberately been chosen for analysis, for two reasons. First, they correspond to the nature of international relations, where the number of asymmetrical encounters vastly exceeds more symmetrical relations; and second, these cases tend to be the most theoretically interesting cases.

In all of the asymmetrical cases, insightful lessons are given to explain how weak and strong can negotiate satisfactorily to both. But beyond that explanation the paradox remains in all cases. Three of the asymmetrical cases involve the United States, often referred to as the world's only superpower and hence a perceived high-power party. In the first case, the United States negotiates with its neighbor, Canada, to establish a free trade area that both sides want, although in different ways and with different degrees of intensity. Yet despite the imbalance in the dependency relationship (and not just in aggregate power), Canada won significant concessions and obtained an agreement advantageous enough to win overwhelming popular endorsement in a subsequent election. In part, this is explained by the fact that both the situation and the tactics of both sides served to level the playing field.

In the second and third cases, the United States negotiates with two Third World aid recipients, trading the quantity of development assistance against certain policy aims that it would like to see adopted by the assisted countries – an end to trade with China for Indonesia and internal economic reforms for Egypt. In the balance, determination played against dependency in both cases, against a background of a relationship that both sides wanted to preserve.

The fourth case is an extended bilateral example, involving the European Community (now Union), a collective heavyweight of heavyweights, and two of its members, France and Spain, negotiating with the smallest state – only semi-sovereign – in its midst, Andorra, for a trade agreement. Classically, agile Andorra was able to play the weighty opponents against each other to achieve its ends. The fifth case pits another giant, India, against its relatively tiny neighbor, Nepal, as they negotiate agreements on their shared rivers. The headwaters position of Nepal obviously helped level the table, but not completely, particularly given the attitudes of the two parties toward each other.

The sixth case, between the Arabs and Israeli at three points during their conflict, is also clearly asymmetrical and so heightens the paradox. The measure of asymmetry at each point is military victory rather than aggregate power, and yet at each point it was the loser who gained negotiated advantages. A search for why the weaker party won takes the analysis outside the bilateral negotiations. The last asymmetrical case tests the propositions and uses the concepts of power on the multilateral level with a negotiation of the strong North against the weaker South at the UN Conference on Environment and Development. The structuralists' paradox is most evident here, since neither tactics nor context was able to work to mitigate the asymmetry. Yet a basic tradeoff was made, to which both parties subscribed. Thus, in these six cases, the basic questions are indicated by the seven propositions in cases of perceived power asymmetry, accompanied by an analysis of power-as-an-action by the two parties to indicate their exercise of power in the negotiating situation.

But the propositions must also be tested against perceived symmetry. The remaining cases are not marked by a pronounced asymmetry, and although symmetry may be a debatable matter anywhere in human relations, both external and intra-party judgments in some cases can agree that the paired-off parties are equal enough to hold each other in check. The strong pair found in the highly ideological and high-power confrontation between Communist China and the United States negotiating to end the Korean War and the weak pair found in low-power parties to the War of the Poor between Mali and Burkina Faso (Upper Volta) in West Africa allow a test of the propositions under conditions where parties try to buttress or break out of their perceived symmetry rather than work within their perceived asymmetry. Although it would be hard to claim that two cases represent the same typicality for symmetry as the seven do for asymmetry, the two are representative enough of the essential features under analysis to be able to challenge or support the propositions.

Notes

[1] We thank the members of the Washington Interest in Negotiation (WIN) Group – Kate Antrim, Francis Deng, Daniel Druckman, Lloyd Jensen, Dean Pruitt, Donald Rothchild, Timothy Sisk, Bertram Spector, and Saadia Touval – and the following students of the Fletcher School of Law and Diplomacy – Yvonne Agyei, Geoffrey Fink, Olaf Groth, Daniel Lieberfeld, Joshua Lincoln, and Valerie McCabe – for their helpful comments on this manuscript. For an earlier statement of the problem and some tentative solutions, see Rubin and Zartman (1995) and Zartman (1997).

[2] Tawney (1931/1952:159) recognized these problems and then dismissed them because their solution was not his concern. His words, however, are incisive:

> Power may be defined as the capacity of an individual, or group of individuals, to modify the conduct of other individuals of groups in the manner which he desires, and to prevent his own

> conduct [from] being modified in the manner in which he does
> not. Everyone, therefore, possesses some measure of power,
> and no one possesses more than a measure of it. Men exercise
> only the power that they are allowed to by other men, so that the
> strong are rarely as powerful as they are thought by the weak,
> or the weak as powerless as they are thought by themselves.

[3] Admittedly, "ability" might be taken to mean "skill and will," two components of power discussed later, although it has never been identified explicitly in this sense. Were it to be so, it would only be a partial definition, since it would exclude another component, resources, also discussed below.

[4] It should be noted that this refinement of the more general question is present in the physics concept as well, leading in that case to a differentiation in notions of energy.

[5] Even force may not be as ultimate a cause as claimed, since it too can be refuted as a cause, even if not as an effect.

[6] Sometimes it is noted that they are not baggage-less humans but usually American students, with a specific social location (Faure et al. 1998:185).

[7] "Effectiveness" in the studies cited refers to a variety of things, primarily consisting of the frequency of mutually cooperative choice behavior or measures of joint outcome or both.

[8] In the Acme-Bolt trucking paradigm, each of two experimental participants is asked to imagine that he or she is in charge of a trucking company, carrying merchandise from a start to a destination, where a portion of the route is only one lane wide; this section of the trip forms the basis of the potential conflict between Acme and Bolt. Pay is determined by the time taken to travel from start to destination, and there is typically an alternative route that is unimpeded but is guaranteed to be rather time-consuming. In some variations of the Acme-Bolt paradigm, subjects are each given a "gate" to control that lies near the beginning of their route; once erected, the gate may not be crossed by the other side, although the participant can move through his or her own gate at will. Deutsch and Lewicki's "chicken game" is a variant of the Acme-Bolt paradigm, in which each side can lock its truck in forward gear.

References

Aggarwal, V.K., and Allan, P., 1983, *Evolution in Bargaining Theories: Toward an Integrated Approach to Explain the Strategies of the Weak*, American Political Science Association, Chicago.

Aranoff, D., and Tedeschi, J.T., 1968, Original stakes and behavior in the prisoner's dilemma game, *Psychonomic Science*, **12**:79–80.

Bell, R., Edwards, D., and Wagner, R.H., eds., 1969, *Political Power*, Free Press, New York.

Bull, H., 1995, *The Anarchial Society*, Columbia University Press, New York.

Crozier, M., 1964, Pouvoir et organisation, *Archives Européennes de Sociologie*, **5**(1): 55–58.

Dahl, R., 1957, The concept of power, *Behavioral Science*, **2**(2):201–215.

Dahl, R., 1976, *Modern Political Analysis*, 3rd edition, Prentice-Hall, Englewood Cliffs, NJ.

Deutsch, M., 1960, The effect of motivational orientation upon trust and suspicion, *Human Relations*, **16**(2):123–138.

Deutsch, M., 1973, *The Resolution of Conflict*, Yale University Press, New Haven, CT.

Deutsch, M., and Krauss, R.M., 1960, The effect of threat upon interpersonal bargaining, *Journal of Abnormal and Social Psychology*, **61**:181–189.

Deutsch, M., and Krauss, R.M., 1962, Studies of interpersonal bargaining, *Journal of Conflict Resolution*, **6**:52–76.

Deutsch, M., and Lewicki, R.J., 1970, "Locking-in" effects during a game of chicken, *Journal of Conflict Resolution*, **14**:367–378.

Deutsch, K.W., and Singer, J.D., 1964, Multiple power systems and international stability, *World Politics*, **16**(3).

Doran, C., 1995, *Systems in Crisis*, Cambridge University Press, New York.

Druckman, D., ed., 1977, *Negotiations, Social-Psychological Perspectives*, Sage Publications, Beverly Hills, CA.

Duffy, G., et al., 1998, Language games, *International Studies Quarterly*, **32**:273.

Dwyer, R.T., and Walker, D.C., 1981, Bargaining in an asymmetric power structure, *Journal of Marketing*, **55**(1):104–115.

Faure, G.O., et al., 1998, *La négociation*, Nathan, Paris.

Fox, A.B., 1959, *The Power of Small States*, University of Chicago Press, Chicago.

Habeeb, W.M., 1988, *Power and Tactics in International Negotiation: How Weak Nations Bargain with Strong Nations*, Johns Hopkins University Press, Baltimore, MD.

Hammerstein, P., 1981, The role of asymmetries in animal contests, *Animal Behavior*, **29**(1):193–205.

Hammerstein, P., and Parker, G.A., 1982, The asymmetric war of attrition, *Journal of Theoretical Biology*, **96**(4):647–682.

Hart, J., 1976, Three approaches to the measurement of power in international relations, *International Organization*, **30**(2):289–305.

Hewitt, P.G., 1985, *Conceptual Physics*, 5th edition, Little Brown, Boston, MA.

Hobbes, T., 1651/1964, *The Leviathan*, Washington Square Press, New York.

Keohane, R.O., and Nye, J.S., 1989, *Power and Interdependence*, 2nd edition, Scott Foresman, Boston, MA.

Kim, S.H., 1991, *Conflict, Negotiation, and Dispute Resolution: An Annotated Bibliography*, PON Books, Cambridge, MA.

Kim, S.H., and Smith, R.H., 1993, Revenge and conflict escalation, *Negotiation Journal*, **9**:37–43.

Knorr, K.E., 1975, *The Power of Nations*, Basic, New York.

Komorita, S.S., and Barnes, M., 1969, Effects of pressures to reach agreement in bargaining, *Journal of Personality and Social Psychology*, **13**:245–252.

Komorita, S.S., and Nagao, D., 1983, The functions of resources in coalition bargaining, *Journal of Personality and Social Psychology*, **34**(1):95–106.

Kritek, P.B., 1994, *Negotiating at an Uneven Table*, Jossey-Bass, San Francisco, CA.

Lawler, E.J., Ford, R.S., and Blegen, M.A., 1988, Coercive capability in conflict: A test of bilateral deterrence versus conflict spiral theory, *Social Psychology Quarterly*, **51**:93–107.

Lockhart, C., 1979, *Bargaining in International Conflicts*, Columbia University Press, New York.

Luterbacher, L., 1999, Political rationalities, in I.W. Zartman, ed., *The Concepts of Politics*, Macmillan, New York.

Maoz, Z., 1989, Power, capabilities and paradoxical conflict outcomes, *World Politics*, **41**(2):238–264.

Maynard Smith, J., 1982, *Evolution and the Theory of Games*, Cambridge University Press, Cambridge, UK.

Michels, R., 1962, *Political Parties*, Free Press, New York.

Michener, H.A., Vaske, J.J., Schleifer, S.L., Plazewski, J.G., and Chapman, L.J., 1975, Factors affecting concession rate and threat usage in bilateral conflict, *Sociometry*, **38**(1):62–80.

Mitchell, C.R., 1995, Asymmetry and strategies of regional conflict reduction, in I.W. Zartman and V.A. Kremenyuk, eds., *Cooperative Security*, Syracuse University Press, Syracuse, NY.

Morgan, T.C., 1994, *Untying the Knot of War*, University of Michigan Press, Ann Arbor.

Morgenthau, H., 1948, *Politics Among Nations*, Knopf, New York.

Murnigham, K., 1985, Coalitions in decision-making groups, *Organizational Behavior and Human Decision Processes*, **35**(1):1–26.

Olson, M., 1965, *The Logic of Collective Action*, Harvard University Press, Cambridge, MA.

Organski, A.F.K., 1968, *World Politics*, Knopf, New York.

Paul, T.V., 1994, *Asymmetric Conflicts: User Initiation by Weaker Powers*, Cambridge University Press, New York.

Pruitt, D.G., and Carnevale, P., 1993, *Negotiation in Social Conflict*, Brooks/Cole, Pacific Grove, CA.

Raiffa, H., 1982, *The Art and Science of Negotiation*, Harvard University Press, Cambridge, MA.

Raven, B.H., and Kruglanski, A.W., 1970, Conflict and power: The structure of conflict, in Swingle, P., ed., *The Structure of Conflict*, Academic Press, New York, pp. 69–109.

Raven, B.H., and Rubin, J.Z., 1983, *Social Psychology*, 2nd edition, John Wiley & Sons, Inc., New York.

Ross, M.C., 1993, *The Management of Conflict*, Yale University Press, New Haven, CT.

Rothman, M.A., 1963, *The Laws of Physics*, Fawcett, New York.

Rothstein, R., 1977, *The Weak in the World of the Strong*, Columbia University Press, New York.

Rubin, J.Z., and Brown, B.R., 1975, *The Social Psychology of Bargaining and Negotiation*, Academic Press, New York.

Rubin, J.Z., and Zartman, I.W., 1995, Asymmetrical negotiations: Some survey results that may surprise, *Negotiation Journal*, **11**(4):349–364.

Rubin, J.Z., Pruitt, D.G., and Kim, S.H., 1994, *Social Conflict: Escalation, Stalemate, and Settlement*, 2nd edition, McGraw-Hill, New York.

Schelling, T.C., 1960, *The Strategy of Conflict*, Harvard University Press, Cambridge, MA.

Simon, H., 1953, Notes on the observation and measurement of power, *Journal of Politics*, **153**:500–516.

Singer, M., 1972, *Weak States in a World of Powers*, Free Press, New York.

Snyder, G., and Diesing, P., 1977, *Conflict among Nations*, Princeton University Press, Princeton, NJ.

Stein, J., and Pauly, L., 1993, *Choosing to Cooperate*, Johns Hopkins University Press, Baltimore, MD.

Stoll, R., and Ward, M., 1989, *Power in World Politics*, Lynn Rienner, Boulder, CO.

Stolte, J., 1978, Internationalization: A bargaining network approach, *Journal for the Theory of Social Behavior*, **8**(2):297–312.

Stolte, J., 1983, The legitimization of structural inequalities, *American Sociological Review*, **48**(2):331–342.

Tawney, R.H., 1931/1952, *Equality*, Unwin, London.

Tedeschi, J., 1970, Threats and promises, in P. Swingle, ed., *The Structure of Conflict*, Academic Press, New York.

Telhami, S., 1990, *Power and Leadership in International Bargaining*, Columbia University Press, New York.

Thibaut, J.W., and Kelley, H.H., 1959, *The Social Psychology of Groups*, John Wiley & Sons, Inc., New York.

von Clausewitz, C., 1832/1968, *On War*, Penguin, New York.

Waltz, K., 1954, *Man, the State, and War*, Columbia University Press, New York.

Waltz, K., 1979, *Theory of International Politics*, Random House, New York.

Wriggins, W.H., 1987, Up for auction, in I.W. Zartman, ed., *The 50% Solution*, Yale University Press, New Haven, CT, USA.

Wrong, D.H., 1980, *Power: Its Forms, Bases, and Uses*, Harper Colophon, New York.

Young, O.R., 1967, *The Intermediaries*, Princeton University Press, Princeton, NJ.

Zartman, I.W., 1971, *The Politics of Trade Negotiations Between Africa and the European Economic Community: The Weak Confront the Strong*, Princeton University Press, Princeton, NJ.

Zartman, I.W., 1974, The political analysis of negotiation: How who gets to what and when, *World Politics*, **26**(3):385–399.

Zartman, I.W., ed., 1987, *Positive Sum: Improving North–South Negotiations*, Transaction Books, New Brunswick, NJ.

Zartman, I.W., 1997, The structuralist dilemma in negotiation, in R.J. Lewicki, R.J. Bies, and B.H. Sheppard, eds., *Research on Negotiation in Organizations*, JAI Press, Greenwich, CT.

Zartman, I.W., and Berman, M., 1982, *The Practical Negotiator*, Yale University Press, New Haven, CT.

Zartman, I.W., et al., 1996, Negotiation as a search for justice, *International Negotiation*, **1**(1):79–98.

Part II

Cases of Asymmetry

This section presents seven cases of asymmetrical negotiations, typical of the most common type in which one party has greater resources and is perceived as being stronger by itself and by its opposite. The first three of these cases – involving the United States negotiating with Canada, Indonesia, and Egypt – feature the remaining superpower, hence the strongest of the individual states; in one case the weaker party is a next-door neighbor, locked in a geographical relationship, whereas in the other two cases, the weaker parties are far away but are part of a political relationship that is important to all sides. In a fourth case, there is an assortment of stronger powers – in descending order, the European Community (now Union), France, and Spain – all pitted against tiny, and not even sovereign, Andorra. Again, to a political relationship is added geographical propinquity. The fifth case involves one of the largest Third World countries, India, negotiating with its small, up-river neighbor, Nepal. In the sixth case, Israel – small, equipped, organized, and motivated – and the Arab states – fragmented, large and surrounding, factious, disorganized – negotiated after battles over the 30 years covered here (and ongoing); the negotiations ended in a clear victory, but the loser was left alive to revive the contest and the victor was unable to achieve a negotiated outcome that was equivalent to the battlefield victory. The equalizing factor that overcame the battlefield asymmetry came from external balancers and relations. Finally, the last case pits the collective strong – the industrialized North or the First World – against the collective weak – the developing South or Third World. There was never any doubt in anyone's mind of the asymmetry in these sets of relationships.

In all cases, negotiation was desired by both sides and a negotiated agreement was in both sides' interest. An alternative means of achieving an agreement through the use of force was ruled out for many reasons – the norms of international relations, the inappropriateness of the means of force to the ends desired, the destructive effects of force on the valued relationship, or, in the Middle East case, the fact that it had already been used inconclusively. Thus, despite its asymmetry, the situation was ideal for negotiation. Indeed, the mutual desire for an outcome and for one that was satisfactory to both sides, for its own sake and for the sake of the ongoing relationship, worked to even the sides a bit. The sides were further evened by allowing the weaker party to press firmly – even audaciously – for the jointly valued agreement and by ruling out harsh retaliation by the stronger party. Nonetheless, these efforts to even the sides did not alter the basic asymmetry between the parties.

Each case had its idiosyncrasies. Some cases were relatively brief or at least specific. The US–Canada Free Trade Agreement was negotiated under a congressional two-year deadline; this is the same amount of time it took to address the US–Indonesian aid issue over trade with the Communist China. The UN Conference on Environment and Development only took a week, although its four Preparatory Committee meetings took place over two years. The trade agreement over Andorra, however, took eight years, marked – and sparked – by a number of contextual changes; the US–Egyptian aid relationship and even some of its salient issues has covered a decade and a half and an agreement is still to be reached; the North and South have been plugging away at development issues for decades; and the India–Nepal tractations over the Ganges water system is an epic tale of folkloric dimensions. Trade, aid, and resource sharing are the various broad issue areas. The Arab–Israeli negotiations punctuated a 20th-century 30-years' war for some participants and a 50-years' war for others.

As a result, outcomes have varied. In most cases, a mutually prized agreement was achieved, and both sides were satisfied with the results. The US–Canada Free Trade Agreement was ratified by the US Congress, supported by a Canadian election that served as a referendum, and then expanded to include Mexico in the North American Free Trade Agreement, with other countries pressing for inclusion as well. Andorra, too, got its trade agreement with the European Community and achieved its goals within it, without any concomitant loss for its negotiating partners. Aid to Egypt and to Indonesia continues, the relationship has been maintained, and troubling issues have been handled with some satisfaction.

Nevertheless, the Himalayan saga goes on without any agreement on the numerous sites that could be turned into hydroelectric and irrigation dams and – as often happens – delay has only made things more complicated, as democratization has brought new criteria of accountability and new parties into the negotiations. The weaker Nepal, which before effectively played its power to delay and deny, has in the process become strengthened by the need to have any agreement run the gauntlet of its opposition parties and pass approval by parliament. But the achievement of a mutually satisfactory result has not been hastened or facilitated as a result, and those agreements that have been achieved are not as satisfying to Nepalese as they are to Indians. Similarly, the North–South dialogue of the deaf continues, with only marginal progress in getting the South to pay attention to environmental issues or the North to get involved in development issues. The outcomes of the Arab–Israeli negotiations kept the defeated party alive at least to negotiate and sometimes to fight another day.

One way of summarizing the relation between behavioral or bargaining power and outcomes is to note that in all cases the strength of the weaker party was a function of the strength of the stronger party's desire for an outcome. If the stronger wanted an outcome badly enough, it would pay for it and the weaker had increased power to name the price, since the stronger could not achieve its goal by force. Usually, this is an overstatement, to be sure: The weak could not name just any price. Nevertheless, it did have the increased ability to get more for its agreement than it previously appeared – binding arbitration that leveled the playing field for the future in the Canadian case, debt forgiveness and less interference in internal inefficiencies for Egypt, unavowed trade with China for Indonesia, treatment as if sovereign and other items such as refusal of unionization for Andorra, and exceptions to environmental norms for the South. In most cases, the now-less-stronger party was quite satisfied with what it got in exchange.

It is noteworthy that each result was usually not so much a loss or shift of benefits from one side to the other as a lessened agreement in general. The scope of the agreement was adjusted to the demands of the weaker side. In exchange for the inclusion of some demands, the scope of the whole agreement was narrowed. Although both sides received more than they would have had without an agreement – the outcome was an improvement on both sides' security point – the agreement was less than it could have been if the maximum demands of the parties had been combined – the outcome was less than Pareto-optimal. Canada gave up its demand for an entirely revised trade relationship in exchange for its juridical dispute settlement procedures; a "little" equalization and improvement rather than a "big" equalization and improvement in the trade relationship was achieved. The North and South did not achieve a broad agreement handling environmental and developmental issues, although in exchange for some specific concessions on each side – some meager development financing measures from the North and some limited and delayed adherence to environmental restrictions from the South – framework agreements and narrower action plans were put into effect. Indonesia and Egypt, and the United States did not achieve full efficient development in exchange for full security cooperation, although some progress was made on both counts, in one area in exchange for the other.

Nepal did not receive full and fair payment – in money or in benefits – for agreeing to the huge dams that Indian needs required, even though it did receive some benefits. Egypt and Israel, on different occasions, did not overthrow the results of the particular war, but they did achieve results that their defeat would not have predicted. The parties accepted what they could agree to and settled for that, getting something for the weak as well as the strong, but gave up the hope of broad encompassing agreements. But, after all, negotiation aims at avoiding the extremes of all or nothing at all, to achieve something for each.

To exchange benefits, both weaker and stronger parties exercised power as actions, and such actions were not restricted to the stronger side. Concessions were attracted, paired, and paid for by actions of the parties, without which the concessions would not have been made. Formulas were established embodying terms of trade – mutual concession areas indicating where actions would elicit appropriate positive counteractions. Not only were actions taken against each other; they were also made – or paid – against the other party's need, against the two parties' relationship, against the asymmetric interdependence of the two sides, or against relationships with an interested third party. Finally, such activities also included inactivities (Bachrach and Baratz 1962), negative uses of power to delay agreement and withhold assent. The balance sheet of these actions in an asymmetrical relationship are drawn in detail in the conclusions, for it shows that certain actions were more generally available to and used by weaker states and other actions were used more often by the stronger parties.

Reference

Bachrach, P., and Baratz, M., 1962, Two faces of power, *American Political Science Review*, **56**(4):947–952.

Chapter 2

Asymmetry in Negotiating the Canada–US Free Trade Agreement, 1985–1987

Gilbert R. Winham and Elizabeth DeBoer-Ashworth

On 3 October 1987, Canada and the United States signed the "Elements" of a Free Trade Agreement (FTA) designed to liberalize the largest bilateral trade relationship in the world. The skeletal agreement concluded a difficult two-year negotiation that had been initiated by the Conservative government of Prime Minister Brian Mulroney. The "Elements" of the FTA were converted into a formal legal agreement by December 1987, and US congressional approval of the deal followed without substantial difficulty. In Canada, acceptance of the FTA was postponed until the Conservative government won a new mandate in the bitterly fought election of autumn 1988.

The FTA is an interesting story from many perspectives. Economically, the Agreement broke new ground by highlighting the importance of services, investment, and energy in a trade agreement, whereas legally the FTA promoted the importance of dispute settlement in establishing a rules-based trading system. However, one of the most interesting aspects

is how Canada, with a medium-sized economy, could single-handedly negotiate a trade agreement with an economic superpower like the United
States. The United States dominates Canada economically, and its population is 10 times Canada's. Strategically, the defense capability of the
United States dwarfs that of Canada, and culturally American literature,
music, and films pervade Canadian markets. Despite these imbalances,
which one might expect to influence the negotiating process, the two
countries concluded an agreement that was effectively subjected to a national referendum in Canada in the 1988 elections. There is no more
severe test that democratic governments can give a diplomatic agreement
than to make that agreement the subject of a national vote. Opponents
of the FTA strongly argued that Canada had been out-negotiated by the
United States: Had they convinced Canadians of this charge, it is unlikely
the Conservatives would have won a new mandate to implement the FTA.

Occasionally, the weaker party, quite the opposite of being over-
whelmed or submissive in a negotiation, actually acquires more concessions than would be expected given its asymmetrical power base. Such
is the situation with certain dispute settlement procedures of the Canada–
US FTA. Canada, as the weaker power, had an interest in engaging the
United States in a rules-based rather than a power-based relationship, and
it viewed a strong dispute settlement mechanism as one way to achieve
this. Essentially, the test of the mechanism was whether it could produce
legally binding results as opposed to results that had to be accepted by
the parties before they could be implemented.

The FTA established binding procedures in two areas. One area is
safeguards [that is, emergency or escape clause action pursuant to Article XIX of the General Agreement on Tariffs and Trade (GATT)]. The
FTA states that if consultations between Canada and the United States
are unsuccessful regarding a trade dispute on safeguards, then that safeguard action shall be taken to binding arbitration. This means that a decision made by an international arbitral panel can hold both Canada and
the United States to its decision, notwithstanding the views of national
agencies. This type of concession is a substantial reduction of the United
States' sovereignty, as well as Canada's. Canadian trade lawyer Debra
Steger remarked: "The ability of an international panel to review and
make binding decisions concerning a country's use of safeguards measures . . . is without precedent in any international agreement" (Steger
n.d.:19). This procedure might have been very important to Canada in

a dispute in the shakes and shingles industry, which actually occurred during the negotiations of the FTA.

An even more important area of binding authority is defined in Chapter 19 of the binational panel reviews, which replaced judicial review by national courts in cases of antidumping and countervailing.[1] Binational panels are five-member committees of trade experts drawn from both Canada and the United States. Their task is to review the antidumping and countervailing actions of domestic agencies and to determine inter alia whether an agency's action was supported by evidence or was in accordance with law. Binational panels have the power to reverse an agency's action, and the decisions of a panel are final and cannot be appealed to a national court. Since the FTA came into existence in 1989, Canada has challenged actions by US agencies in over 40 cases, of which about half have resulted in a partial or complete reversal of the agency's action. In sum, binational panels are unique in international trade law and they represent an important step toward a rules-based relationship. In a world of sovereign nations, the panels are regarded as a significant concession by the stronger party to the weaker party.

This chapter addresses the following question: How did Canada manage to get binding dispute settlement included in the FTA, considering that the provision constrains the sovereignty of the United States, recognized as the more powerful partner in the negotiations? The theme that developed is one in which power, while seen as an asymmetrical (HL) relationship at a high level, does not appear in negotiations as a finite constant, but as actions that can change depending on the issue, the negotiating partner, and the international context. The actions available to one partner to move another are greatly affected by issues, parties, and context, and this is especially true for small states. Systemic factors (such as the international context of negotiations) set important parameters that small states must take into account in formulating their strategy. Systemic realities provide the important backdrop of the international system that promotes or discourages negotiation. Once a situation that facilitates small state/large state negotiation exists, the relationship between the negotiating parties and the issue being negotiated become paramount.

To explore these themes more fully we examine successively the perceptions and positions taken by Canada and the United States. In the conclusion we return to the question of Canada's success in achieving binding dispute settlement and attempt to explain the outcome based on the available evidence.

2.1   Canada's Position

The Canadian position on the FTA negotiations had a long history growing out of the realization of its international vulnerability and increasing dependence on the US market. Because Canada's small population
inhabits a large land mass, production of goods for a domestic market
has had limited potential. To maintain a reasonable standard of living
Canada has had to export. During the first half of this century Canadian exports focused on Great Britain, whose percentage of foreign investment in the Canadian economy was 85% in 1900 (Morici 1991:22).
The United States in contrast owned only 14% of foreign investment in
Canada. However, since World War II the US share of foreign investment, as well as Canadian exports to the United States, has increased to
more than 75% (Morici 1991:22). The FTA, therefore, was not so much a
recognition of export dependency as an acceptance that the United States
had become Canada's dominant economic interest.

   The historic process of deciding that Canada's interests lay with the
United States reveals the prominence and high-level attention the Canadian government invested in this issue. Discussions regarding free trade
and the relationship with the United States have not always ended in
closer economic ties; however, there is no denying that on the Canadian
side the issue has attracted mass concern, and successive governments
have treated it as an issue deserving consideration at the highest level.
The Laurier government of 1911, for instance, negotiated a reciprocity
(free trade) agreement with the US government. This provoked a heated
domestic debate and caused Sir Wilfred Laurier to lose an election to Sir
Robert Borden of the Conservatives. Although the issue of free trade was
often raised during the depression of the 1930s and later after World War
II, the only major success at reaching an agreement was the Canada–US
Automotive Products Trade Agreement (the Auto Pact) of 1965. Once the
Auto Pact was implemented, trade in the automotive sector increased 24
times until more than one-third of all US–Canadian trade is in this sector
(Trezise 1988:16–23). So while the topic of free trade remained a sensitive issue, the Canadian economy was becoming increasingly dependent
on the US market for its major exports.

   Incentives to negotiate the existing FTA grew out of the unstable economic conditions in the 1970s, which were followed by the 1981–1982
recession. The Liberal government of Pierre Trudeau decided that, in
light of the economic recession, work needed to be done to uncover the
roots of Canada's economic malaise. As a result a Royal Commission was

established, under the chairmanship of Donald Macdonald, with a mandate to find the sources of Canada's problems and to make recommendations for future economic policy. The Macdonald Commission carried out the largest reevaluation of its kind in Canadian history. The findings of the Commission indicated that Canada's difficulties lay firmly in its trade policy (Macdonald 1991:155–161). Not only was Canada the most trade-dependent nation of the major countries in the Organisation for Economic Co-operation and Development (OECD), but its economic profile was also analogous to some resource-exporting developing countries (External Affairs 1983:26). To make the Canadian economy more competitive and to increase manufacturing, large economies of scale were needed; one of the Commission's main policy suggestions, therefore, was for Canada to negotiate bilateral free trade with the United States (Winham 1988:17).

The Macdonald Commission had been established by a Liberal government, but its findings were embraced in 1985 by the ruling Conservative party of Brian Mulroney. The Commission's report tended to fall in line with the ethos of the Conservative government, which wished to rely more on market forces rather than government intervention to stimulate the economy. Additional studies undertaken by the Mulroney government tended to reaffirm the Macdonald report's findings, and as a result the government decided to initiate a free trade negotiation with the United States (External Affairs 1985a).

The need for freer trade was also driven home to Canada by the rise of protectionism in the United States. The economic reevaluation illustrated Canada's reliance on the United States; however, at the same time, strong protectionist forces were running through America. These forces found their outlet in formal complaints of unfair trading practices that often resulted in the use of countervailing duties and other penalties being directed toward Canadian companies (Schott and Smith 1988:42). The worry about US countervailing actions, coupled with a renewed realization of Canada's dependence on the American market, resulted in market access – protected from arbitrary trade remedies – being a major Canadian concern in a free trade agreement.[2]

The formal decision to pursue a free trade agreement with the United States was announced by Prime Minister Mulroney in the House of Commons on 26 September 1985. The Canadian initiative was brought to US President Ronald Reagan, who in turn handed the matter over to Congress. While waiting for congressional approval on the American side, the Canadian government lost no time in establishing a new bureaucracy to deal specifically with obtaining a free trade agreement. The prime minister appointed Simon Reisman, former senior official from the Department of Finance, as the chief negotiator. Reisman was given authority to establish a large ad hoc organization called the trade negotiations office (TNO). The TNO was given access to the highest levels of government and reported directly to the Cabinet. During the next 16 months this organization negotiated hard to achieve a deal with the United States (Bowker 1988:17). The official goals of Canada in the bilateral negotiations were to (External Affairs 1985a:25–27):

1. Enhance access to the US market by eliminating tariffs and liberalizing nontariff barriers and to attempt to remove US discrimination in federal and state procurement, product standards, patents, and copyrights.
2. Secure access to the US market by limiting the effects of US trade remedy laws and obtaining possible exemption from the US safeguard measures aimed at third countries along with an agreed-upon definition of the countervailing subsidy.
3. Enshrine these negotiated measures in a strong agreement with an effective dispute settlement mechanism.
4. Maintain policy discretion in sensitive sectors such as cultural industries and foreign investment.

The combination of a clear plan and the negotiators' access to the highest levels of government were the strengths of the Canadian position. During the months of negotiations Canadian officials could count on an immediate response from their government whenever US negotiators reacted negatively to a Canadian initiative. The many trade disputes that were running alongside the negotiations made the negotiators, in tandem with the politicians in Ottawa, solidify their opinion that the dispute settlement mechanism was the most important concession to be achieved.[3] The negotiators and the government were working together in a way that did not exist on the US side. As a result, the Canadian contingent was very aware of why Canada was negotiating (market access) and what specifically they wanted from the deal (protection through a dispute settlement mechanism).

The Conservative government saw the FTA as an absolute need for Canadian economic survival. Such was their commitment that in Canada's 1988 national elections the Conservatives were willing to let their government stand or fall on the issue of free trade (Pammett 1989). By the time the election campaign was in full swing the "Elements" of the FTA had already been signed (External Affairs 1987). The negotiations had been arduous, and one of the most common complaints from Reisman was that Canada could not get the United States to take the negotiations seriously. The issue of a dispute settlement mechanism was seen as paramount by the Canadians and next to nonnegotiable by the Americans. Because Canada had placed so much importance on the dispute settlement, it regarded the lack of response from the United States as intransigence on *the* fundamental element of the Canadian position. Therefore, on 23 September 1987, Reisman walked away from the table and suspended the free trade talks. This action, in effect, pushed the negotiations up on the American side to the governmental level that existed in Canada. Provoked by this diplomatic crisis situation, the US side quickly handed responsibility over to Treasury Secretary James Baker, who was very influential with various US agencies as well as with the president.

Considering the efforts made to reach an agreement on dispute settlement, once this had been achieved the Conservatives would not back away from the agreement even with national elections looming. In the end the Conservatives were successful in winning 170 of the 295 seats in Parliament on 21 November 1988 (Doern and Tomlin 1991:238). This election then paved the way for ratification of the FTA, which subsequently was approved and implemented in 1989. The Canadian negotiating team had been successful in reaching the goal laid down by its government: Canada had a free trade agreement complete with a dispute settlement mechanism.

2.2   United States' Position

The FTA negotiations were not a policy watershed for the United States in the same way they were for Canada. The initiative for the negotiations came from the Canadian side. Because of the more passive role taken by the United States during the early period of negotiations, the Americans lacked a grand scheme for the negotiations and they were happy to let Canada do the leg work. It was not that the United States was against an agreement; it was that the US government recognized that an over-enthusiastic response might stimulate a nationalistic response on the Canadian side and, therefore, poison the negotiations before they got started.

The history of Canadian angst toward free trade does not have a parallel in the United States. Since World War II, Americans have been more interested in liberalizing trade internationally rather than just on a regional basis. The US Congress accepted the bilateral approach reluctantly, not so much because it liked the idea of freer trade with Canada as because it had become disillusioned with GATT. After the failure of the 1982 GATT ministerial meeting, many members of Congress felt that entering into negotiations with Canada could be both a wake-up call to the European Community and a low-budget fallback in case the GATT talks broke down completely (Schott 1983). Even after President Reagan received approval to conduct the Canada–US free trade negotiations, his administration treated the deal as something alongside GATT, and not as something to supplant it.

The FTA gave the United States an opportunity for clearing up some minor trade irritants between itself and Canada. It also allowed a certain degree of experimentation regarding the liberalization of areas such as investment and services that had been stumbling blocks for the broader multilateral talks of GATT (Schott and Smith 1988). The trade "irritants" experienced by the United States were some of the few clear-cut reasons for agreeing to negotiate a trade deal with Canada. Canadian policies in the decade prior to the negotiations had stymied US investment in certain sectors through policies of screening and regulating foreign investment and also through the treatment of foreign-owned firms under the National Energy Policy (Leyton-Brown 1985).

Beyond the notion that the Canada–US talks offered a chance to resolve some trade problems between the two states, the incentives to negotiate were less clear. The United States was not dependent on the Canadian market in the same way that Canada was dependent on the United States. "One party's power is another party's dependency" (Pruitt and Carnevale 1993:131). Even though Canada was the United States' largest trading partner it accounted for less than 20% of total US trade (Winham 1988:20). However, ideologically the Reagan administration did not want to smother another country's attempt at trade liberalization, especially since this was precisely what the United States had been trying to achieve internationally. Nevertheless, the free trade negotiations remained a Canadian initiative and as such were not a goal that the United States had specified for itself.

The above reasons explain why Reagan requested "fast-track" approval for a trade negotiation with Canada, but the meager 10–10 vote of the Senate Finance Committee also showed that Congress doubted the usefulness of the deal.[4] In reality the worries of US policymakers were closer to home. The huge US deficit and the domestic problems it created were seen as issues of vital importance by Congress, and President Reagan's foreign-policy request for fast-track approval was seen as a poor attempt to sidestep this major debate in the United States (*Toronto Globe and Mail* 1986). There were also criticisms regarding the lack of a focused international trade policy for the United States.

Whatever the reasons may have been in 1986, one thing is clear; in the grand scheme of things, the Canadian negotiations were expendable in contrast with the other broader problems in the United States. Even the Reagan administration, which had gone to Congress for fast-track approval for free trade, did not place these negotiations high on its agenda, and Congress was even less interested.

The subordinate nature of the free trade negotiations in the United States was reflected in the type of organization used to set up its negotiating team. Peter Murphy, a former US textile negotiator and then US ambassador to GATT, was made chief negotiator. However, Murphy's access to administrative backup, information, and high levels of government was minimal. He had full-time access to only one other officer, William Merkin of the Office of the US Trade Representative (USTR). The two of them could rely only on specialized help from many different US government departments and were not given the political authority to cut through normal bureaucratic resistance, which their Canadian counterparts had (Winham 1988:25).

Once fast-track approval had been given and the negotiations began, public debate on the issue within the United States almost disappeared. The closer the negotiations came to finishing, the more the differences between the US and Canadian teams came to the fore. While the Canadian side had secure access to senior officials, such was not the case for the Americans. Canada also continually tried to raise the process to a higher political level whenever possible. The Canadians took advantage of the summit meetings between President Reagan and Prime Minister Mulroney, as well as the Venice Economic Summit in June 1987, by pressing for a dispute settlement mechanism and other issues.

The US response to Canadian pressure was mixed. In President Reagan's State of the Union address in January 1987 a reference was made to a need to complete a "historic free-trade agreement" between Canada and the United States (Gherson 1987). This statement seemed to suggest that at least the talks were on the administration's agenda. However, in August when talks were the most intense a lengthy *New York Times* summary of the US administration's priorities never mentioned the Canada–US trade talks, even though interviews were held with senior White House staff members.

It was this lack of interest that was perceived on the Canadian side as intransigence and prompted Canada to suspend the talks. Canadian negotiator Reisman was intensely critical of the strategy employed by the United States, saying "there was nobody really in charge in the United States" (Waddell and Lewington 1987). This comment did not help the negotiations and deepened the existing dislike of Reisman by the American team. However, the result of the Canadian walkout was to push up the talks within the US administration and Treasury Secretary Baker took responsibility for the negotiations. The American lack of enthusiasm for a binding dispute settlement contributed to the Canadian walkout, creating a diplomatic crisis. The US negotiators' position was an awkward one; the ball was in their court, but only by giving in on dispute settlement could they get the Canadians to come back to the negotiating table.

Many Americans, not without reason, accused Canada of grandstanding. Nevertheless, the Canadian tactic of walking away from the table did make the US administration take a hard look at the proposed agreement; US leaders recognized that not only would the deal be to their benefit, but if the free trade talks failed the image of the Reagan administration would be dealt a damaging blow. The upshot of the breakdown in free trade talks on 23 September 1987, was a flurry of activity on the American side to try to salvage something. Treasury Secretary Baker spent the following two weeks attempting to find a solution to the deadlock that would be acceptable to both parties. The intensity of the negotiations during this period was reminiscent of a marathon, and it was not until Baker's offer to Canada was accepted, just before a midnight deadline on 3 October 1987, that the free trade deal had any kind of certain future.

What made a deal possible was Canadian concessions on a number of issues, such as tariffs, investments, and financial services. Canada also backed away from trying to negotiate a subsidies code. Once this flexibility had been exhibited, chances were good that something could be salvaged from the talks regarding antidumping and countervailing, and that a dispute settlement could be worked out to deal with them.

The United States had, in effect, managed to gain some control over the Canadian trade irritants, which had been one of the main reasons for

US agreement to negotiate. Because the United States was the receptor – not the initiator – of the talks, its conception of what an agreement should be was narrower than Canada's. The Canadians treated the agreement almost as a positive rights-based economic constitution between the two countries. For Canada the FTA meant a new special relationship. The American conception was much more modest. The US officials aimed at removing a number of Canadian government trade-related practices that were causing friction between the two countries.

In the final analysis it was likely that the increasing political desire of the United States for an agreement, coupled with its perception that the agreement was not a big deal, allowed Canada to sell a binding dispute settlement mechanism whose principal aim was to protect Canada's existing access to the US market. In the final marathon session, after Treasury Secretary Baker took over the negotiations, the Americans recognized that the existing deal offered by Canada – ranging from autos to energy and investment – went a long way toward removing the trade irritants that the United States disliked. If the United States rejected this offer, it would undercut the hard-nosed position that US negotiators had taken in GATT. They had clearly stated that, in the absence of a multilateral deal in the Uruguay Round, the United States would proceed with bilateral agreements with its major trading partners. In this context the United States had a great deal at stake in concluding a deal with Canada, and this gave Canada the opportunity to win an important concession from the United States.

2.3 Analysis

In the case of the Canada–US FTA, the international system was one in which a country that knew itself to be weaker could propose and enter into an economic negotiation with a neighbor that knew itself to be stronger to set up an agreement that would be beneficial to the stronger party as well as itself. Canada being the smaller power did, however, have initial confines within which it had to work. Before going to the United States, therefore, it had to determine if its request would have been seen as reasonable by the United States and larger international communities (such as GATT). The suggestion of a free trade agreement, however, fell in line with the trade strategy of the United States and was not against the rules of GATT. The structural background of a negotiation, although not sufficient to predict success or failure, is very important in determining whether a negotiation would be possible at all. In the case of the FTA, the international system was not an impediment to negotiation, and agreement regarding certain norms such as liberalization of trade helped push the United States toward accepting Canada's offer to negotiate.

Once a situation exists that allows for negotiation, the relationship between the negotiating parties and the issue being negotiated become of primary importance. The asymmetrical relationship between Canada and the United States would seem on the surface to leave Canada in a very weak negotiating position. However, a superpower like the United States has a myriad of concerns. Its foreign policy is intrinsically multilateral. Even though its resources are many times larger than those of Canada, the United States cannot lift allocation of resources from other international projects and turn its full weight against Canada. As Jonsson (1981:249) has pointed out, many failures in predicting negotiation outcomes based on the power of the parties can be attributed "to the mistaken belief that resources useful in one issue-area will be equally useful in a different one." The United States, during the FTA negotiations, theoretically had many resources to call upon; however, its administration was more concerned with problems with GATT and its own domestic agenda vis-à-vis the government deficit. Canada and the FTA were not high among US foreign-policy objectives.

Although it was frustrating for Ottawa that the FTA was not a high foreign-policy priority for Washington, the situation nevertheless created an advantage for Canada. The US global presence and multilateral concerns did not allow that nation to be as assertive in negotiation as it might have been. As Andrew (1970:53) astutely pointed out in the 1970s, "Possibly the main advantage a small power's foreign minister has over his great power colleague is that he is not obliged to adopt a position on every international issue that arises." This observation still holds true in the 1990s. Canada had much more freedom than the United States to concentrate on the free trade negotiations because it had fewer and smaller international responsibilities. The comprehensiveness of the Macdonald Commission report and the focus of the Conservative government on the FTA could not have been replicated in the United States. Asymmetry of power is often inversely linked to asymmetry of attention. For example, US negotiator Murphy was able to command far fewer political and bureaucratic resources than his Canadian counterparts. Not only was an entire new bureaucracy established in Canada for the FTA negotiations, but the politicians in Ottawa were briefed and prepared in a way that did not exist in Washington.

The level of concentration given to a negotiation is an important element. The cohesion of the Canadian federal government and its bureaucracies allowed it to present a relatively unified facade to its US negotiating partners. The United States had its attention deflected by other concerns, such as internal debate on the general direction of US trade policy and external discussions on policies such as the need to demonstrate that the United States could make progress in trade liberalization through bilateral agreements at a time when multilateral negotiations in GATT were moving slowly. In comparison with Canada, the US negotiating effort came across as disjointed, thus occasioning Reisman's comment lamenting that there did not seem to be anyone in charge in the United States.

Hoffman (1978:215) put it well when he recognized that a powerful state has "to disperse its attention over a huge number of chessboards and players and cannot always keep its own internal bureaucratic coalitions together." The Canadian government, however, recognized that the United States was its major game. Without the US market, Canada's standard of living would suffer. Because of the perception by the Canadian government that an agreement was of vital importance, it was able to exert all its effort to obtain a deal, and it was willing to take the risk of pushing hard to get an agreement on a binding dispute settlement mechanism. By contrast, the United States expended less effort on the negotiations, and it did not perceive the negotiations as raising issues of high stakes for the US system.

Given all these points, the reasons for Canada's success in negotiating binding dispute settlement into the FTA become clearer. First, the international context of the negotiations was conducive to initiatives toward liberalizing trade. Even though this did not guarantee Canadian success at the bargaining table, it did allow for smaller power actions. Second, the Canadian government made use of this initiative by establishing its goals through internal research such as the Macdonald Commission report and, therefore, focusing on the issue of free trade to gain secure access to the US market. Third, the relationship between the United States and Canada allowed for a more focused Canadian effort toward the United States, while the United States was preoccupied with its larger international and domestic concerns. In sum, Canada was able to define legitimate and defensible goals in the eyes of its negotiating partner, and to pursue those goals in a focused and determined manner.

Not every small state will have the same success as Canada. However, by recognizing the importance of these three points – international context, issue focus, and relationship with a larger power that may have concerns elsewhere – a small state can take actions and make substantial gains toward reaching goals that at first glance would seem impossible.

2.4 Conclusion

The FTA negotiations were an example of bargaining between parties with asymmetrical powers. In this case, power asymmetry was probably an aggregate perception, more important in the period prior to the negotiations than during the negotiations. For example, it is likely that the use by the United States of antidumping and countervailing duty measures against Canada encouraged the latter to negotiate in order, as the Canadian government said, to *secure* the access to the US market it had already achieved. Of course, Canada could have retaliated with antidumping and countervailing duties against US products, but the discrepancy in size between the two economies meant such action would have little deterrent effect. Thus, in the prenegotiation phase, the United States appeared to take actions based on its superior power, which had some effect in encouraging a weaker party to negotiate; there is evidence that this power tactic was recognized by Canadian leaders and that it led to a desire to negotiate a resolution to this problem.

Once the negotiations began, the situation at the bargaining table was rendered less asymmetrical than that which was perceived in the overall relationship; in other words, a threshold was crossed in which a perceived asymmetric economic-power relationship did not automatically translate into an asymmetric negotiating-power relationship. The reason for this is that in economic negotiations the goal is usually to establish an agreement from which both parties can gain, and therefore the main power resource that a party can rely on is the power to say "no." Both small and large countries can take advantage of this power, for it is based not on economic size, but on the attractiveness of the respective offers and the extent to which the parties lose their indifference toward a prospective agreement. On this dimension, the Canadians – motivated in part by self-interest – offered the Americans an attractive package, which in turn increased Canada's bargaining leverage in the negotiation.

Anecdotal evidence shows that the parties perceived they had crossed a power threshold when they commenced negotiating. First, during the FTA negotiations two independent agencies of the US government took a highly visible countervailing duty action against Canada's major lumber exports. This action was untimely, it was not intended by US negotiators, and it was nearly fatal to the negotiations. Both sides undertook efforts to minimize the incident, and *both* claimed it underscored the need to establish a better understanding, as well as a dispute settlement system, between Canada and the United States. Thus, what might have been perceived by both sides as a power action before the negotiation was instead viewed by both as an unfortunate accident during the negotiations. Second, it is probable the Canadian government perceived it had achieved a situation of relative power with the United States, largely owing to the attractiveness of its offers on energy, investment, and market access (i.e., all areas where the United States had concrete interest groups pushing specific negotiating demands). The perceptions of Canada's power in this particular context, situation, and relationship led the US government to raise its negotiating effort to the Cabinet level to accommodate specific Canadian demands on dispute settlement. The Canadian strategy was risky, but it was born of a careful assessment of the negotiating power Canada was able to muster in this unique circumstance.

Two other elements increased Canada's power as the parties crossed the threshold into formal negotiations. One entailed the manner in which the United States entered the negotiations, and the other entailed the manner in which Canada negotiated once the process was under way. The United States entered the process partly to demonstrate to its GATT partners that it was willing to conclude trade-liberalizing agreements with other countries willing to do likewise. This strategy was undoubtedly intended to put pressure on the Europeans and the developing countries to be more accommodating in the GATT negotiations, but it also put pressure on the United States to accommodate Canadian demands, lest it appear that the United States was bluffing over its willingness to negotiate sub-GATT deals. It appears both sides appreciated the importance of these systemic/external constraints on the US position, and this gave the Canadians more power to undertake the risky strategy of a walkout to obtain a concession on dispute settlement.

Second, the Canadian delegation entered the negotiations with the intention of creating fundamentally changed trading rules between the two countries, but it gradually dropped back from this position when it recognized such change would be unacceptable to Congress. As an alternative, Canada redefined its negotiating goals and focused its demands on dispute settlement. It is probable that this concentration of effort created a more powerful negotiating position, much in the way that the principle of mass creates the perception and thus the reality of power in armed conflict. Against this display of determination on the part of the weaker party, the stronger party was obliged to accept an accommodation or suffer the loss of an otherwise attractive agreement.

In the Melian dialogue, the Greek historian Thucydides has the Athenians claim that negotiation is only appropriate between equals (Thucydides 1960:265–274). In one sense this principle is surely incorrect, for the weak (including the Melians) often negotiate with the strong. But in another sense Thucydides is correct, for negotiation presupposes that both sides have something of interest to give the other side, or else there would not be a negotiation. Thus negotiation tends to create an equality in the currency of interest-seeking behavior. When the United States commenced a negotiation with Canada, it put itself in a position of becoming interested in what an ostensibly weaker party had to offer. As a result, the power relationship at the bargaining table allowed for specific actions or exercises of power that rendered the negotiations less asymmetric than might be assumed from perceptions based on the comparative size of the two countries' economies.

Notes

[1] Antidumping and countervailing are legal actions that can result in increased customs duties. They are initiated by domestic companies against imports. An antidumping case exists when imported products are sold more cheaply than in the country of origin. A countervailing case exists when imported products benefit from subsidies provided by foreign governments. Antidumping and countervailing are actions in administrative law and can be reviewed and overturned by a reviewing court (or a binational panel).

[2] US trade remedies against Canada rose to 51 between 1980 and 1986. From these cases, more than 75% of the preliminary rulings by the US International Trade Commission (ITC) went against Canada. For a detailed discussion see Doern and Tomlin (1991:68).

[3] Two of the prominent cases that became major irritants during the negotiations were US actions against Canadian cedar exports (shakes and shingles) pursuant to GATT and the countervailing suit taken against Canadian softwood lumber imports.

[4] "Fast track" is a US legislative procedure whereby Congress commits itself in advance to approve or disapprove expeditiously and without amendment a forthcoming trade agreement with another country. Failure to get fast-track approval would have killed the prospects for the FTA. The narrow Committee vote, in which a tie counts as approval of the FTA, was partly explained by opposition in Congress to the administration's trade policy in other areas, which had little to do with US–Canada relations.

References

Andrew, A., 1970, *Defence by Other Means: Diplomacy for the Underdog*, Canadian Institute of International Affairs, Toronto, Canada.

Bowker, M.M., 1988, *On Guard for Thee: An Independent Review of the FTA*, Voyageur Publishing, Hull, Quebec, Canada.

Canada–US Trade Negotiations: A Chronology, n.d., Government of Canada, Ottawa, Canada.

Doern, G.B., and Tomlin, B.W., 1991, *Faith and Fear: The Free Trade Story*, Stoddart Publishing Co. Ltd., Toronto, Canada.

External Affairs, 1983, *A Review of Canadian Trade Policy*, Department of External Affairs, Ottawa, Canada.

External Affairs, 1985a, *Canadian Trade Negotiations*, Department of External Affairs, Ottawa, Canada.

External Affairs, 1985b, *Competitiveness and Security: Directions for Canada's International Relations*, Department of External Affairs, Ottawa, Canada.

External Affairs, 1987, *The Canada–US Free Trade Agreement*, The International Trade Communications Group, Ottawa, Canada.

Gherson, G., 1987, Reagan's signal brings trade talks out of obscurity, *Toronto Financial Post*, 2 February.

Goldmann, K., 1979, The international power structure: Traditional theory and new reality, in K. Goldmann and G. Sjöstedt, eds., *Power, Capabilities, Interdependence*, Modern Political Series, Volume 3, Sage, London.

Hart, J., 1976, Three approaches to the measurement of power in international relations, *International Organization*, **30**(2):289–305.

Hoffmann, S., 1978, *Primacy or World Order*, McGraw-Hill, New York.

Jonsson, C., 1981, Bargaining power: Notes on an elusive concept, *Cooperation and Conflict*, **16**:249–257.

Leyton-Brown, D., 1985, *Weathering the Storm: Canadian–US Relations, 1980–1983*, Canadian–American Committee, Toronto, Canada.

Macdonald, D., 1991, A leap of faith: The Canadian decision for free trade, *American Review of Canadian Studies*, Summer/Autumn:155–161.

Morici, P., 1991, *A New Special Relationship: Free Trade and the US–Canada Economic Relations in the 1990s,* Centre for Trade Policy and Law, Carleton University, Ottawa, Canada.

Pammett, J., 1989, The 1988 vote, in A. Frizzell, J. Pammett, and A. Westell, eds., *The Canadian General Election of 1988*, Carleton University Press, Ottawa, Canada.

Pruitt, D.G., and Carnevale, P., 1993, *Negotiation in Social Conflict*, Brooks/Cole, Pacific Grove, CA.

Rothstein, R.L., 1968, *Alliances and Small Powers*, Columbia University Press, New York.

Schott, J.J., 1983, The GATT ministerial: A postmortem, *Challenge*, May/June.

Schott, J.J., and Smith, M.G., eds., 1988, *The Canada–United States Free Trade Agreement: The Global Impact*, Institute for International Economics, Washington, DC.

Steger, D.P., n.d., *An Analysis of the Dispute Settlement Provisions of the Canada–US Free Trade Agreement*, Paper prepared for the Business Council on National Issues, Ottawa, Canada.

Thucydides, 1960, *The Peloponnesian War*, Penguin, New York.

Toronto Globe and Mail, 1986, The senators relent, editorial, 24 April.

Trezise, P.H., 1988, At last, free trade with Canada? *The Brookings Review*, **6**(1), Winter.

Waddell, C., and Lewington, J., 1987, Canada, US plan bid to salvage trade talks, *Toronto Globe and Mail*, September.

Winham, G.R., 1988, *Trading with Canada: The Canada–US Free Trade Agreement*, Priority Press Publications, New York.

Zartman, I.W., 1971, *The Politics of Trade Negotiations Between Africa and the European Economic Community: The Weak Confront the Strong*, Princeton University Press, Princeton, NJ.

Chapter 3

US–Indonesian Negotiations over the Conditions of Aid, 1951–1954

Timo Kivimäki

The Communist takeover of China in 1949 led to new priorities for US assistance in Asia (Bachrack 1976). The takeover immediately increased American readiness to contribute to anti-Communist causes in Southeast Asia. The countries of Southeast Asia became more valuable to the United States as a bloc (*Bangkok Post*, 18 February 1950:1). The takeover also pointed out the importance of those countries closest to China. Top priority was given to countries in the offshore island chain between China and the United States: Aleutian Islands, Australia, Caroline Islands, Formosa (today Taiwan), Hawaii, Hong Kong, Japan, Marshall Islands, New Zealand, and the Philippines [Foreign Relations of the US (FRUS), Department of State, 13 February 1952:45–51; 6 April 1953:285–298; 21 December 1954:1056–1061]. The continental nations closest to China including Burma (today Myanmar), Thailand, and the other states of Indochina, were almost as important in the Asian containment effort (*Bangkok Post*, 18 February 1950:1). At a conference of top foreign-policy officials in Bangkok, Thailand, in February 1950, Indonesia's importance in the containment effort became associated with the so-called leapfrog theory, which played a far less significant role in American thinking than the domino theory. According to the leapfrog theory, the Communists might try their next offensive in Indonesia, because no one expected the United States to pay much attention to countries behind the "front line" (Jones 1973:38).

The new US priorities were reflected in legislation that conditioned aid policies to the rationales of the US role in the Cold War. In the Mutual Security Act of 1951, Congress committed the administration to making humanitarian aid to foreign countries conditional on their support of US long-term interests. Eligibility for US military assistance required contributions to the defense of the "free world" (Mutual Security Act, Section 511a). That military commitments were demanded in exchange for military assistance created a problem for Indonesia, which was a neutral country but needed some assistance for its constabulary, police, and army. More specifically, at issue was the amount of aid to be given: Economic assistance, which could be received without extensive commitments, was highly desired by the developmentalist circles of Indonesia's leadership. An important issue at the bargaining table was Indonesia's commitment to defending the "free world": How was it to be defined, and how public did the Indonesian leadership have to be about this commitment? On the one hand, if the issue were to become a matter of public debate, the Indonesian government would find it extremely difficult to persuade the Parliament to ratify military commitments (Cochran's report, in FRUS, Department of State II, 7 January 1952:246–248). On the other hand, if Indonesian commitments were to be concealed from the Parliament, political parties would not consider themselves committed to the containment effort (*Congressional Record*, pp. 10837–10838).

The general Congressional conditions for economic assistance were somewhat vague (Mutual Security Act, Section 511b), but the United States insisted that without a balanced military–economic agreement it would not grant any assistance to Indonesia (FRUS, Department of State II, 22 February 1952:272–274; 9 April 1952:280–281). Thus, without military commitments Indonesia could not obtain economic assistance. In addition to general conditions, specific conditions were created regarding trading strategic materials with the Communist bloc. On 17 May 1951, the United Nations Political and Security Committee passed a resolution, adopted the following day by the United Nations (UN) General

Assembly, calling for termination of trade involving strategic materials with China. The UN rationalized its decision on the grounds that China had helped the aggressors against UN troops in Korea. Simultaneously, the United States tried to impose strict sanctions against the Communist bloc by conditioning certain privileges (aid, loans, preferential access to certain products) to agreements not to trade strategic materials with China, Eastern Europe, and the Soviet Union.[1] Compliance with the embargo's regulations became a specific way for Indonesia to prove its contribution to the defense of the "free world."

For the United States, embargo policies were a part of Cold War power politics, and they were possible in the UN context only because of the temporary withdrawal of the Soviet Union and the exclusion of China from the Security Council. Even though both Indonesia and the United States wanted to maintain their mutually beneficial relations, Indonesia, a neutral country in need of any possible export earnings, did not want to accept the Cold War-related trade commitments that had become a condition of US friendship. As compensation for partial compliance, Indonesia demanded extensive US assistance in stabilizing the world market prices of rubber and tin, commodities exported by Indonesia whose demand was reduced because of the embargo. In addition, Indonesia demanded substantial compensations in the form of foreign aid and political support in its relations with its former colonial master, the Netherlands.

Negotiations to solve the problem of economic and military aid were initiated between US Ambassador to Indonesia Merle Cochran (1950–1953) and Indonesia's Foreign Minister Subardjo in late 1951. Cochran and Subardjo concluded an agreement on 5 January 1952; however, the agreement did not receive support from the Indonesian Cabinet, which refused to present it to the Parliament for ratification. The focus of negotiations shifted to Washington, where a new agreement was finalized between the State Department and Indonesia's Ambassador Ali Sastroamidjojo. Issues concerning the relationship between aid and Indonesian compliance with the UN embargo remained after the general agreement on the terms of aid was concluded in Washington. The incompatibility of military and economic aid objectives created a conflict of interests whose negotiated settlement provides an interesting case for the study of asymmetrical negotiations. In particular, an analysis of the aid negotiations provides the theory of asymmetrical bargaining with a case against models suggesting that asymmetry in resource power necessarily implies bargaining leverage.

3.1   Power and Negotiation

A comparison of the power resources of the United States and Indonesia in the early 1950s immediately shows a disparity that was evident to both parties. While Indonesia was a weak and economically underdeveloped country (although populous and full of fighting spirit), the United States was a military, political, and economic giant. Provided that Indonesian decision makers fulfilled the minimal criteria of rationality (that is, that they would choose policies based on the desirability of their outcomes) and that US resources could be channeled into areas where Indonesia had strong interests, the United States could, through punishments and rewards, make obedience more desirable than disobedience for Indonesia. The degree to which an agent is able to affect the target's preferences of the target (through actions to manipulate outcomes) is often called the intensity of power (Harsanyi 1958:378–385). Converting resources into something that could affect Indonesia's subjective preferences was the first obstacle confronting the ability of the United States to exercise power over Indonesia: Even if American calculations of Indonesia's need for foreign aid indicated that Indonesia should have been more exposed to US dollar diplomacy, the value calculations were made by Indonesian leaders and people whose preferences differed from those expected by the United States. An outstanding example of this can be seen in US estimates of Indonesia's dependence on US aid (see, for example, Cochran's report, in FRUS, Department of State 1951:692) contrasted with the fact that, in the end, the Indonesian government was "fully prepared to face up to the consequences of [termination of US aid]" (FRUS, Department of State 1952–1954:440). Thus, the US–Indonesian relationship was one of perceived power asymmetry (high-low, HL) where the total level of power was dampened by preference variations.

Whether the United States had the power to make Indonesia fulfill the conditions of aid and obey the embargo regulation depended on two factors: the intensity of US power actions and the intensity needed to persuade Indonesia. Both depended on the degree to which the United States would be able to manipulate outcomes affecting Indonesia's utilities and how much influence on these preferences was needed. These factors in turn depended on how undesirable the consequences of obedient behavior were for Indonesia.

The mediation between power intensity and effect power was the second element that weakened the power of resource-rich United States vis-à-vis Indonesia.[2] Certain characteristics of US–Indonesian interaction and Indonesian strategic orientations tended to increase the intensity of power needed to affect Indonesia's policies. For instance, Indonesia's nationalistic culture involved norms against yielding to the demands of external powers. This, obviously, meant that obedience, as such, was costly for Indonesia, and therefore the United States was required to delicately manipulate outcomes (punishments or rewards) to influence Indonesia's policies. In addition, due to the asymmetry of relations, issues handled in US–Indonesian negotiations were vital to Indonesians (decisions on the independence and neutrality of Indonesia's trade policies) but rather extraneous and secondary to Americans. Therefore, it seemed natural that a great deal of effort had to be made to persuade Indonesia to make concessions on vital issues, whereas much less was needed to affect policies on secondary issues. These observations seem to confirm the more general thesis about the defensive power (ability to resist external influence) of weak nations (Goldmann 1979:115–140).[3]

The third and final obstacle in the conversion of US resources to power in negotiations is related to characteristics and limitations specific to the aid and embargo negotiations. According to Habeeb (1988), power can be divided into general aggregate power, which refers to total power resources, and issue-specific power, which refers only to actions based on resources relevant in a particular negotiation. The United States' issue-specific power in the aid and embargo negotiations was mainly based on economic resources of a different sort. With regard to aid, the United States was in a position to do what it liked. Furthermore, because of the size of the American market and the wealth and economic political power of the federal government, the United States was able to manipulate the demand for Indonesian commodities by limiting US synthetic rubber production (Rubber Producing Facilities Disposal Act of 1953, approved on 7 August 1953:67 Stat: 408), by making commodity purchasing contracts and stockpiling Indonesian commodities,[4] by not opposing the rubber stabilization conference in May 1953 (FRUS, Department of State 1952–1954:378–379), and by launching programs to help market Indonesian commodities (National Security Council meeting 124/2, 5 August 1953, FRUS, Department of State 1952–1954:392). The greatest limitation on the United States' issue-specific power was that the dispute was not serious enough to justify the use of coercive threats.

The general image of the United States as a powerful nation was a tremendous obstacle to US–Indonesian cooperation. The very strength of the United States was perceived by the nationalist Indonesians as a threat to their sovereign independence. According to Howard P. Jones, a US ambassador to Indonesia (1973:42), this nationalist fear made it very difficult for Americans to exercise power, to cooperate, or even to appear in public with Indonesian officials in the 1950s. Nonetheless, the ability to reward obedience for accepting specific issues obviously made it easier for the Americans to strike a deal. At the same time, the ability to compensate has a built-in inflationary factor in negotiations: if one is able to pay handsomely for concessions, one is also more inclined and expected to do so. When the United States was considering whether to compensate Indonesia for compliance by manipulating the international rubber and tin markets with more than adequate stockpiles, the fact that the United States was not facing economic problems made the American National Security Council (NSC) more generous toward Indonesia. At one point Secretary of State John F. Dulles explicitly proved this point by responding to Secretary of Treasury George M. Humphrey's complaints about "the heavy weight on US taxpayers" of this generosity by reminding him that the United States had more important concerns than "unemployment here and there in the United States" (FRUS, Department of State 1952–1954:390–393). This rationale also applied to considerations of how much aid was to be given to Indonesia.

On the basis of this discussion, it can be concluded that power resources do not necessarily imply negotiation success; only an empirical analysis of the actions that make up the negotiations can reveal why in this case strength was a weakness and weakness a strength. Even an enumeration of the vulnerabilities of asymmetrical interdependence provides only the starting point for the analysis of bargaining interactions.

3.2   Indonesian Perceptions

Although Indonesia was a nonsocialist country and valued the UN's role in the decolonialization of the world, Indonesian leaders did not feel particularly committed to either the defense of the "free world" or the UN's Chinese embargo. Nor were they supportive of US legislation, such as the Kerr Amendment and the Battle Act, which were even stricter in their regulations than the UN resolution. The Kerr Amendment and the Battle Act restricted US assistance to countries trading strategic materials, as defined by US officials, not only with China, but also with all members of the Communist bloc. In contrast, the UN embargo resolution left the definition of strategic materials to individual member nations and was directed only against China. Indonesia, for example, did not initially define rubber as a strategic material, and when the United States was finally able to persuade it to include rubber in that category, Indonesia reserved the right to reclassify it at any time. In 1948 Indonesia defined its role in the world as independent and neutral in the power struggles between East and West (Hatta 1976). In fact, only after considerable persuasion did Indonesia agree to abstain from voting on the question of the Chinese embargo in the UN Political and Security Committee: The Indonesian foreign minister, other members of the Indonesian government, and the Indonesian delegate to the UN were believed to be against the embargo. From their perspectives, it was not in Indonesia's interests to comply with the embargo of Communist countries.

US military strength was not a motive for Indonesia to comply with the embargo. On the one hand, use of military force in this issue was naturally ruled out. On the other hand, as a neutral country, Indonesia was not seeking security in an alliance with the United States. According to an American assessment, however, Indonesians believed that the United States would defend Indonesia against a serious threat, even though Indonesia was not prepared to give anything in exchange for the ultimate security guarantee. Reports of US–Indonesian negotiations on the embargo of Communist bloc countries reveal that this expectation of defense assistance did not soften Indonesia's line.

However, the Indonesian perception of US economic and political strength had a definite influence on Indonesia's negotiation behavior. For many years, Western-minded circles within the Indonesian political elite rationalized their compliance with Western values – democracy, anti-Japanese collaboration (during World War II), concentration on development – by arguing that the United States was economically and politically very powerful and therefore the only nation that could help Indonesia.[5] As the United States began to emerge as a world leader, American goodwill and responsibility for Indonesia's well-being began to be taken for granted. For example, nowhere in the reports of Indonesia's key negotiator, Ambassador Ali Sastroamidjojo or in the reports of the US State Department was it stated that the Indonesians found it peculiar that the United States would compensate Indonesia for losses caused by the UN embargo. On the contrary, this was generally accepted and, as the United States did not face any economic problems, Indonesians expected Americans to be generous with their compensations.

The Indonesian perception of US economic strength and economic capacity to expand globally mobilized Indonesian nationalism in a way that made Indonesia determined not to yield. Any attempts to make American aid or purchases of rubber and tin conditional on political or trade–political obedience were met with rigid opposition by the nationalists and the revolutionaries in Indonesia. This opposition was society-based – a grassroots movement of popular nationalism that could not be dealt with by bribing people in the political elite. Even if this popular nationalistic sensitivity was partly manipulated and stirred up by the political elite and especially the press as conjectured by the Americans (Cochran's report, in FRUS, Department of State 1951:681, 666), it could not be controlled later by the elite political leaders. This society-based nationalism made it hard for the political leadership to publicly commit Indonesia to support the rubber embargo of China (FRUS, Department of State 1951:668, 679, 683). Secret commitments were difficult to make because the ultranationalists of the political elite capitalized on Indonesian nationalism in their political efforts by publicizing all issues that were sensitive to the nationalist movement. Compliance with the Kerr Amendment and the Battle Act prohibiting export of strategic materials to the Soviet Union and Eastern Europe was felt to be even more embarrassing by the Indonesian elite given the domestic political situation, because these restrictions were being unilaterally imposed by the powerful United States. Mostly as a result of this nationalistic grassroots input into Indonesia's decision-making system, Indonesia was never able to yield to the US position enough to make a permanent commitment to include rubber on the list of strategic materials prohibited to be exported to China. Indonesia committed itself to the UN embargo in a general sense (FRUS, Department of State 1951:656). However, in the beginning Indonesia used its right to determine which materials it regarded to be strategic by omitting rubber from its list of strategic materials (FRUS, Department of State 1951:679). Later, Indonesia included rubber in its list, but at the same time it reserved the right to alter the list if necessary. The determination of the Indonesian elite increased with regard to restrictions on trade with other Communist countries: The Indonesian elite could never be imposed upon to restrict trade with Eastern Europe or the Soviet Union (Ambassador Cumming's report on 5 July 1954, FRUS, Department of State 1952–1954:440).

Indonesia's perceptions of its economic weakness also influenced its bargaining behavior in the embargo issue. Because of its economic problems, Indonesia would have welcomed export earnings from any country. Earlier, Indonesia did not trade with China; however, two months before the UN resolution on the embargo, China had offered to trade tungsten and rice for 50,000 tons of the 700,000 tons of rubber produced annually in Indonesia, or more than 7% of Indonesia's total rubber production (FRUS, Department of State 1951:650). Three years later, according to Indonesian sources, China was still willing to exchange rice for up to 50,000 tons of rubber. This figure was, however, considered an exaggeration by the US NSC (FRUS, Department of State 1952–1954:473). These additional export earnings were given added weight because of Indonesia's dependence on rubber production, which in 1953 accounted for about 3.3% of all export earnings and almost 0.8% of the Government of Indonesia's receipts (calculated from FRUS, Department of State 1952–1954:382). Also, the opening up of new markets for natural rubber would have been welcomed by Indonesians, who produced 40% of the world's rubber between 1951 and 1953 during a period of global oversupply and declining prices. Moreover, Indonesia needed additional rice from China. Tin sales were an important component of Indonesia's trade with Eastern Europe, even though its trade with Eastern Europe was more modest than its trade potential with China and it was less dependent on its production of tin than its production of rubber. In addition, Indonesia was, perhaps, more interested in the import side, of the tin trade, for example, the import of cheap automobiles, available from East European markets (FRUS, Department of State 1951:711). For the economic technocrats and development-oriented politicians, the economic value of trade, mainly the value of imports available from Communist countries, was an important factor contributing to the disadvantages of complying with American requests to impose an embargo on Communist economies.[6] Under these economic conditions, the weaknesses of the Indonesian economy increased the costs of yielding and thus made Indonesia more determined not to yield.

Members of Indonesia's leadership did not have a uniform perception of the country's economic realities. According to Vice President Mohammad Hatta and Chief of Staff of the Indonesian Armed Forces Abdul Haris Nasution, Indonesia's political leadership at the time of the embargo negotiations was divided into two groups: (1) the developmentalists, including two key negotiators (Vice President Hatta and Ambassador and later Prime Minister Ali Sastroamidjojo),[7] and one of the two most important parties, the Masjumi (Moslem party); and (2) the revolutionaries/nationalists, including President Sukarno and the other major party, the Nationalists (Nasution, interviewed by Ambassador Howard P. Jones in 1969, *Jones Papers*, box 66; Hatta and Anak Agung, interviewed by Jones in 1968, *Jones Papers*, box 92). This division was reflected in the dual structure of the Indonesian presidency. For Vice President Hatta, Indonesia's most important objective for the future was to develop a sound economy; in contrast, President Sukarno remained convinced that anticolonial struggle was Indonesia's most important task.

In the eyes of the developmentalists, Indonesia's main task was to concentrate on developing its economy in the world economy. The value of aid was much greater for the developmentalists than for the revolutionaries. Therefore, commitments defined in Section 511a of the Mutual Security Act and in relation to the UN embargo of China were considered tolerable by Foreign Minister Subardjo, Prime Minister Sukiman, and two other developmentalist Cabinet ministers, Leimena and Wibisono (Cochran's Report, in FRUS, Department of State II, 22 February 1952:270–272).

At the same time, the nationalists were more concerned with continuing the anticolonial struggle and were less enthusiastic about allowing world capitalism to penetrate Indonesia. President Sukarno and his nationalist supporters did not know much about economic matters (CIA: Background information on Sukarno, *Jones Papers*, box 102). Sukarno found that foreign aid could easily be used in a subversive fashion (FRUS, Department of State 1951:616), and according to many American and Dutch estimates he was not really interested in the economic well-being of his people (Stikker 1965; Jones 1973). At times when dealing with revolutionaries it seemed that Ambassador Cochran was more concerned with the health of the Indonesian economy than the Indonesians themselves (the same conclusion was drawn by Hilsman 1967:365, 401; see also Hilsman 1971). For this reason, it was sometimes impossible for the United States to use assistance to compensate Indonesia for concessions stemming from the Cold War.

For those in the nationalist and revolutionary circles of Indonesia's political elite, independence of trade policy and the refusal to commit to alliances were political principles closely related to Indonesia's jealously guarded new independence. For these circles none of the economic quid pro quos offered by the United States could compensate for the sacrifices inherent in Indonesia's compliance. These nationalistic political costs, in addition to the economic costs, both increased by Indonesia's weakness, were extensively used by Indonesia as bargaining leverage in its efforts to demand compensations or exceptions to Indonesia's compliance (Foreign Minister Mukarto, in FRUS, Department of State 1952–1954:436–437).

In addition to the perceptions of the political leaders, the perceptions of Indonesian people, especially those of rubber smallholders, had an important effect on US–Indonesian negotiations. Rubber export earnings directly influenced the livelihood of 12.5% of Indonesians, mostly rural and poor. Due to the poor state of the Indonesian economy, any additional decline in the demand for rubber in world markets and the consequent decline in prices would cause many smallholders to distrust the capitalist market economy and the US-led world markets. As a result, the more Indonesia had to yield on the rubber issue, the more probable the increase in revolutionary and anti-American reactions in Indonesian society (see the NSC's estimate on this, in FRUS, Department of State 1952–1954:378– 379). This anti-American reaction was also partly caused by Indonesia's perception of US strength: the United States was the biggest market for rubber and, therefore, the price was considered to be heavily dependent on US actions (FRUS, Department of State 1952–1954:378–379). As well, the United States was blamed for the unpopular embargo, because of the country's perceived power in the UN and because of certain US legislation such as the Battle Act and the Kerr Amendment (FRUS, Department of State 1952–1954:392–393). The rise of anti-Americanism not only influenced the Indonesian military elite's determination not to yield too much, but, what is perhaps more important, it also affected the US–Indonesian bargaining through US perceptions about the need to persuade Indonesia to join the embargo and to compensate Indonesian rubber smallholders for their losses, the latter effect Schelling (1960) terms coercive deficiency (see Dulles, in FRUS, Department of State 1952– 1954:445).

While Indonesia's perceptions of its weakness made it more determined not to participate in the embargo, those perceptions also made it more suspect to accept some agreement that could ensure it compensation in the form of US aid and purchases of tin and rubber. Evidently, development-oriented circles felt that Indonesia was dependent on development cooperation with the United States. Additionally, the structural power of the globally oriented United States was perceived by the developmentalists as a motive for Indonesian compliance, since it was felt that US influence among the Western allies would make it easy for Indonesia to compensate the losses caused by the embargo with an improved

position in Western trade (FRUS, Department of State 1951:692). This
sense of dependence led Indonesia to agree to include rubber, for the time
being, on its list of strategic materials not to be exported to China. The
decision was made in June 1951 by Sukiman's Cabinet, which was considered development oriented.[8] The Indonesian decision was explicitly
regarded as quid pro quo for the US decision to make an exception to the
Kerr Amendment and not to discontinue aid to Indonesia, even though
Indonesia was continuing its trade of strategic materials (mainly tin) with
the Communist bloc (FRUS, Department of State 1951:671, 681–687).

3.3   US Perceptions

If we look at the effects of the perception of the weakness of Indonesia
on US bargaining behavior, we immediately find some examples of the
model of desperate bargaining described by Fox (1959), Lockhart (1979),
and Vital (1967). Because Indonesia was relatively unimportant in US
policy planning, the United States was not determined to concentrate its
efforts in demanding that Indonesia make concessions. While Indonesia
was motivated by the nationalistic spirit of its society, the United States
failed to use the leverage of US public opinion in the negotiations. In
the beginning of the negotiations, US Secretary of State Dean Acheson
tried to use this argument to persuade Indonesia to join the trade embargo
by warning that "US public opinion [had become] increasingly aroused
by casualties resulting from operations in Korea" and that US hopes that
"Indonesia will not subject itself to risking [the] approbation of US public by [an] untoward move in opening new trade channels "toward the
Communist bloc" (FRUS, Department of State 1951:648). However, as
the signing of Indonesia's trade agreements with Eastern Europe and the
Kerr Amendment exception granted by the United States were not no-
ticed by the US media and public opinion, this rationale for Indonesia's
compliance lost its credibility. The United States could not reciprocate
with society-based bargaining strategies even though these strategies had
become the most important source of leverage for Indonesia. The limited
importance of Indonesia made it difficult for officials in charge of US–
Southeast Asian policies to persuade the rest of the US foreign policy administration to grant special conditions and compensations to Indonesia.

     The US sense of overall power in world affairs affected the US–
Indonesian negotiations mainly through the American vision of its role

as a hegemonic nation in the world system. As one of the most powerful nations in the world, the United States saw its role as a leader of the Western world, and as such it felt responsible for international order. A clear expression of this sense of responsibility was the heated discussion during the 1950 election campaign, on "who lost China," as if the freedom of China had belonged to one of the American administrative branches (Acheson 1969; Bachrack 1976:3–7; Truman 1956:401). The United States' need for, and dependence on, Indonesian cooperation on the Communist embargo issue resulted from the fact that the Americans interpreted their power to include global responsibility for the containment of Communism.

The United States became increasingly convinced of its global military and economic obligation to contain Communism and, therefore, increasingly determined to demand Indonesian participation in the defense of the "free world" in general and in the anti-Communist embargo in particular. This determination made it more difficult for the United States to resolve the US–Indonesian conflict of interests by making the Americans hard bargainers. This effect was especially visible in the policies of Ambassador Cochran (1950–1953), who, for other reasons, was unwilling to compensate Indonesia generously for compliance (Cochran's report, in FRUS, Department of State 1952–1954:281). Cochran's determination partly served as his insurance against the suspicions of anti-American activity in the State Department during the McCarthy era and was used as a proof of his patriotism against such allegations (FRUS, Department of State 1951:598). While this sense of responsibility increased US determination, it also made the United States more prepared to compensate Indonesia for its compliance with US anti-Communist alliance and trade policies. This preparedness was obviously generated by the US sense of the need to cooperate with all non-Communist powers, including Indonesia, to make the alliance and the trade embargo effective. The US Congress and the Economic Cooperation Agency (ECA) were especially anxious to persuade Indonesia to take the Western view on the trade issue.[9] This preparedness to compensate obviously made it easier for the United States to cooperate with Indonesia, but simultaneously it softened the US negotiation stance on Indonesia.

Whereas the trade and military realities of US leadership increased US determination to demand Indonesian compliance, political realities reduced it.[10] The US leadership position required legitimacy, and it needed to be perceived as beneficial by such "subordinates" as Indonesia.

This same conclusion – that the United States had to soften its approach toward subordinates because of problems with the legitimacy of its leadership – in a US–European context can be found in neorealist and neo-Gramscian analysis.[11] An aggressive imposition of military conditionality and the embargo requirements on Indonesia were seen as detrimental from the point of view of political power. First, it could hamper the society-based, spontaneous goodwill and the positive image of the United States in Indonesia (see reports by Ambassador Cummings and President Eisenhower, in FRUS, Department of State 1952–1954:443–444, 392). Second, it was felt that Indonesia's political elite needed to be committed to the US side for reasons originating from the concerns over US leadership. If the United States was too demanding, it would be suspected that the pro-US forces had lost some of their power within the Indonesian decision-making process, as was the case in 1952 (FRUS, Department of State 1951:679; FRUS, Department of State 1952–1954:443–444). This dependence on some minimal relations to justify its leadership definitely weakened the American bargaining position vis-à-vis Indonesia. Along with the rise of revolutionist anti-Americanism between 1952 and 1954, this endeavor to maintain at least some relations with Indonesia finally resolved the conflict of interests between Indonesia and the United States as the president, the secretary of state, and the US ambassador to Indonesia started to see the US insistence on the embargo of Communist countries as politically too costly to the American leadership. The exclusion of rubber and tin from the American list of strategic materials would "result in net advantage to the 'free world' through increased political and economic stability" in Indonesia (FRUS, Department of State 1952–1954:395, see also pp. 393, 441). According to Cumming's report, throughout the negotiation process the Indonesian side had counted on this American dependence on "minimal terms":

> I also believe that he [Ali Sastroamidjojo] is banking very strongly
> on the possibility that the US will not take any retaliatory action
> under Battle Act because of adverse effect on public opinion in
> Indonesia and Southeast Asia. [FRUS, Department of State 1952–
> 1954:439]

US dependence on at least some sort of relations with Indonesia was also increased by the fact that US economic interests were global. During the time of the embargo negotiations, Indonesia was developing legislation on regulating economic activities in Indonesia, including regulations concerning the activities of foreign investors. The Indonesian Cabinet periodically reminded the Americans that imposing conditions that were too strict (such as conditioning aid) would create an anti-American reaction among Indonesians and, in turn, would influence investment regulations. In an anti-American climate the Indonesian Cabinet would be forced to draft more nationalistic investment legislation than it wanted (Sudarpo, in FRUS, Department of State 1951:674). With these arguments Indonesia was able to sway American investors with fixed assets in Indonesia to their side in the embargo issue because it was in the interests of those investors to try to avoid provocations of anti-Americanism in Indonesia (FRUS, Department of State 1951:687–690).

The US perception of its strength and role as the leader of the Western order, together with its perception of Indonesia's economic weakness, lessened the United States' determination to bargain with Indonesia on concessions with minimal compensations. That the United States did not face any economic problems was, in addition to the pressing strategic concerns, the main reason President Dwight D. Eisenhower and Secretary of State Dulles did not have sympathy for the Secretary of Treasury's complaints to the NSC in 1954 about the costs of US compensations (FRUS, Department of State 1952–1954:390–393). This disregard for US compensations (concessions in negotiations) obviously made it easier for the United States to maintain good relations with Indonesia (minimal objectives of the United States in the negotiations), but also weakened the US bargaining position.

In addition to the disregard for the costs of US compensations, the United States' sense of responsibility for the stability of the Western order gave it an additional political reason for providing assistance, but this element did not contribute to the reasoning behind compensation for Indonesia's compliance.

It is possible that in the long run Indonesia would have developed, even without ECA assistance, the skills and knowledge needed to overcome the underdevelopment of the country. In view of the critical situation at that time and the Communist efforts to spread their influence in Southeast Asia, the time element was of great importance. The United States, therefore, chose to do everything in its power to speed the consolidation of this, the fifth largest nation in the world (ECA officer's report, in FRUS, Department of State 1951:761).

The threat of Communist rebellions among the rubber producers can be seen as the main motivation to increase aid projects that would enhance the livelihood of rubber smallholders, improve the quality of Indonesian rubber, make the rubber industry more self-sufficient, improve rubber-marketing projects, and increase the entire paramilitary assistance program (FRUS, Department of State 1951:676, 692–693; 1952–1954:378–379, 472, 476). This same fear justified the trade-related concessions (extensive stockpiling, concessionary prices, restraints in US global commodity policy, limits on US production of synthetic rubber, etc.) that were resisted by private business circles in the United States.[12] The US bargaining leverage with Indonesia naturally deteriorated because the United States had motives to grant concessions even if Indonesia did not give anything in return. This willingness to grant concessions did not help the United States to strike a deal easily with the Indonesians; the Indonesians were aware of this weakness (caused initially by US resource power) and wanted to use it fully to their own advantage.

Different issues at the negotiation table were perceived slightly differently within the delegation of US negotiators and between the actors they represented. For Congress, the Mutual Security Act (MSA) was a guarantee that taxpayers' money would not be spent on strategically less profitable countries.[13] In the US–Indonesian military aid negotiations, congressional legislation strengthened US invulnerability with respect to cooperation with Indonesia: Congress cared little whether Indonesia was ready to make certain military commitments in exchange for US military assistance. Therefore, in bargaining terms, Congress was not dependent on cooperation, but it was very determined about the US terms. Congress was responsible for cutting the cost to the public, not for implementing the strategy of containment of Communism. For Congress and the ECA, which was acting under congressional mandate, the US bargaining position was extremely rigid: Indonesia had to make a public commitment if it was to receive military aid, no matter how hard it would be for the Indonesian Cabinet.[14]

Secretary of State Dulles and his supporters in the US government used the MSA as an incentive for countries to join Western defense pacts. Dulles' influence in the State Department increased US determination concerning Indonesian military commitments: Dulles badly wanted Indonesia's contribution to his collective defense concept in Southeast Asia (Feith 1967). For Dulles, this meant that to obtain military assistance, Indonesian leaders had to publicly defend their position on the military commitment issue. In addition, Dulles' determination to address questions of the distribution of benefits can be explained by his institutional position as the man who was, along with the president, responsible for the containment of Communism. This input in the US–Indonesian negotiations, along with the "invulnerability" of Congress, toughened US bargaining at the beginning of the MSA negotiations with Indonesia.

According to Herbert Feith (1967), an Australian research fellow, Cochran had sympathies for Dulles' containment policy and, therefore, was willing to negotiate the Indonesian assistance agreement on the basis of MSA Section 511a instead of Section 511b. In several of his reports to the State Department, Cochran demanded support for his insistence on concluding a military assistance agreement. Cochran wanted to maintain the leverage congressional legislation was giving him to persuade Indonesia to take a first step toward the Western alignment (FRUS, Department of State II, 18 February 1952:266–268). Like Dulles, Cochran favored demanding strict Indonesian compliance with the regulations of the embargo. At the same time, however, he and Dulles supported extensive American compensation for Indonesia's costs for joining the embargo.

The least powerful component of the US side related to bargaining was leadership of the State Department. On the one hand, Secretary of State Acheson and his staff in the Asian branches were interested in economic assistance and assistance to the Indonesian constabulary, making the State Department anxious to offer contributions. On the other hand, Acheson and acting Secretary Allison did not feel the need to bind Indonesia to the Western defense system. Moreover, they felt there was political risk of pushing neutral nations too far in their commitments and, therefore, were not anxious to demand concessions from Indonesia in exchange for American aid (Acheson to Cochran, in FRUS, Department of State 1952–1954, 1 May 1952:282; *New York Times*, 25 February 1952; Pauker n.d., box 28; Feith 1967).

3.4   Negotiation Process

When negotiations between Ambassador Cochran and Foreign Minister Subardjo began, Indonesia gained no direct advantages from the radical antiforeign feelings of the newly emancipated Indonesian public; negotiations were kept secret and the public did not know about plans to move closer to the Western bloc. However, Cochran had to consider these antiforeign feelings, as it was clear to him that the United States also wanted the Indonesian Parliament to commit to the agreement. Cochran wanted

Parliament to decide on ratification of the agreement without prior political debate on the matter (FRUS, Department of State 1952–1954, 7 January 1952:246–248). This course would have enabled those politicians who felt the need for military assistance to defend and vote for the ratification without committing political suicide. Publicity before the ratification would have enabled the anti-American parliamentarians to stir up suspicions that their adversaries were under foreign influence.

Maintaining secrecy was not all Cochran was forced to do to avoid weakening the position of pro-American members of the Cabinet. Political commitments that were to be acceptable in exchange for military assistance had to be made as loose as possible within the limits of congressional legislation (FRUS, Department of State II, 7 January 1952:246–248). According to Cochran, the United States had to move extremely cautiously concerning Indonesia's association with the West (FRUS, Department of State 1952–1954, 10 February 1953:356–360). The Cochran–Subardjo agreement, which was signed on 5 January 1952, was extremely advantageous to Indonesia, compared with deals signed with other Southeast Asian countries: According to Foreign Minister Subardjo, Indonesia did not have to commit to any defense treaty or to any external defense commitments (AP, 22 February 1952; Pauker n.d., box 28). When Subardjo got into trouble within the Indonesian Cabinet, Cochran insisted that US assistance be declared as support for independence and sovereignty, whereas the MSA would have required supporting the strength of the "free world" (FRUS, Department of State 1952–1954, 11 February 1952:255–259; 12 February 1952:262–264). At this point, Assistant Secretary of the State Department F.W. Smith pointed out that those parts of the US–Indonesian MSA agreements that were too advantageous to comply with the original legislation should not be stressed in public, as they would bring the credibility of the legislation into question (FRUS, Department of State 1952–1954, 15 February 1952:265–266). Yet, because the new aid contract was secretly negotiated under the new Cold War framework, it was widely criticized.

As a result of internal Cabinet conflicts and revelations by ECA officials in Indonesia, the Subardjo–Cochran agreement became public (FRUS, Department of State 1952–1954, 12 February 1952:259–265). The Indonesian ultranationalist revolutionaries and the public became aware of it before it went to the Parliament. At this stage Ambassador Cochran demanded that the Indonesian Cabinet defend in Parliament its very modest military concessions to the United States, despite the domestic political price (FRUS, Department of State 1952–1954, 18 February 1952:266–268, 22 February 1952:272–274; 2 September 1952:310–313). However, even though this was not done, the domestic price of the negotiation became too high. Subardjo was fired as Foreign Minister on 12 February 1952, and the pro-US developmentalist Sukiman Cabinet was forced out on 22 February 1952 (Sastroamidjojo 1979:231). New negotiations on aid were initiated as the new, less pro-American Cabinet refused to present the Subardjo–Cochran agreement to the Parliament. This time Indonesians insisted that negotiations be held in Washington (FRUS, Department of State 1952–1954, 8 May 1952:284–288) in an obvious effort to avoid Cochran and to use the weaker bargaining position of the State Department's leadership. An obviously humiliated Cochran was allowed to participate in these negotiations, but his personal influence was greatly reduced. Sastroamidjojo, who represented Indonesia in the new negotiations, wanted to change Indonesia's commitment from MSA Section 511a to MSA Section 511b, which contained requirements for economic assistance. For the revolutionary, new Indonesian government, losing military grants was more attractive than paying the domestic political costs of yielding on military commitments (Section 511a). According to Secretary of State Acheson, the United States could agree to separate the Cochran–Subardjo agreement into two different agreements, one for technical and economic assistance and the other for purchases of military and constabulary equipment (FRUS, Department of State 1952–1954, 1 May 1952:282; 6 June 1952:290–291; 30 July 1952:305). For Acheson and other Europeanists in the State Department, Indonesia's radicalization as a consequence of imposed military commitments was less acceptable than artificial military commitments.

With the exception of military grants and a guarantee of support for its claims in any future dispute with the Netherlands, Indonesia was able to gain all the political terms it wanted in the Washington negotiations while giving practically nothing in return. New agreements on continued technical and economic assistance to replace the Cochran–Subardjo agreement were concluded on 5 January 1953, and signed on 12 January 1953. In accordance with the new agreement, in addition to economic assistance, US deliveries of equipment to the Indonesian constabulary, police, and army, originally negotiated by Hatta and Cochran on 15 August 1950, continued on a redisbursement basis. However, despite advantageous terms, Indonesia lost in the volume of US aid and the quality of its relationship with the United States.

The needs of the Indonesian constabulary, police, and army were not an obstacle to the US–Indonesian aid relationship. Nor was the issue of the UN's China embargo. Officially, Indonesia agreed not to sell to China; however, there were strong suspicions that it was secretly exporting goods to China. According to some Indonesian scholars and officials interviewed for this study, exports probably continued secretly without interruption throughout the embargo period. The State Department suspected the secret trading (FRUS, Department of State, 12 March 1951:616; 1 June 1951:669–671), but as the US resources for Indonesia had already been cut because of policies of supporting only allies and because of Indonesia's unwillingness to accept foreign aid, a further cut in economic aid (US$3.5 million in 1951 and 1952) would probably have damaged US prestige in Indonesia more than it would have hurt Indonesia's economy.

In 1953, during the Eisenhower administration, the US took an even less persistent attitude toward the blockade. At the time there was more solid evidence supporting the suspicions that Indonesia was actually selling rubber to China (FRUS, Department of State 1952–1954:435). The NSC, which had become the center of power in the US foreign policy process, discussed the issue at some length in the summer of 1953. It became clear that President Eisenhower opposed the Battle Act, which made the United States enforce the unpopular UN embargo by using aid as a positive sanction (National Security Council's 171st meeting, FRUS, Department of State 1952–1954:388–394). The embargo idea was more acceptable to the new Secretary of State, John Foster Dulles, but as the United States had become the principal guarantor of the economic stability of the non-Communist countries, it was necessary for the United States to take care of the interests of Indonesian producers of strategic materials. The United States had already made an extremely unprofitable agreement with the Indonesian government to buy tin from Indonesia for three years, even though their own tin stockpiles were more than adequate (National Security Council 124/2 Progress Report of Indonesian Section, FRUS, Department of State 1952–1954:372–383). Programs to help Indonesian rubber smallholders were also under way (FRUS, Department of State 1952–1954:449–450, 452–455). In the NSC, Secretary of State Dulles had to defend this economically disadvantageous policy with Cold War arguments against the attacks of the Secretary of the Treasury. Because Cold War questions were perceived as much more urgent than economic issues in wealthy America, other members of the NSC had more sympathy for Dulles' reasoning than for economic arguments (National Security Council's 171st meeting, FRUS, Department of State 1952–1954:388–394).

3.5 Conclusion

The general dynamics of US–Indonesian negotiations show that all major movements toward a solution could be derived from changes in the relative determination and dependence of the negotiators. Whatever increased Indonesia's determination not to yield also contributed to Indonesia's increasing bargaining leverage and made the negotiators less flexible to find a cooperative solution. Also, whatever contributed to US dependency on some type of negotiated solution weakened the United States as a bargainer and increased its flexibility to agree on a solution. The bargaining part of this observation exemplifies game theoretical bargaining models (Ellsberg 1968; Harsanyi 1956, 1958, 1961; Nash 1950, 1953; Shapley and Shubic 1954; Zeuthen 1930), which are taken into a context of minimal rationality expectations (Kivimäki 1993:17–26). The determination component of bargaining leverage is interpreted in game theoretical models as the size of the difference between the utilities that the agent gets from a solution on its own terms and from the solution on the terms of the opponent. Obviously, if the opponent's solution is almost as desirable as the one suggested by the agent, the agent is not very determined to get his or her way. Correspondingly, the dependence component is interpreted as the distance between a negotiated solution and a failure to achieve any solution (security point).

The most important direct influence of power resources in the negotiation process was that US economic wealth made the United States less willing to offer a tough bargain for the compensations that were to serve as quid pro quo for Indonesia's compliance. Therefore, the direct impact of US power was not contributing to the United States' ability to exploit the weaker party. Indonesia's weakness could have made it very dependent on US compensations, and this could have exposed Indonesia to exploitation. However, because of Indonesia's nationalism, US aid was not highly valued. In addition, because Indonesia's weakness contributed to its increasing determination to receive fair compensation for its lost export earnings, Indonesia was not exposed to exploitation.

Since there would not have been an easy way to define a 50–50 deal between unequal negotiators, it is fair to say that power asymmetry did not directly contribute to the complexity of the negotiations and, there-fore, did not directly make negotiations more difficult. However, the difficulties and inflexibilities of US–Indonesian negotiations during this period were indirectly caused by the reaction of Indonesian society to resource asymmetry. Because US policies were of vital importance for Indonesia, and because of the Indonesian fear that America's economic power could force Indonesia to compromise its independence, Indone-sia's negotiation stance on compliance was extremely rigid. The United States did not act exploitatively and Indonesia certainly did not act sub-missively. Even though Indonesia's terms of agreements were very good, this society-level sensitivity made it difficult for the Indonesian govern-ment to seek more cooperation with the United States. The public con-troversy forced the pro-American Sukiman Cabinet to resign, and the Wilopo Cabinet had to resign within a year after assuming power as a result of divisions in the army caused by the Cochran–Subardjo deal. In the Sastroamidjojo Cabinet, the strongest opponents of Communism, economic nationalism, and ultranationalism, the Masjumi, and the PSI, were completely left out of the coalition ("Budjardjo: History of Devel-opment of Cabinets in Indonesia 1957," Pauker n.d.:50–57). The new Cabinet included several ministers whom the United States suspected of having Communist sympathies including the Defense Minister (NSC Progress Report 124/2, in FRUS, Department of State 1952–1954:372–383). Radical anti-American sentiments continued to rise among the In-donesians. According to Howard P. Jones, political counselor of the US embassy (1954–1958) and ambassador (1958–1965), after the Cochran affair the Indonesian political climate was so filled with suspicion against the United States that for several years no Indonesian army officers or po-litical leaders dared to appear in public with US officers (Jones 1973:42).

In addition to the society-level implications of resource asymmetry, global-power political contexts also conditioned the interpretations of the meaning and impacts of power in the US–Indonesian negotiations. The most important of these indirect implications was related to the Amer-ican perception of its role as the guarantor of stability in the Western world. This made the United States vulnerable to a variety of Indonesian bargaining strategies, which can be seen as different uses of the "Soviet Card" or the "China Card." The logic of the "Soviet Card" implies that the more the United States pressed Indonesia for concessions and the less the United States was willing to grant compensations, the closer Indone-sia moved toward the Communist camp and the greater the erosion of the United States' position as the world leader. On the one hand, the use of the "Soviet Card" was quite intentional. According to Ambassador Cochran, a frustrated US negotiator, the Indonesians "are now threatening to do business with Commies if we do not meet their trade demands as well as terms on which they are willing to accept our taxpayers' money." On the other hand, the Indonesian negotiation strategies were also, and perhaps more effectively, using the "Soviet Card" passively and unintentionally: US reduction of aid and imposition of conditions automatically caused a reduction of American prestige and an increase in revolutionary sentiment in Indonesian society.

Because of its dependence on abstract strategic concerns and on the legitimacy of its position, the United States had to abandon many of its self-interests. This is extremely evident in a comparison of reports by the Secretary of Treasury in the NSC and the Secretary of State to the Indonesia policy administration on the public and private economic interests of the United States with the reports by the NSC on strategically motivated American actions in relation to the US–Indonesian negotiations. While both the private and public economic interest groups wanted to reduce tin and rubber stockpiles, President Eisenhower ordered an increase in US stockpiles to help Indonesians. Although the private and public economic groups strongly opposed purchasing contracts for large purchases of rubber and tin from Indonesia, the US government signed contracts that were highly beneficial for the Indonesian tin and rubber producers without informing US industries. At the same time, the US government frustrated domestic industries and the Secretary of Treasury by not acting against international plans to strengthen cooperation between rubber-producing countries. Finally, while the private sector urged a 50% increase in US synthetic rubber production capacity to lower world rubber market prices,[15] strategic considerations forced Congress to agree on the Rubber Producing Facilities Disposal Act (Acheson's report, in FRUS, Department of State 1951:657–659; National Security Council meeting memorandum, in FRUS, Department of State 1952–1954:372, 378–379, 406).

The US–Indonesian negotiations over aid in the early 1950s began with a situation of perceived asymmetry based on the resource possession of the two parties. Once bargaining began, however, the weaker side exercised power as actions, based on resources, perceptions, relations, and roles, to produce much more symmetrical results than the initial asymmetry would have suggested were possible. In summary, Indonesia exploited its relationship with the United States and the United States submitted. But this competition undermined cooperation and made negotiations inefficient.

Notes

[1] Kerr Amendment, Section 1302(a) of the Third Supplemental Appropriations Act of 1951 (became law on 2 June 1951) and the Battle Act, Mutual Defense Assistance Control Act of 1951 (approved on 26 October 1951).

[2] Effect power is understood here within the context of utility theoretical basic assumptions of minimal rationality. Therefore, effect power of A on B over action x implies a tendency of B to always do x when the utility for A of the consequences of x is bigger than the disutility for A of the costs of exercising power on B. This formulation avoids the tautological nature of Dahl's (1965) definition of power (in which power is defined by using an almost synonymous term ability).

[3] For a discussion of the vitality of interests of small powers and the model of desperate bargaining, see Fox 1959; Habeeb 1988:21–23, 131–132; Lockhart 1979:93; Vital 1967.

[4] See, for example, the Wilson–Sumitro rubber contract of 7 April 1951 (FRUS, Department of State 1951:638–639) and the three-year tin contract of March 1953 (FRUS, Department of State 1952–1954:378–379).

[5] Former Prime Minister Sutan Sjahrir argued that Indonesia's declaration of independence in 1945 had to be sufficiently anti-Japanese, democratic, and capitalistic to attract US attention (Kahin 1952:147; Sastroamidjojo 1979:108). The same argument was given in the Political Manifesto of the Indonesian government at the Indonesian National Convention in 1948. Similar arguments were given by former Education Minister Roeslan Abdulgani (1964:31–38).

[6] For this assessment see Sastroamidjojo (1979:232); see also Chief of the Economic Section of the Indonesian Foreign Ministry Zarin Zain (FRUS, Department of State 1951:711).

[7] Even though Sastroamidjojo was the chairman of the Nationalist party, he was considered by the US Ambassador in Indonesia, the NSC, and the CIA to be a developmentalist (FRUS, Department of State 1952–1954:372–377; CIA, Background information on Ali Sastroamidjojo in *Jones Papers*, box 102). For a similar assessment by Ambassador Cochran, see FRUS, Department of State (1951:366–367).

[8] See "Budjardjo: History of Cabinets in Indonesia 1957," Pauker, n.d., box 50/7; see also Cochran's estimate (FRUS, Department of State 1951:689).

[9] See, for example, Lacy's memorandum of talks with the head of the Economic Cooperation Agency, mission in Indonesia, Allen Griffin, in FRUS, Department of State (1951:598–602); and the debate related to the Mutual Security Assistance Bill 1951, *Congressional Record*, 82nd Congress, 1st Session, vol. 97, part 8, 10 August 1951:10837–10838.

[10] The concept of hegemonic leadership used is that of the neorealist (Haas 1983:29; Kindleberger 1970, 1973–1986; Krasner 1981; Snyder 1984; Stein 1984) and neo-Gramscian conceptual systems (Augelli and Murphy 1988:58–60, 122–124; Cafruny 1990:103–106; Cox 1983; Femia 1981; Gill 1986; Gramsci 1971:56, 161, 377; Ikenberry and Kupchan 1990:49–50; Wight 1977). It refers to a stable state of matters (order) where an agent, or the normative system the agent is promoting, is obeyed by other agents and where the leading agent accepts responsibility for maintaining the order. In this definition three elements characterize the state of matters: order characterizes the relationships and the system; obedience characterizes the behavioral patterns of the subordinates; and responsibility characterizes the qualities of the leader.

[11] See Ikenberry (1989). For conclusions that the United States has to soften its stand to make its leadership look beneficial for the subordinates, see Krasner (1981) and Krasner (1982).

[12] For evidence of this conflict between "strategic, power political" interests and the private business interests, compare Acheson's report of the business interests, in FRUS, Department of State (1951:657–659) with the strategic interests of the National Security Council, in FRUS, Department of State 1952–1954:372, 378–379, 406.

[13] See the debate related to the Mutual Security Assistance Bill 1951, *Congressional Record*, 82nd Congress, 1st Session, Vol. 97, part 8, 30 August 1951:10837–10838.

[14] The Cochran-Sukiman agreement was leaked to the press by ECA officials. The Economic Cooperation Agency was apparently less concerned with Indonesia's need for military assistance, and it was also more insistent concerning the commitments Indonesia had to make in reciprocation (FRUS, Department of State, 12 February 1952:259–261).

[15] This was, of course, also in the interest of the Department of Treasury, which wanted to fight inflation.

References

Abdulgani, R., 1964, *Heroes Day: The Indonesian Revolution*, Jakarta, Indonesia.

Acheson, D., 1969, *Present at Creation: My Years in the State Department,* New York.

Augelli, E., and Murphy C., 1988, *America's Quest for Supremacy and the Third World*, London.

Bachrack, S.D., 1976, *The Committee of One Million: "China Lobby" Politics 1953–1971*, New York.

Cafruny, A.W., 1990, The Gramscian concept of declining hegemony: Stages of US power and the evolution of international economic relations, in D.P. Rapkin, ed., *World Leadership and Hegemony: International Political Economy Yearbook*, Volume 5, Lynne Rienner, Boulder, CO.

Cox, R.A., 1983, Gramsci, hegemony and international relations: An essay in method, *Millennium: Journal of International Studies*, **12**(2):162–175.

Dahl, R.A., 1965, The concept of power, in D. Singer, ed., *Human Behaviour and International Politics*, Rand McNally, Chicago, pp. 372–328.

Ellsberg, D., 1968, *The Theory and Practice of Blackmail,* Rand, Santa Monica, CA.

Feith, H., 1967, Note on the effects of US policies, private paper file, Hoover Institute, Stanford University, Stanford, CA.

Femia, J.V., 1981, *Gramsci's Political Thought: Hegemony, Consciousness and the Revolutionary Process*, Clarendon Press, Oxford, UK.

Fox, A.B., 1959, *The Power of Small States: Diplomacy in World War II,* University of Chicago Press, Chicago.

Gill, S., 1986, US hegemony: Its limits and prospects in the Reagan era, *Millennium: Journal of International Studies*, **15**:311–336.

Goldmann, K., 1979, Tension between the strong and the power of the weak: Is the relation positive or negative? in K. Goldmann and S. Sjöstedt, eds., *Power, Capabilities, Interdependence*, Modern Political Series, Volume 3, Sage, London.

Gramsci, A., 1971, *Selections from the Prison Notebooks of Antonio Gramsci*, translated by Q. Hoare and G. Nowell Smith, International Publishers, New York.

Haas, E.B., 1983, Regime decay, conflict management and international organizations 1945–1981, *International Organization*, **37**(2):189–256.

Habeeb, W.M., 1988, *Power and Tactics in International Bargaining: How Weak Nations Bargain with Strong Nations*, Johns Hopkins University Press, Baltimore, MD.

Harsanyi, J.C., 1956, Approaches to bargaining problems before and after the theory of games, *Econometrica*, **24**:144–156.

Harsanyi, J.C., 1958, Measurement of social power, opportunity costs and the theory of two person bargaining games, in D. Singer, ed., *Human Behaviour and International Politics,* Rand McNally, Chicago.

Harsanyi, J.C., 1961, On the rationality postulates underlying the theory of co-operative games, *Journal of Conflict Resolution*, **5**(2):178–196.

Hatta, M., 1976, *Mendayung Antara Dua Karang* (Rowing between two streams), Speech, 2 September 1948, at Jogjakarta, Indonesia.

Hilsman, R., 1967, *To Move a Nation*, Garden City, MI.

Hilsman, R., 1971, *The Politics of Policy-Making in Defense and Foreign Affairs*, New York.

Ikenberry, J.G., 1989, Rethinking the origins of American hegemony, *Political Science Quarterly*, **104**(3):375–400.

Ikenberry, J.G., and Kupchan, C.A., 1990, The legitimation of hegemonic power, in D.P. Rapkin, ed., *World Leadership and Hegemony, International Political Economy Yearbook*, Volume 5, Lynne Rienner, Boulder, CO.

Jones, H.P., n.d., *Jones Papers*, Hoover Institute Archives, Stanford University, CA.

Jones, H.P., 1973, *Indonesia: A Possible Dream*, Singapore, Malaysia.

Kahin, G.McT., 1952, *Nationalism and Revolution in Indonesia*, Cornell University Press, Ithaca, NY.

Kindleberger, C.P., ed., 1970, *The International Corporation*, MIT Press, Cambridge, MA.

Kindleberger, C.P., 1986, *The World in Depression 1929–1939,* University of California Press, Berkeley, CA.

Kivimäki, T., 1993, *Distribution of Benefits in Bargaining Between a Superpower and a Developing Country: A Study of Negotiation Processes Between the United States and Indonesia,* Finnish Society of Sciences and Letters, Helsinki, Finland.

Krasner, S.D., 1981, Power structures and regional developing banks, *International Organization*, **35**(2):303–328.

Krasner, S.D., 1982, American policy and global economic stability, in W.P. Avery and D.P. Rapkin, eds., *America in a Changing World Political Economy*, Longman, New York.

Lockhart, C., 1979, *Bargaining in International Conflicts*, Columbia University Press, New York.

Nash, J., 1950, The bargaining problem, *Econometrica*, **18**(1):155–162.

Nash, J., 1953, Two person cooperative games, *Econometrica*, **21**(1):128–140.

Pauker, G.J., n.d., *Pauker Papers*, Hoover Institute Archives, Stanford University, CA.

Sastroamidjojo, A., 1979, *Milestones on My Journey: The Memoirs of Ali Sastroamidjojo, Indonesian Patriot and Political Leader*, C.L.M. Penders, ed., University of Queensland Press, St. Lucia, Queensland, Australia.

Shapley, L.S., and Shubic, M., 1954, A method of evaluating the distribution of power in a committee system, *American Political Science Review*, **48**:787–792.

Snyder, G.H., 1984, The security dilemma in alliance politics, *World Politics*, **36**(4):461–495.

Stein, A.A., 1984, The hegemon's dilemma: Great Britain, the United States, and the international economic order, *International Organization*, **38**(2):355–386.

Stikker, D.U., 1965, *Men of Responsibility*, Harper & Row, New York.

Truman, H.S., 1956, *Memoirs*, Volume 2, *Years of Trial and Hope*, Doubleday, Garden City, NJ.

Vital, D., 1967, *The Inequality of States*, Oxford University Press, Oxford, UK.

Wolf, C. Jr., The Indonesian Story, Indonesian national convention, working committee (1948), Political manifesto of Indonesian government 1.11.1945, translated by Charles Wolf, pp. 172–175.

Wight, M., 1977, *Systems of States*, Leicester University Press, Leicester, UK.

Zeuthen, F., 1930, *Problems of Monopoly and Economic Warfare,* G. Routledge & Sons, Ltd., London.

Chapter 4

US–Egyptian Aid Negotiations in the 1980s and 1990s

William M. Habeeb

The US–Egyptian relationship since the signing of the Camp David Accords in 1979 has been characterized by two major factors: the massive amount of US economic and military assistance that has been provided to Egypt and Egypt's position as one of the keystones of US political and strategic policy in the Middle East. These factors are, of course, intimately interdependent and thus, broadly speaking, define the perceived asymmetry and interdependent relationship between the United States and Egypt. To say that the United States and Egypt are interdependent is merely to acknowledge that both sides would incur costs if the relationship were broken (Keohane and Nye 1989); it does not imply that both sides are equally (or symmetrically) dependent upon each other.

In the case of the United States and Egypt, each side had demonstrated an ability to live without the other. For most of the period between

1952 and the early 1970s, the two countries were adversaries if not out-right enemies. Very little US aid flowed to the Cairo government, and Egypt was more an obstacle to, than a supporter of, US Middle East policy. It was only after the October 1973 Middle East War that the United States and Egypt each made conscious policy choices that gradually converged into an interdependent relationship. This convergence process has been recounted and analyzed well by others, and it is not the purpose of this chapter to reexamine it (see Quandt 1977, 1986; Telhami 1990). It is sufficient simply to note that US–Egyptian interdependency is one deriving from the policy choices of the two actors; its maintenance, therefore, is dependent upon each actor's assessment of the continued policy relevance of the relationship and the benefits deriving therefrom. Each actor must believe that it has enough power within the relationship to achieve at least some of its preferred outcome.

An interdependent relationship is seldom static. Interdependence implies mutual issues; where there are mutual issues, there are usually differing positions; where there are differing positions, there is bargaining; where there is bargaining, there is the exercise of power. Therefore, an interdependent relationship – even a contrived one, such as the US–Egyptian relationship – is characterized by bargaining and the mutual exercise of power. Thus, it is likely to be a dynamic relationship, in which each side attempts to exercise power to enhance its benefits.

The purpose of this chapter is to analyze the bargaining relationship between the United States and Egypt over the issue of US economic aid to Egypt. This objective is tantamount, however, to analyzing the nature of the US–Egyptian interdependency for, as noted above, US aid to Egypt is one of the principal defining elements of the relationship. As such, this is more a macrolevel analysis of a bargaining relationship than a microlevel analysis of a particular negotiation interaction. After addressing the question of bargaining power – how it is manifest in US–Egyptian bargaining over aid – and each side's respective sources of power, an overview of the history and extent of US economic aid to Egypt is provided. A hypothesis about the power structure of the relationship is offered. The changing terms of trade of the US–Egyptian aid relationship are then analyzed, and how the terms of trade at any given time reflect the balance of bargaining power between the two sides is assessed. Finally, to test the hypothesis, three micro issues within the macro issue of the US–Egyptian aid relationship are investigated.

4.1 Power in a Bargaining Relationship

Central to understanding the dynamics of a bargaining relationship is the concept of power:

> Negotiation analysis is concerned with explaining outcomes. Explaining outcomes involves searching for causation, since negotiation outcomes are the result of a causal process. ...If explaining outcomes involves searching for causation, explaining causation involves seeking a notion of power. [Habeeb 1988:10]

Moreover, because negotiation involves at least two sides, it is important to understand the power balance between them. Understanding the power balance is not only critical for explaining outcomes; it also helps explain the terms of trade of a bargaining relationship (terms of trade in negotiation are discussed in more detail below).

The power balance between states is best understood if a distinction is made between structural power (resources and capabilities) and behavioral power (actions using these resources). Structural power, moreover, is best analyzed at two levels: the aggregate level and the issue-specific level. At the aggregate level, structural power refers to the national resources and capabilities of a state. At the issue-specific level, structural power refers to "an actor's capabilities and position vis-à-vis another actor in terms of a specific mutual issue" (Habeeb 1988:19, et passim). For example, the ability of the United States to provide Egypt with hundreds of millions of dollars in economic aid is an element of US aggregate structural power; Egypt's ability to offer the United States certain military-base rights on Egyptian territory is an element of Egypt's issue-specific power (i.e., Egypt's relevance to the issue of US strategic interests in the Middle East).

Behavioral power refers to actions in which actors employ their resources (both aggregate and issue-specific) to bring about preferred outcomes. It is manifest in the tactics actors use during the negotiation process.

At the level of aggregate structural power, the US–Egyptian aid relationship is asymmetrical (high-low, HL) and is perceived in this way by both sides. The United States possesses far greater resources and capabilities than Egypt, including the capability to provide hundreds of millions of dollars in economic aid. Egypt's power in the bargaining relationship and Egypt's ability to achieve its preferred outcome must therefore derive from its issue-specific power resources and its skill at using them.

More specifically, bargaining outcomes in the US–Egyptian aid relationship are a function of the interplay between real and perceived Egyptian leverage over US objectives in the Middle East and real and perceived US leverage over Egyptian economic and foreign policy. Egypt's ability to maximize its negotiation outcome at any given time is a function of both its importance to US policy objectives in the Middle East and the state of its economy. Egypt's power in the relationship is, thus, enhanced the more vital Egypt is (or is perceived to be) to US policy objectives in the Middle East and the less need Egypt has for US economic assistance. Conversely, Egypt's power in the relationship is reduced if Egypt becomes less critical to US objectives in the region and if its need for US economic assistance becomes greater. Clearly, perceptions of power asymmetry (HL) play an important role in the US–Egyptian relationship – especially from the perspective of Egypt, the structurally weaker power. Egyptian policy toward the United States seeks to maintain the perception that Egypt is vital to the achievement of US objectives in the region and that US assistance to Egypt is a justified reward to an ally and not charity to a pauper.

As previously noted, US power over Egypt derives from US aggregate structural power – specifically, the United States' ability to provide high levels of economic assistance. This economic assistance has been provided during a period in which US and Egyptian policy objectives in the Middle East have largely coincided, which raises the question of whether US aid is an action that has brought about policy changes in Egypt (thus revealing the exercise of power) or is rather a reward for policy changes that Egypt would have made anyway but were pleasing to the United States.

Heba A. Handoussa (1984:84), an Egyptian scholar who reflects the views of a large portion of the Egyptian intelligentsia, argues that Egypt made "substantive political and military concessions" in exchange for US aid. She further claims that because of US aid Egypt's credibility as a nonaligned state was destroyed, its trade and aid relationships with the East bloc renounced, and much of its aid and export markets in the Arab World lost when it signed the Camp David Accords (Handoussa 1984:89).

Moreover, Handoussa (1984:84), argues that "the objectives of US aid do not closely coincide with those of Egypt." Egypt's objectives, she says, are social equity, a strong public sector, central planning at least at the sectoral level, and rapid economic growth by means of exports. She claims that the US aid program has not supported these objectives, especially export-led growth and production: "Egypt ... was initially led to understand that it would get long-term economic support aimed at growth and development," whereas the United States "considers the substantial aid it delivers to Egypt as a means to feed the population and provide it with basic services and, thus, maintain domestic stability as an end in itself." As a result, Handoussa (1984:90) argues, Egypt will become increasingly dependent on the US aid relationship.

Handoussa's points raise a question: To what degree does the aid relationship itself widen the power asymmetry inherent in the relationship? The displacement explanation of aid argues that massive aid to Egypt has discouraged domestic investment and production and has imposed alien values and consumption patterns. Undeniably, US aid to Egypt helps determine Egypt's development and economic strategies. The Egyptian left and other critics of the government argue further that Egypt's dependence on aid has allowed the United States to "buy" Egypt's participation in US policy objectives (see discussion in Weinbaum 1986:49–67).

An extension of this point of view has led some to conclude that the purpose of US aid is to bring about control over Egypt's political and economic policy. Robert Springborg (1989:258) theorizes a very aggressive US policy objective vis-à-vis Egypt, with aid as the source of power and the lever of policy change: "Foreign aid and increasing indebtedness have gone hand in hand and in so doing created vulnerabilities that the United States immediately seized upon" to make economic policy demands. Springborg focuses principally on US pressure for Egyptian economic reform which, as discussed in detail below, was only one of the terms of trade in the US–Egyptian aid relationship. His view is also based on the *dependencia* model, which would posit that the goal of US involvement in Egypt is to pave the way for penetration of Egypt by multinational corporations.

Yet the real issue is not one of economic dependence. After all, there is no evidence of dependence in the classical sense (i.e., there has been no US exploitation of Egyptian markets or goods and, in fact, relatively little penetration of Egypt by US multinational corporations, other than those participating in projects funded by the US government). Rather, the real issue is one of political dependence: Has US aid to Egypt over the past 15 years allowed the United States to bring about policy changes in Egypt that are compatible with US objectives in the Middle East but that Egypt would not otherwise have undertaken?

As always, proving causation is difficult. In the case of the United States and Egypt, although the potential for US policy leverage would appear to exist, it is difficult to identify specific Egyptian policy changes that are the result of US leverage. President Anwar Sadat chose to visit Jerusalem in 1977 and pursue a peaceful resolution to Egypt's conflict with Israel prior to any promises of economic aid, although he may have anticipated such a reward. Although President Hosni Mubarak must have known that his decision in 1990 to commit Egyptian forces to the war with Iraq would symbolize Egypt's importance to US policy in the region (and thus enhance Egypt's economic benefits), there were other factors related to the balance of power in the Arab world which would likely have led him to the same decision.

Instead of leading Egypt to initiate policies it otherwise would not have, the massive US aid of the ensuing years is more likely to have served to keep Egypt safely ensconced in the pro-American camp and to discourage Egypt from taking policy positions that would have clearly been unacceptable to the United States. But it is hard to do more than speculate on how Egyptian policy may have differed over the past 15 years had the United States not been providing assistance.

Some have argued that Egypt's power and leverage in the aid relationship with the United States derive from its implicit ability to pursue policies antithetical to Washington's interests. For example, Denis Miller (1984:77) writes; "If the US does not come forth with sufficient aid that Egypt wants, then Egypt would make things rougher for US vital interests in the Middle East." This position is hard to support for several reasons.

For one, how would Egypt do this, especially in the post-Cold War era, when there is no other superpower to threaten alliance with? Moreover, would making things "rougher" for US vital interests in the Middle East be compatible with Egypt's own policy objectives in the Middle East? Under the Sadat/Mubarak government, Egypt is essentially a status quo power – one that favors a negotiated settlement to the Israeli–Palestinian conflict, conservative rule in the oil-producing states of the Gulf, and control of the spread of Islamic fundamentalism. Threatening to subvert US interests in the Middle East would thus not only be an unwise way to keep the aid flowing; it would also undermine Egypt's objectives in the region.

If Egypt's policies are essentially the same regardless of whether the US provides aid, then what leverage does Egypt have in the bargaining relationship over aid? Egypt's fundamental source of power is not only its continued pursuit of policies desired by the United States, but also its fundamental economic vulnerability, which threatens the stability of a regime that the United States very much favors. In dialogues over aid, Egypt has never failed to remind the United States of both its importance and its vulnerability, a tactic which Thomas Schelling (1960:37) has coined "coercive deficiency." As Marvin Weinbaum (1986:64) observes, "A Cairo government that complains strongly enough and implies that its ability to succeed (and survive) is at stake has during the history of the US aid program received most of what it sought." Alfred Atherton (1988:20), a former US ambassador to Egypt, described the difficulty the United States has had in attempting to condition even a small portion of its aid on Egyptian economic reforms:

> The United States' own strategic interests require it to recognize the domestic political constraints on how far and fast Egypt can go in adopting economic reform measures that, in purely economic terms, are logical and desirable. ... There are thus limits on the "leverage" theoretically inherent in US aid to Egypt.

The US–Egyptian aid relationship is clearly an asymmetrical one, at a moderately high level. The United States, as dispenser of approximately US$20 billion in economic aid alone since 1976, has played a vital role in maintaining social order in Egypt and perhaps even in maintaining the Sadat/Mubarak government in power. Moreover, the relationship is driven by US foreign policy needs, as well as Egyptian domestic political needs. The United States needs and desires a strong and friendly Egypt to protect its interests in the Middle East. If Egypt were not so strong, it would not matter if it were friendly, and US aid would probably be a fraction of what it is. Similarly, if Egypt were both strong and friendly but US interests in the Middle East either changed or lessened in importance, US aid to Egypt would also be a fraction of what it is. But if Egypt did not need the economic support for its economy and its government, offers of US aid would have no attraction.

As long as Egypt is vital to US interests, and as long as the interests of the United States and Egypt are in rough harmony, Egypt will have leverage in the aid relationship. Because Egypt's vulnerability is a source of power, the Cairo government has been able, at times, to go against US policy objectives, especially in the areas of economic reform and relations with Israel, by pleading that its social or political stability would be threatened by alternative policies.

Table 4.1. US economic aid to Egypt (in million US$)

Fiscal year	Total	Grants	Loans
1976	695	205	490
1977	700	205	495
1978	750	157	593
1979	1050^a	800^a	250
1980	865	585	280
1981	850	780	70
1982	771	771	
1983	750	750	
1984	750	750	
1985	750	750	
1986	750	750	
1987	815	815	
1988	815	815	
1989	815	815	
1990	815	815	
1991	815	815	
1992	815	815	

^{a}Includes US$300 million "peace dividend" after the peace agreement with Israel.
Source: United States Agency for International Development, Annual Budget Submission for Fiscal Years 1976–1992.

4.2   US Economic Aid to Egypt

The provision of significant US economic aid to Egypt began in 1975, co-inciding with the US-mediated disengagement agreement between Egypt and Israel. During the first several years, the aid was principally ear-marked for balance of payments support and war reconstruction; nearly 70% was in the form of loans (see *Table 4.1*). After President Sadat's path-breaking trip to Jerusalem and the subsequent US-mediated Camp David Accords, the United States enhanced its aid program to Egypt both quantitatively and qualitatively. In US fiscal year (FY) 1979, two-thirds of US economic aid to Egypt was converted to grants, and an additional US$300 million "peace dividend" was awarded. By FY 1982, all US economic aid to Egypt was in the form of grants; by FY 1987, the amount had stabilized at US$815 million.

One is immediately struck by the remarkable consistency in the US aid levels to Egypt after FY 1980. It is apparent that whatever the bargaining dynamics between the two countries, the bargaining outcome – at least the overall amount of aid – has remained very much the same for over a decade. This does not mean, however, that the terms of trade remained the same, nor that the bargaining process that produced the outcome was conducted with equal ease in each year. Although the outcome has been consistent – even static – the process of achieving that outcome has been dynamic. As shown below, there have been four distinct terms of trade in the US–Egyptian aid relationship, and each has involved a different negotiation process.

Moreover, aggregate amounts of aid reveal nothing about the form the aid takes. US economic assistance is provided in forms ranging from outright cash transfer to long-term financing of development projects. In the case of Egypt, the vast majority of US aid has been for specific projects, despite the Egyptian government's often-stated desire to receive more aid in the form of cash. Finally, some issues related to US–Egyptian bargaining over aid are not reflected in the aid-level figures, such as the issue of debt relief, which has figured prominently in the US–Egyptian negotiation process.

4.3 US and Egyptian Positions

As noted above, the United States and Egypt converged toward a bargaining relationship out of choice. In other words, the US–Egyptian interdependency was a conscious creation intended to fulfill specific objectives of each side. The relationship, and the interdependency, will thus continue providing that it remains a win–win relationship. Each side must achieve, to a substantial degree, its objectives in the bargaining process.

It should be noted from the outset that US objectives in its relationship with Egypt are not the result of a homogeneous policy process. The US administration's objectives and policy toward Egypt have not always been supported by Congress. In this chapter, the US position and objectives are defined as those that emerge from the internal US policy-making and bargaining processes (those processes, however, are not irrelevant to our study, as they reveal trends and attitudes in the relationship).

US objectives in its aid relationship with Egypt are directly related to US interests and objectives in the Middle East, which historically have been the prevention of Soviet penetration of the region (now, of course, no longer an issue), the advancement of the Arab–Israeli peace process, and the protection of Western access to Middle Eastern oil. As the largest and militarily most powerful Arab state, Egypt has been critical to achieving these objectives. The first two objectives could not have been achieved at all without Egyptian collaboration. Peace between the Arab world and Israel requires Egypt's participation to succeed; no other Arab state is so indispensable to peace. Similarly, Soviet penetration of the region was dealt a fatal blow when Moscow lost its foothold in Egypt; no other Arab state could substitute. The third objective – access to Middle Eastern oil – is secured in part because of Egypt's control of the Suez Canal and support for Arabian Peninsula states. An Egypt hostile to the United States would make reliable access to oil problematic.

One analyst has described the situation quite bluntly:

> The US extends aid to Egypt basically out of its own self-interest to maintain a greater degree of peace and stability in the Middle East. Elements of exchange are present here. Egypt gains from aid, and the US gains from more certainty in the Middle East. [Miller 1984:77]

US officials have been explicit about the role aid to Egypt plays in achieving these objectives. The US Agency for International Development (USAID), in response to questions posed by the House Foreign Affairs Committee, said the purpose of US economic aid to Egypt is "to support Egyptian economic and political stability, viewed as essential to achieving a comprehensive peace in the Middle East" (United States Congress, House of Representatives, Subcommittee on Europe and the Middle East of the Foreign Affairs Committee 1988:206).

Michael Stone (1984:35), former director of the USAID mission in Cairo, has noted that the purpose of the US aid program in Egypt is to create a "stronger Egypt," which in turn will do two things: make Egypt better able "to provide effective leadership in the peace process in the Middle East" and render Egypt "better able to be a strong friend of its allies."

At times, another US objective – free-market economic reform in Egypt – has also been introduced into the US–Egyptian bargaining process over aid. Yet, as demonstrated below, the overriding US objective in the relationship remains the political and security alliance with Egypt.

The immediate Egyptian objective in its aid relationship with the United States is obvious: the aid relationship provides Egypt with badly needed economic assistance that is necessary, in the minds of many Egyptians, to maintain social and thus political stability. But Egypt has other objectives, as well. For example, it became clear to Egyptian leaders after the October 1973 Middle East War that a closer relationship with the United States was more likely to bring about Egypt's own regional political objectives: an end to the state of war with Israel, a return of the Israeli-occupied Sinai Peninsula, and a prominent leadership role for Egypt in the region.

Shibley Telhami (1990:105) adds a twist to this last objective. He argues that Sadat, in choosing to become dependent upon the United States for economic aid and military support, was trying to rid Egypt of its growing economic, and thus political dependence, on other Arab states. In this way, Egypt would regain its dominant political role within the Arab world and within the region.

4.4   The Changing Terms of Trade

Most bargaining relationships operate under an implicit set of terms of trade or formula, the specific amounts of the items exchanged representing the detailed application of the formula (Zartman 1978). That is, most bargaining relationships are an exchange of values: each side provides something of value to the other –X in exchange for Y (Axelrod and Keohane 1986; Keohane and Nye 1989:253–254). If the value of one or the other party changes, then either the terms of trade of the bargaining relationship change or the relationship comes to an end. The bargaining process centers on determining how much X for how much Y. These exchanges are bilateral actions by which each side exercises power over the other – it is a mutual relationship unless some clear sequencing can indicate an initiator and a responder.

In the case of the US–Egyptian bargaining relationship, the underlying terms of trade, as alluded to above, are US economic aid in exchange for Egyptian policy decisions that promote US political and strategic objectives in the Middle East. However, attempts have been made to change or modify this formula, mostly initiated by the United States. A chronological history of the terms of trade in the US–Egyptian aid relationship reveals that, despite these initiatives to change the terms of trade, the basic underlying exchange has remained intact.

Substantial US economic aid to Egypt began in the years immediately following the Sinai disengagement agreements. By allowing the United States to mediate these agreements and by preventing the Soviet Union from playing a role in the process, Egypt had implicitly cast its lot with Washington. US aid increased in FY 1977 and FY 1978 (see *Table 4.1*) following Sadat's trip to Jerusalem and the initiation of the Camp David process. After the signing of the Egyptian–Israeli peace agreement in 1979, aid was qualitatively improved by being transformed to largely grant aid.

The terms of trade during this period were in part "aid in exchange for peace with Israel" and in part "aid in exchange for altering the strategic balance" (i.e., precluding a Soviet role in the peace process and denying Moscow a major outpost in the Middle East).

In the early 1980s, under the Reagan administration, US aid levels to Egypt increased both quantitatively and qualitatively as a result of the Reagan administration's emphasis on bolstering regional allies in the struggle against Moscow; the aid became all-grant in FY 1982. The terms of trade could be redefined as "aid for strategic consensus," referring to the Reagan administration's desired policy of creating a network of allies in the Middle East that shared the US objective of thwarting Moscow's ambitions (in fact, US foreign assistance throughout the world was, at the time, based principally on the recipients' roles in the war against communism).

According to one US State Department official who was involved in US–Egyptian aid negotiations, "Sadat was totally in synch with US strategic concerns" and was "very persuasive" in arguing Egypt's critical role in defending US strategic interests.

From the US perspective, this new set of terms of trade seems to have pushed aside, if not displaced, the earlier "aid in exchange for peace with Israel." For example, there was no significant change in aid levels during the Israeli invasion of Lebanon in 1982, when Egypt essentially "froze" its relations with Israel, withdrew its ambassador from Tel Aviv, and harshly criticized Israel's actions.

Midway through the Reagan presidency, yet another set of terms of trade began to compete with "aid for strategic consensus" as the basis of exchange: aid in exchange for Egyptian economic reform. This formula was consistent with the Reagan administration's global crusade to promote the establishment of capitalist free-market economic systems, which was labeled "the new orthodoxy of development," by some (see Springborg 1989:256, for a discussion of this concept and how it applies to US aid to Egypt).

As a result of this new set of terms of trade, serious differences were introduced into the US and Egyptian perspectives about the aid relationship for the first time. Egypt strongly resisted complying with US demands for economic reform, which essentially mirrored the structural adjustment demands of the International Monetary Fund (IMF) and the

World Bank. Egyptians saw this not only as patronizing, but as an effort by the United States to use its aid as leverage to bring about economic policy changes, as opposed to a reward for an ally that was critical to US regional interests. Some Egyptians saw this new policy as reflective of collusion among the United States, the IMF, and the World Bank.

Egypt preferred that its contribution to the exchange be based on its strategic, not economic, policy for several reasons. First, there was the sensitive issue of parity with Israel. US aid to Israel had never been conditioned on economic reform, even though the Israeli economy in the 1980s was in many ways as statist as the Egyptian economy. Second, even at more than US$800 million per year, US aid to Egypt could in no way make up for the hardship Egyptians would endure if the full program of IMF-mandated reforms were implemented (the program included an end to food and energy subsidies, as well as the privatization of state-run enterprises, a major source of employment). In short, Egypt simply did not want to carry out the reforms. Finally, Egyptian officials felt that the "aid for strategic consensus" exchange had the potential to be more enduring and did not require them to take policy positions that they would not otherwise have made.

Nevertheless, despite Egypt's opposition, the "aid for economic reform" exchange gained popularity in the United States, especially among members of Congress, who began to scrutinize Egypt's economic policies and criticize the administration for pouring aid money into what appeared to be a bottomless pit, and within USAID, where proponents of economic development and reform far outnumbered advocates of Egypt's strategic role.

Yet ultimately, US actions revealed that the underlying objective of US aid to Egypt remained the strategic one, which meant that the United States did not push Egypt so hard on economic reforms that it would risk threatening government or regime stability. In fact, in 1989 US officials placed so much pressure on the IMF to reach a standby agreement with Egypt, despite Egypt's failure to carry out the required reforms, that several IMF officials resigned in protest. Moreover, neither the administration nor Congress actually took steps to reduce Egypt's aid levels.

Discussing this period in the relationship, a former USAID official recalled with frustration how the Egyptian negotiating team "would run over to the State Department when the going got tough" in negotiations with USAID. The Egyptians knew that the State Department would be receptive to arguments about the strategic importance of the relationship.

They also correctly believed that the State Department would ultimately prevail over USAID.

But because of the simultaneous existence of two conflicting terms of trade, tension in the aid relationship grew until the Iraqi invasion of Kuwait in 1990. In the words of a USAID official "Egypt must have had a direct line to God," for the invasion muted the voices in Washington that advocated a tough line against Egypt on economic reform. Egypt was the first and most militarily important Arab state to join ranks with the United States against Iraq, and Egyptian President Mubarak personally persuaded other Arab states to join the coalition. The result was that the overriding terms of trade – "aid for strategic consensus" – quickly reassumed their primary role, and US criticism of Egyptian economic reforms (or lack thereof) virtually ceased. Moreover, the United States carried out its part of the exchange by not only providing the regular amounts of aid, but by offering an additional gift of nearly US$7 billion in bilateral debt relief.

All three formulas (aid for peace with Israel, aid for strategic consensus, and aid for economic reform) have been cumulative, with each seeming to carry more or less weight at various times, but with the underlying "aid for support of US policy" being the definitive exchange.

This fact becomes clear in the wording of the International Security and Cooperation Act of 1985 (known as the Foreign Aid Bill). Although this act was passed during a period in which the "aid for economic reform" terms of trade seemed to be growing in popularity, Congress nevertheless wrote:

> [A]ll United States foreign assistance to Egypt is provided in the expectation that the Egyptian Government will continue in its efforts to bring peace to the region and that it will continue to support and fulfill the provisions of the Camp David Accords and the Egyptian–Israeli Peace Treaty. [Reprinted in United States Congress, Senate Committee on Foreign Relations and House Committee on Foreign Affairs 1991]

Is it any wonder that Egypt felt free to resist US demands for rigorous economic reform?

In the wake of the Gulf War, Egypt has faced uncertainty about what new terms of trade may emerge. In the conclusion to this chapter, we speculate on how the nature of the bargaining exchange may evolve in the late 1990s and beyond. But first, to see more clearly how the terms of trade and each side's elements of power work, we briefly analyze three micro issues within the macro bargaining relationship.

4.4.1 The issue of parity with Israel

Since the beginning of the US–Egyptian aid relationship, many Egyptians have argued that Egypt and Israel should receive equal treatment; this has never, however, been the case. Israel received a greater "bonus" at the time of the Egyptian–Israeli peace agreement (this was explained in part by US officials as compensation for the costs of Israeli withdrawal from the Sinai), and when US economic aid to Egypt stabilized at US$815 million in FY 1987, aid to Israel was set at US$1 billion.

Israel has also received other advantages in its aid program that did not accrue to Egypt. For example, as early as 1982, Congress indicated that US economic aid to Israel should never be less than the annual debt repayment (interest and principal) Israel owed the United States (United States Congress, Senate Committee on Foreign Relations 1982:7–9). This stipulation became codified in the FY 1987 Foreign Assistance Appropriations Act, in effect guaranteeing Israel a minimum amount of aid every year. By comparison, Egypt has no legislatively mandated guarantee of economic aid. Indeed, Congress launched an investigation in 1987 when it suspected that Egypt may have used some of its cash transfer to pay off military debt owed to the United States (United States Congress, House of Representatives, Subcommittee on Europe and the Middle East of the Foreign Affairs Committee 1988.)

Finally, Israel's economic aid from the United States is awarded in the form of a direct cash transfer, with no stipulations on how the aid is to be used. The bulk of Egypt's economic grant is in the form of slow-disbursing project assistance, allocated for specific development projects that are designed and managed by USAID.

Egyptian officials have frequently pointed out this disparity and requested more equitable treatment. Mostafa El-Said (1984:16), at the time Egyptian Minister of the Economy, wrote: "The Americans should give us all the aid in cash. We are in a better position to make the best use of it. ... This is done for Israel. Why shouldn't it be done for Egypt?"

One way Egypt's second-class treatment can be explained is the special relationship between the United States and Israel, and the strong support that exists for Israel within the US Congress. Representative Lee Hamilton, then Chair of the House Foreign Affairs Committee's Europe and Middle East Subcommittee, rejected an argument by an administration witness in favor of allowing Egypt to use its economic aid to pay off its military debt to the United States: "I am concerned about your assumption that what the Congress signaled its intent to be with respect to Israel would also apply to Egypt. I just don't think that recognizes the reality of what happens up here [in Congress] with respect to Israel" (United States Congress, House of Representatives, Subcommittee on Europe and the Middle East of the Foreign Affairs Committee 1988:25). The bottom line is that Egypt, Israel, and the United States interact in a triangular relationship in which Egypt is the weakest side.

Another explanation, however, is that the United States had determined that it could get what it wanted out of its bargaining relationship with Egypt (which, as we have identified it, is a politically stable ally in the Arab world) without granting to Egypt the same largess it bestowed upon Israel. US aid to Egypt merely needed to be at sufficient levels to serve the dual and interconnected purposes of helping to maintain both social stability in Egypt and the Sadat/Mubarak government in power. Given this explanation, which is based on the two sides' bargaining power, one would argue that Egypt would have received greater benefits in its aid program if it appeared to be confronting economic or social instability. In fact, in January 1977, the United States quickly shifted US$190 million of Egypt's aid from slow-disbursing capital development projects to fast-disbursing commodity aid after Cairo was wracked by violent food riots (Weinbaum 1986:37).

4.4.2   The issue of increasing the cash component of Egypt's aid

As noted above, the bulk of Egypt's economic assistance from the United States is provided in the form of project assistance; only a relatively small portion has been awarded as a cash transfer (sometimes described as balance of payments support). The debate over the cash-transfer issue not only reveals the power balance of the aid relationship, but also reflects the relationship's changing terms of trade.

As echoed in Minister El-Said's statement, many Egyptian officials have expressed that the cash component of US economic assistance should represent a larger portion than it has. In fact, the cash component of US assistance has never been greater than US$115 million (with the exception of the "peace dividend" after Camp David). Moreover, beginning in FY 1985, all cash transfers to Egypt were to be disbursed "in conjunction with the achievement of economic reforms" (letter from Jay Morris to Lee Hamilton, reprinted in United States Congress, House of Representatives, Subcommittee on Europe and the Middle East of the Foreign Affairs Committee 1988:69–73), thus reflecting the "aid for economic reform" terms of trade. The US foreign aid bill for FY 1986 and FY 1987 required that the cash transfer to Egypt be provided "with the understanding that Egypt will undertake economic reforms ... additional to those which would be undertaken in the absence of the cash transfer" (see United States Congress, Senate Committee on Foreign Relations and House Committee on Foreign Affairs 1991). According to an official at USAID who was involved in the US–Egyptian dialogue, this new stipulation in the foreign aid bill was a "seminal event" in the relationship, for it reflected the strong desire by Congress and USAID to promote the economic reform agenda. It also demonstrated that although there was no desire to change the overall aid levels to Egypt, there was a willingness to use cash transfer as a leverage over Egyptian policy.

In response to the slow progress in economic reform, the United States in FY 1988 and FY 1989 withheld all cash transfers to Egypt (while maintaining the overall aid level at US$815 million). The justification given by Administration officials was the lack of any "substantial progress" in Egypt's ongoing negotiations with the IMF. The official State Department position was given at a press conference: "Release of the cash funds is not formally tied to an agreement between Egypt and the IMF," but cash transfer "would be most productively applied in support of an economic reform program which could command broad international support, including the support of the IMF, the World Bank and other major donors" (Charles Redman, State Department Press Spokesperson, 8 March 1989). An internal USAID document explained the decision to withhold the release of the cash as follows:

> AID's policy dialogue with the government [of Egypt] has been friendly, but not easy. For example, the [government of Egypt] did not undertake macroeconomic reforms sufficient to justify the annual release of cash transfer in FY 1988. There is still strong resistance to changing policies that have characterized the economy and society for thirty years. [USAID Egypt 1989]

Representative Hamilton was even more pointed, arguing that the Administration should be "much, much tougher and stronger in demanding and insisting" on economic reform from Egypt (*Washington Post*, 8 March 1989:A26).

In 1987, Representative Hamilton commissioned a study by the US General Accounting Office (GAO) on the issue of Egypt's cash transfer. The resulting report (United States General Accounting Office 1987), which has four principal conclusions, argues strongly in favor of the "aid for economic reform" terms of trade. Specifically, the report found that: cash transfers should be linked to "real reform progress"; cash transfers have been based on the "conflicting objectives" of offering political support as well as leverage for economic reforms; cash disbursements should be made "only after specific agreed-upon reform actions are taken"; and cash transfer decisions have often been made on political, not economic, grounds. On this last point, the report mentioned the transfer of US$115 million in 1987, a year in which Egypt lapsed out of compliance with its IMF program.

The report concludes that, while "the primary overall objective of US assistance to Egypt has been to support the peace process in the Middle East," this objective has sent the wrong signal to Egypt – specifically, that its cash transfer is an entitlement regardless of its progress on reform.

At the same time, other voices in the US policy-making process were warning that linking US assistance to economic reforms risked undermining the more important terms of trade in the relationship, "aid for strategic consensus." Senator Robert Kasten, a strong congressional supporter of Egypt, reminded his colleagues during a 1989 Senate hearing that US support for Egypt is based on the Camp David Accords and Egyptian support for US efforts to seek a Middle East peace. The United States, Senator Kasten said, must not push Egypt to the point of "threatening its political stability."

In the end, the "aid for strategic consensus" terms of trade prevailed, and Egypt's US$230 million in cash transfer for FY 1988 and FY 1989 was eventually released (after several highly touted Egyptian reform initiatives). But the brief history of this issue demonstrates how the changing terms of trade that characterized much of the 1980s often caused confusion in the bargaining relationship.

4.4.3   The issue of debt relief

The third issue in the US–Egyptian bargaining relationship over aid pertains to Egypt's military debt to the United States. While it is unrelated to the annual allocation of US economic assistance, the provision of US debt relief to Egypt is nevertheless a form of economic aid, and the bargaining over debt relief is similar to that over economic grant aid.

Egypt began receiving large quantities of US arms in 1979. These arms were provided on credit, at commercial interest rates (some as high as 14%). Israel received arms from the United States on the same financial terms. In 1985, both countries' military aid was converted into grants, in acknowledgment of the high cost of advanced military weaponry and in line with the Reagan administration's emphasis on building a strategic consensus among allies in the Middle East. Debt from earlier purchases, however, remained a financial obligation for both Egypt and Israel. Both countries asked for debt relief – or better yet, debt forgiveness – but these requests were rejected by the United States at the time.

In 1988, Israel accepted a US-structured plan to refinance its debt at lower interest rates. Egypt, however, refused to refinance and again asked for debt forgiveness. Egypt also slipped into arrears on repaying its debt. In 1989, Egypt fell one year behind in debt payments and risked enforcement of the Brooke amendment, a law that stipulates that any country more than one year in arrears in paying its military debt would be ineligible to receive any military or economic aid from the United States. It was saved from the penalty of the Brooke amendment by the Bush administration, which "discovered" some previously allocated funds to Egypt that were being held in escrow at the US Treasury; these funds were counted against Egypt's debt payments (see Quandt 1990:28–29). The US position thus appeared to be somewhat contradictory: keep Egypt from slipping into default on its debt payments and becoming ineligible for all aid, but avoid granting Egypt any degree of debt relief. This seeming contradiction was in fact a reflection of the two competing terms of trade: "aid for economic reform" and "aid for strategic consensus."

The Egyptians, of course, emphasized the importance of the latter terms of trade. In a document prepared in 1988 for distribution to members of Congress, the Egyptian government argued that "the [military] debt has become a destabilizing threat to Egyptian and regional security.... . This debt burden could be fatal to Egypt's hopes in the face of its current massive balance of payments crisis" (Government of Egypt 1988).

With the threat of war in the Persian Gulf in August 1990, the contradiction in the terms of trade in the US–Egyptian aid relationship was resolved in Egypt's favor. Specifically, "aid for strategic consensus" once again became the dominant terms of trade.

Within hours of the outbreak of hostilities between Iraq and Kuwait, Egypt clearly indicated that it intended to play a leadership role in coalescing the Arab world behind US initiatives against Iraq. Within weeks, the United States was proposing to forgive Egypt's entire military debt of approximately US$7 billion. The reasons US officials gave for this sudden willingness to forgive Egypt's debt clearly reveal how the terms of trade had changed due to Egypt's newly enhanced strategic importance to US policy in the Middle East.

Deputy Secretary of State Lawrence Eagleburger testified before Congress to offer justification for providing the massive debt relief. The arguments he made are instructive. He began by arguing that "President Mubarak's stand in the Gulf crisis can be compared ... to Egypt's decision to sign a peace treaty with Israel in 1979" (Congress:237). In other words, Egypt's support of Operation Desert Shield was equivalent in importance to the Camp David Accords in its support of US regional and strategic objectives. "Without Egypt," Eagleburger said, "we can't make [Operation Desert Shield] work" (Congress:288).

Eagleburger continued: "Between 1984 and 1990, the burden of servicing Egyptian [military] debt became the largest political irritant in US–Egyptian relations" (Congress:238). A somewhat cynical, yet accurate interpretation of this passage would be that even though the debt issue was a political irritant, it was not resolved until the United States could not afford a political irritant in its relations with Egypt.

In his conclusion, Eagleburger stated clearly that the strategic terms of trade had overridden the economic terms of trade:

> Let me make it perfectly clear, however, that we were not prepared to seek cancellation of Egypt's [military] debt on the basis of [economic] factors. Our decision to do so now is solely related to the unique circumstances, and in particular to the urgent political and military challenges Egypt is facing as a consequence of the ongoing crisis in the Gulf. [Congress:239]

He added, "The forgiveness of [military] debt, in short, will not lessen in any way our commitment to engaging the Egyptians on ... structural [economic] reforms" (Congress:239–240). In other words, Eagleburger was promising a return to the economic reform terms of trade as soon as the Gulf crisis ended.

The Egyptians were, of course, eager to encourage this renewed emphasis by the United States on the strategic terms of trade. Mohammed Abdel Moneim, President Mubarak's press spokesperson, said that Egypt's position in the Gulf crisis demonstrates that "now the whole world – the US, Europe, and even the Arabs – realize that a strong Egypt is a stabilizing element in the region" (quoted in Miller 1990).

Even as the debt was being forgiven, some in Congress maintained that the competing terms of trade – "aid in exchange for economic reform" – should rule the aid relationship. Representative Hamilton, in response to the Administration's arguments for debt relief, said that "we should hold to the conditionality of reform. I want to see us go harder rather than easier" (quoted in Friedman 1990). Nevertheless, Congress approved the Administration's debt relief proposal. In addition, the United States lobbied hard among the Paris Club countries for global forgiveness of Egypt's bilateral debt; in the end, 17 nations forgave more than US$20 billion in Egyptian debt (*New York Times*, 27 May 1991:1), out of a total debt of just less than US$50 billion (World Bank Development Report 1991.)

4.5 Conclusion

Several conclusions about the US–Egyptian bargaining relationship are worth noting. The terms of trade in the bargaining relationship have been controlled more often by the United States than by Egypt. Egypt's preference would have been to sustain the "aid for Camp David" terms of trade into perpetuity. The intrusion of the economic reform issue was not welcomed by Cairo and was ultimately resisted largely because of a contextual event (the Iraqi invasion of Kuwait). This situation confirms proposition 2 on asymmetrical negotiation in the introductory chapter, indicating that the stronger power will behave exploitatively.

Egypt's "weakness" is that its need for US economic aid is critical and unchanging. By contrast, the United States' need for what Egypt offers in exchange for aid has oscillated, subject largely to contextual factors and events that are only marginally in Egypt's control. Thus, Egypt must constantly remind the United States of its importance and of the importance of the relationship, whereas the United States does not need to convince the Egyptians of their need for US assistance.

Nevertheless, because both sides share a strong motivational orientation, as well as common goals in the regional context, Egypt has succeeded in at least maintaining high levels of aid, even if it has had to struggle to receive this aid in the form it wants and with as few strings attached as possible. Thus, the underlying terms of trade (aid in exchange for strategic consensus) have remained strong enough to counterbalance

Egypt's asymmetry in the relationship, and, when both sides have committed to these terms of trade, Egypt has even been able to diverge substantially from US regional policy without doing damage to the aid relationship (examples are Egypt's "cold peace" with Israel until the Oslo negotiations and then again in mid-1997, and its rather warmer relationship with Libya).

Egypt's challenge in its aid relationship with the United States will continue to be to achieve its objective (high levels of aid) through the most advantageous terms of trade (aid in exchange for strategic consensus). The reason these terms of trade are the most advantageous for Egypt is that they only require Egypt to do what it would probably do anyway (i.e., pursue policies that are supportive of US interests in the region).

But in light of the end of the Cold War and the new era in Israeli–Arab peace, Egypt finds itself in a less indispensable position than formerly. Cairo must thus seek new ways to define "strategic consensus" – such as mutual resistance to Islamic extremism – and resist definitions that would require it to dramatically alter domestic policies – such as mutual commitment to multiparty democracy and free-market economics.

A comprehensive Middle East peace agreement, which is no longer a fantasy, would deal another blow to Egypt, at least in terms of its bargaining power in its relationship with the United States over aid (in many other ways a comprehensive agreement would benefit Egypt). For Egypt, the ideal situation is a peace process that is sufficiently promising to cause the United States to value Egypt's continuing stability and mediating role, but not so promising that Egypt's role becomes less necessary.

Even with a comprehensive Arab–Israeli peace agreement, US attention will continue to focus on the Gulf and on stable oil prices and oil supply. It would, thus, behoove Egypt to try to transform the terms of trade into "aid for assistance in maintaining Gulf stability." In the wake of the Gulf War, there has been some thinking along these lines in US policy circles. A postwar study prepared by the US GAO notes that "from the US point of view, it would be better for Egypt than the United States to provide security in the Middle East" (United States Government, General Accounting Office 1992:22). Louis Cantori (1992:64–65) notes that the "Damascus Declaration" after the Gulf War (March 1991) would have given Egypt a prominent role in Gulf security, and that this would have ensured continued high levels of US support for Egypt. However, the Saudis dropped the idea, or let it die, out of fear of too prominent an Egyptian role.

Another US government analyst, Stephen Pelletiere (1992:17), links the Islamic threat with the Gulf security requirement. He notes that Egypt is one of the most threatened states in terms of Islamic agitation, is critical to US interests in the region, and should thus be the focus of US aid and support: "US interests in the region require – at a minimum – stable, friendly regimes in Egypt and Saudi Arabia; they are the regions' centers of gravity."

William Quandt, a long-time observer of US–Egyptian relations, believes that "there is going to have to be a postcrisis means for keeping Iraq from throwing its weight around too much in the region. The most important and interesting potential is in Egypt playing more of a role in Gulf security and getting paid to do so" (quoted in Curtius 1990).

The key question for Egypt is whether these trends in US security thinking will evolve into new, and more stable terms of trade in bargaining over US economic assistance. Even if it does, however, factors exogenous to the US–Egyptian relationship – such as federal budgetary pressures, declining domestic support in the United States for foreign aid programs, and an administration less interested in international politics – will probably lead to an eventual decrease in US aid levels to Egypt. This situation does not mean that the bargaining relationship will cease, only that the value of the outcome (from Egypt's perspective) will be diminished.

References

Atherton, A.L., Jr., 1988, *Egypt and US Interests*, Johns Hopkins Foreign Policy Institute, Washington, DC.

Axelrod, R., and Keohane, R., 1986, Achieving co-operation under anarchy, *World Politics*, **39**(2):239–243.

Cantori, L., 1992, The Middle East: Political trends and their implications for US force structure, in United States General Accounting Office, Papers Prepared for GAO Conference on Worldwide Threats, Government Printing Office, Washington, DC.

Curtius, M., 1990, Bush will press to cancel Egypt's $7.1 billion arms debt, *Boston Globe*, 5 September:1.

El-Said, M., 1984, in E.L. Sullivan, ed., *Impact of Development Assistance on Egypt*, American University, Cairo, Egypt.

Friedman, J., 1990, Bush officials lobby Congress to cancel Egypt's military debt, *Christian Science Monitor*, 14 September:1.

Government of Egypt, 1988, *White Paper for 1988*, Government of Egypt, Cairo, Egypt.

Habeeb, W.M., 1988, *Power and Tactics in International Negotiations: How Weak Nations Bargain with Strong Nations*, Johns Hopkins University Press, Baltimore, MD.

Handoussa, H.A., 1984, Conflicting objectives in Egyptian–American aid relationship, in E.L. Sullivan, ed., *Impact of Development Assistance on Egypt*, American University, Cairo, Egypt.

Keohane, R.O., and Nye, J.S., 1989, *Power and Independence*, 2nd edition, Scott Foresman, Boston, MA.

Miller, D., 1984, Egypt and the US: An aid or trade relationship? in E.L. Sullivan, ed., *Impact of Development Assistance on Egypt*, American University, Cairo, Egypt.

Miller, J., 1990, Mideast tensions: Gulf crisis produces surge of Egyptian confidence, *New York Times*, 11 November:14.

Pelletiere, S.C., 1992, *Mass Action and Islamic Fundamentalism: The Revolt of the Brooms*, Strategic Studies Institute, US Army War College, Carlisle, PA.

Quandt, W.B., 1977, *Decade of Decisions*, University of California, Berkeley, CA.

Quandt, W.B., 1986, *Camp David*, The Brookings Institution, Washington, DC.

Schelling, T., 1960, *The Strategy of Conflict*, Harvard University Press, Cambridge, MA.

Springborg, R., 1989, *Mubarak's Egypt: Fragmentation of the Political Order*, Westview Press, Boulder, CO.

Stone, M., 1984, in E.L. Sullivan, ed., *Impact of Development Assistance on Egypt*, American University, Cairo, Egypt.

Telhami, S., 1990, *Power and Leadership in International Bargaining*, Columbia University Press, New York.

United States Congress, House of Representatives, Subcommittee on Europe and the Middle East of the Foreign Affairs Committee, 1988, *Hearing: Agency for International Development Policy on the Use of Cash Transfer: The Case of Egypt*, 100th Congress, 1st session, Government Printing Office, Washington, DC.

United States Congress, House of Representatives, Subcommittee on Foreign Operations, Export Financing and Related Issues of the Committee on Appropriations, 1991, *Hearings*, 102nd Congress, 1st session, Government Printing Office, Washington, DC.

United States Congress, Senate Committee on Foreign Relations and House Committee on Foreign Affairs, 1991, *Legislation on Foreign Relations Through 1990*, Government Printing Office, Washington, DC.

United States Congress, Senate Committee on Foreign Relations, 1982, *Report on the International Security Enhancement Act of 1982*, Senate Report 464, 97th Congress, 2nd session, Government Printing Office, Washington, DC.

United States Congress, Senate Subcommittee on Foreign Operations of the Committee on Appropriations Hearing on Administration's Request for Foreign Assistance in Fiscal Year 1990.

United States General Accounting Office, 1987, *Use of Cash Transfers to Support Economic Policy Reforms in Egypt*, Government Printing Office, Washington, DC.

United States General Accounting Office, 1992, *Perspectives on Worldwide Threats and Implications for US Forces*, Report to the Chairmen, Senate and House Armed Services Committees, Government Printing Office, Washington, DC.

USAID Egypt, 1989, *FY 1990 Action Plan*, 15 March, Cairo, Egypt.

Weinbaum, M.G., 1986, *Egypt and the Politics of US Economic Aid*, Westview Press, Boulder, CO.

Zartman, I.W., 1978, *The Negotiation Process: Theories and Applications*, Sage Publications, Beverly Hills, CA.

Chapter 5

The Andorra–European Community Trade Agreement Negotiations, 1979–1987

Guy Olivier Faure and Patrick Klaousen

The European context offers a wide variety of unexpected negotiations. Among them the agreement between the European Community (EC) and Andorra is practically unknown, like the principality of Andorra itself. However, the agreement is characterized by a number of unique features that are of particular relevance to the study of power under conditions of considerable asymmetry. The story of the EC and Andorra negotiations could provide the material for a new fable, in the manner of La Fontaine, whose title could be "The Lion and the Snail." The former possesses overwhelming capacity of action. The latter appears helpless, unable to make any substantial contribution; even its survival greatly depends on the goodwill of the other party. But who gets his way at the end of this fable?

These negotiations, initially purely economic, reveal multiple situations within which power factors, drawn from very different sources, are at play. In our working definition, power is the action one party takes to influence the behavior of others – that is, to increase the probability that others will respond in certain ways. The intention here is to orient the inquiry toward both the causal aspects of power and tactical actions that enable power to be implemented and that, as a consequence, influence it. We have found it useful to draw lessons of efficiency in the exercise of power by referring to the conditions of such exercises and to the situational context. We conclude by drawing some theoretical implications from the previous observations.

If we consider the asymmetrical distribution of capacities, would such a power situation lead to an accurate prediction concerning the results of the negotiations as indicators of the power distribution? Is the real situation as imbalanced as it appears if one takes data such as the gross national product (GNP) of a country or level of armament? In other words, what is the true nature of the power exercised by each party in the negotiations? On what grounds is this power based? What are its main components? A second type of question can then be raised, concerning the relevance of the available resources to the particular issue. The fundamental investigation would then bear upon the distribution of power among actors on those issues.

When the process starts, the weaker party's inferiority leads it to look for a means of achieving a better position. Several types of tactics are available to serve this purpose. The first type is at the structural level and consists in searching for allies, coalition building, introducing third parties as mediators, and choosing the level at which the discussion is to take place, be it economic, legal, or some other level. The second type of tactic is to develop actions integrated in the general movement of the negotiation to restore a better power balance. It is of interest to inventory the various means implemented in the EC–Andorra negotiations and to assess their effectiveness in relation to the final outcome.

The resolution of a conflict through negotiation can be viewed as a joint search for a new equilibrium acceptable to each party to the dispute. The game played by Andorra was conceived within a multilateral rationale, taking into account the geographical situation of the principality. The EC–Andorra negotiations are a highly asymmetrical case, with the EC, France, and Spain – multiple parties perceived as structurally powerful – dealing with Andorra, a weak micro-state (HHHL). This chapter aims at demonstrating that the outcome of a negotiation cannot be explained, and furthermore predicted, from the mere perception of the resource distribution among the actors, but that perception allows for the exercise of power as actions. As a consequence this case radically challenges the deterministic assumption that equates perceived structural power with the final outcome (see propositions 1 and 2 in the introductory chapter).

5.1 The Parties to the Agreement: European Community, Andorra, and the Outsiders

The European Union (EU) – at the time of the negotiations the European Community – is, above all, an intergovernmental organization. When Spain and Portugal joined in January 1986, the EC comprised 12 member states and influenced the economic destiny of 320 million inhabitants, spread over about 772,000 square miles. Moreover, the EU is the largest world trade power, in value and in volume. Since 1965 the Community has led a single institutional structure endowed with a legal personality. EU action is guided by a logic of integration of the member states' economies, and its long-term objective is the establishment of a supranational entity. On that account, the EC stood uphill from Andorra in the extremely asymmetrical relationship in the negotiations between the two parties.

A remnant of Charlemagne's Empire located high in the heart of the Pyrenees, Andorra, 180 square miles and with 50,000 inhabitants, among whom only 25% are nationals, is a self-administrated territory, juridically independent. Andorra's official language is Catalan and nationals travel abroad with an Andorran passport. However, its small size and its complex institutional structure have generated a relationship of dependence toward its powerful neighbors, France to the north and Spain to the south. Andorra's territory is an enclave in two ways: it has no outlet to the sea; and since Spain joined the EC in 1986, Andorra has been surrounded by the EC's customs union territory. On the eve of World War II, Andorra was a poor mountain economy from which, for centuries, whole generations had to expatriate themselves to France or to Spain to make a living. Hard work and a keen sense of business applied to new opportunities from the development of mass tourism have greatly transformed the economy in a few decades. Today, Andorra's economy is basically built on both retail trade and tourism. An important banking sector has recently been developed, along with light industry and agriculture devoted almost exclusively to growing tobacco. As a result, Andorra's economy produces very little of what it needs. The very low tax rate leads one to compare Andorra to a huge duty-free shop, whose prosperity is mostly built on the maintenance of exemption from customs duties and value-added tax (VAT). Andorra's new wealth is built on the wave of shopping tourism. Annually 10 million visitors take the *route du pastis* (taken from the name of a French liquor made from anise). Over the years, this Andorran practice enraged the French and Spanish governments, which were losing important tax revenue.

The interference of the outsiders – France and Spain – in the negotiations between Andorra and the EC was largely due to economic reasons. Almost all of the goods that enter Andorra are reintroduced into these two countries in the luggage of travelers, but the market shares of French and Spanish exporters to Andorra have been on a downward trend. Given that 90% of the customers in Andorran shops come from France and Spain, there is no doubt that both the increasing deficit of their balance of trade and losses in their tax collection have led these two countries to consider Andorra's arrangement a breach in their customs protection system. Moreover, Spain's interference in the negotiations was also guided by social considerations. Approximately 75% of Andorra's population is made up of immigrants, three-quarters of whom are Spanish nationals. These immigrants hold the majority of the unskilled jobs. During the negotiations, Spanish trade unions pointed out that Andorra's social legislation was 50 years behind that of Spain, and that Spanish nationals working in Andorra make up an underclass shamelessly exploited by Andorran company managers.

Andorra's trade was ruled by two parallel agreements with its powerful neighbors, France and Spain. The integration of Spain into the EC drastically modified the previous situation, for the agreements were no longer between the principality and two sovereign countries but between Andorra and the EC. The goal of the negotiations was to modify the earlier treaties to adapt the trade regime to EC regulations.

If France and Spain not only had good reason to intervene in the negotiation, they also had the means to act. As explained below, each sat on both sides of the negotiation table, the European side and the Andorran side.

The EU's external responsibilities are mainly shared by the Commission of the European Communities and the European Council. The Commission has the power to initiate and carry out negotiations, but the Council is the final decision maker. The Council is made up of representatives of the governments of the 15 member states. Each state usually sends one of its government ministers. Its membership thus varies with the subjects under discussion. The foreign minister is regarded as his or her country's main representative to the Council, but other ministers also meet frequently for specialized Council meetings. When the Commission produces and submits a draft agreement to the Council, any member state has the right to raise an objection. Since, within the Council, the Andorra–EC agreement is a matter primarily concerning France and Spain, an objection from these two countries would have frozen the whole process. However, as decisions passed by the Council on this matter do not require unanimity, neither France nor Spain is entitled to merely veto the draft agreement.

A brief presentation of Andorra's institutional system is useful to understand some of the surprising aspects of the negotiation process. This small, independent, political entity is called a principality because it is jointly governed by two "coprinces": the President of France and the bishop of Urgell. The bishop and his staff are often called the *Mitre* and reside in the Séo de Urgell, a little Spanish town located 10 kilometers south of Andorra. Consequently, neither the French president nor the Spanish bishop has ever resided in Andorra or shared a sense of community with the Andorrans. Each coprince has a representative in the valleys, called the French *viguier* for the French president and the *Mitre's viguier*. The coprinces hold sovereign power over Andorra, except on economic and social matters. Since 1981, Andorra has had a nationally elected Parliament called the "Council of the Valleys"; at the conclusion of each election, the Council of the Valleys appoints an Executive Council, which is responsible for implementing the policies defined by the Council of the Valleys.

To assess the dependence of Andorra on its neighbors, one must determine to what extent France, through the French coprince, is unofficially, but in very concrete terms, involved in the management of Andorra's public affairs. Even if the influence of Spain in the Andorran institutional system is not as strong as the influence of France, one must take into account that the *Mitre* occupies a very limited role in Spain. Admittedly, with regard to Andorran affairs, the *Mitre* is institutionally independent of Spain. Nevertheless, Spain has real influence because the bishop of Urgell is a Spanish citizen residing in Spain. Furthermore, Spain uses the *Mitre*'s representation in the Council of the Valleys as a Spanish consulate, where its nationals working and residing in Andorra can find administrative assistance. Lastly, the French and Spanish governments can exert economic pressure directly by restricting the customs policy on the export of goods from Andorra or tourists' access to the country.

5.2 The EC–Andorra Agreement as an Epiphenomenon of the Accession of Spain to the EC

The negotiations for the accession of Spain and Portugal to the EC started in February 1979 in Brussels. Discussion of the problem of Andorra's customs regime was scheduled on the agenda for 3 December. Therefore, to say that the Andorran customs problem was considered a minor problem is an understatement. Beginning in 1867, Andorra's trade was ruled by two parallel agreements, one with France and one with Spain. As long as Spain was not a member state of the EC, it would have been an aberration, for technical reasons, to substitute an Andorra–EC agreement for the Andorra–France agreement alone. The Commission opened the Andorra file in 1979, during the negotiations for the access of Spain to the EC. This action led the French and Spanish customs authorities to comply with the Rome Treaty, by substituting the Andorra–EC agreement for the two 1867 agreements.

The prenegotiation phase started in December 1979 and ended with the adoption by the European Council of the proposal to authorize the Commission to start the Andorra–EC negotiations in June 1985. What is symptomatic of the minor importance of the Andorra–EC agreement is that the Council agreed to it by means of a provision of the Spain–EC accession agreement signed 12 June 1985. Hence, the prenegotiation phase took five years – that is, until Spain's accession was completed. These five years left the actors (parties and outsiders) with enough time to develop their positions in the Andorra–EC negotiations.

5.3 The Marginalization of France

Although Andorra is an independent entity and its citizens travel with an Andorran passport, its legal status remains an enigma. Nevertheless, there is no doubt that Andorra is not regarded as a state. As such, to participate at the international level, the principality needed the mediation of a state. According to custom, Andorra's external relations are within the jurisdiction of the coprinces. It was established that France would represent

Andorra in relations with the outside world and negotiate agreements on its behalf. Until the 1980s, this situation raised few problems, notably because of the insignificant diplomatic activity of the principality and of the minor importance of the agreements concluded on its behalf. From the start of the prenegotiation phase, the French foreign office, which is entrusted by the French coprince with the care of Andorran affairs, behaved as the only legitimate mediator between Andorra and the EC.

The position of the French diplomats in this situation can be summarized in two points. First, French authorities considered France the only state able to negotiate on behalf of Andorra. France is the state most closely involved in the management of Andorran affairs, and the French coprince, who can veto the decisions taken by Andorra in external relations, would never accept the mediation of another state. Second, French diplomats were determined to play a leading role in the Andorra–EC relationships. To that end, even if the *Mitre* had to be invited to sign the agreement by the French coprince, France was not prepared to share its seat at the negotiation table with an Andorran authority. French diplomats wanted to negotiate alone on Andorra's behalf.

One reason for this attitude is that the room for maneuver from the legal point of view is narrow. The French have a paternal attitude toward the Andorran leaders and its diplomats. This attitude is coupled with a prejudice against Andorran political leaders viewed as moneymakers. The *Mitre*'s understanding of Andorran affairs made it a clever player in the game. Nevertheless, due to the asymmetry in political influence that exists between the French and episcopal coprinces, French diplomats, consciously or not, consider the *Mitre* with condescension.

5.4 Andorran Perceptions

In Andorra, the beginning of the prenegotiation phase coincided with the creation of the Executive Council. When the Council of the Valleys was informed of the renegotiation plan of the 1867 agreements, it entrusted the Andorran Executive Council (AEC) with attending to Andorran interests because, even if external relations were within the jurisdiction of the sole coprinces, economic matters, which were the main issues of the negotiations, were within the responsibility of the Council of the Valleys. Andorran leaders were soon convinced that the EC would not take advantage of its size and would offer Andorra a customs regime containing the advantages of the 1867 agreements.

Two factors prompted the AEC to participate actively in the negotiations. First, this new institution wanted to prove its efficiency. Second, and more important, the AEC mistrusted French mediation; an interview with Andorran leaders and French civil servants revealed that France perceived Andorra's prosperity as an almost cancerous outgrowth, useless to the economies of its neighbors. After that interview, the AEC understood that France wanted to press for an Andorran–EC agreement that would force Andorra's economy to substitute holiday tourism for shopping tourism. Consequently, at least concerning the customs regime, the AEC was worried about the idea of entrusting Andorra's interests to French diplomats.

The bishop of Urgell delegated the exercise of his office to his staff. The latter exercised limited though real power. The staff knew that the *Mitre* existed as a coprince only as long as Andorrans considered it this way, or, in other words, as long as Andorrans needed to remind the French coprince of its existence. Hence, the preoccupation of the *Mitre* was to prove to Andorrans that it still could be useful to them. In Brussels, the Commission paid almost as much attention to the proposals of the *Mitre* as to those of France, but the AEC did not receive any notice from the Commission. Consequently, the AEC and the *Mitre* decided to collaborate as the blind man and the paralytic. Thus, the *Mitre* helped the Andorran Executive Council to become a party in the negotiations. In return, the AEC provided the *Mitre* with the possibility, within the negotiations, to champion a cause that would allow it to continue to challenge the French diplomats. Admittedly, having to resort to the mediation of the *Mitre* troubled the AEC. Yet, compared with the opaque screen erected by France between the Commission and the Andorran Executive Council, the mediation of the *Mitre* was regarded as a transparent, though somewhat distorted, screen. However, the mediation of the *Mitre* was the only means by which the AEC could officially offer a proposal.

The prenegotiation period coincided with the negotiation of Spain's own accession to the EC. Therefore, from the Spanish point of view, Andorran affairs were a minor issue compared with accession. When the EC raised the renegotiation of the French and Spanish customs agreements with Andorra, Spanish diplomats, who were extremely busy at the time, tried unsuccessfully to postpone the issue. Nevertheless, when France claimed to impose its mediation as the only legitimate one, Spain, though in the same situation as France with regard to problems posed by the growth of Andorran economy, sided with the AEC and the *Mitre*. The reason for this attitude lay in the diplomatic tensions resulting from matters that were extraneous to the Andorran issue.

The negotiations lasted from June 1985 to June 1990. After having obtained from Spain an agreement, in principle, on the renegotiation of the Andorran customs regime, the Commission decided to wait until Spain's accession process was completed. The Commission took advantage of the prenegotiation period to become familiar with Andorran affairs. In fact, the EC civil servants contented themselves with receiving information sent to them and made allowances between pressures coming from France, the *Mitre*, unofficial AEC envoys, and Spain. Consequently, the Commission was becoming informed about its role.

The first difficulty the Commission confronted in the negotiations with Andorra was finding a single counterpart endowed with negotiating capacity. To solve this problem, the Commission asked the three components of Andorra to deal with their differences by drafting a memorandum stating the Andorran position. The essential condition to any satisfactory result was to keep French diplomats out of Andorran affairs. As long as France was a party to the Andorran internal negotiation – sometimes speaking on behalf of the French coprince, sometimes speaking on behalf of French administration – Andorra would remain a "kingdom divided against itself" and would not be able to contribute constructively.

The breaking of the coalition formed by France and the French coprince in late 1985 was, therefore, the first step of the negotiations. The AEC officials' mistrust of French diplomats led Andorran leaders to insist on being present at the negotiation table. But, how could they possibly end the diplomatic monopoly of France? France was even denying AEC the right to direct contacts with the Commission. As it did for the *Mitre*, France refused to participate in common meetings with the Commission or to recognize outcomes of those meetings. In short, French diplomats refused to sit at the negotiation table with other interested parties. A major problem resulted from the French coprince's tacit refusal to establish a clear-cut position on his legal status toward Andorra. If he had declared himself head of the Andorran state, the *Mitre* would have done the same; on the other hand, as a sovereign state, Andorra would have been able to negotiate without the mediation of France. But, because of legal factors related to the constitutional status as French president, the French coprince did not dare to declare this.[1] Finally, the AEC managed to break the diplomatic monopoly of France. It took advantage of the French coprince's silence. Betting on the abstruse nature of Andorra's legal status, the AEC undertook to give substance to the idea that Andorra was a state. The fiction worked so well that the Andorran citizens began to believe it. The AEC and surreptitiously the *Mitre* enhanced this strategy by appealing to the patriotism of the Andorran citizens and calling for the right of Andorrans to self-determination. The anti-French sentiment reached such a degree that the French coprince had to be kept informed of the development of the situation.

A turning point in the negotiations occurred when the Commission stated that it was prepared to recognize Andorra as a state; this was considered by the Commission the most convenient solution regarding the EC legal order. The actions of the Commission gave credibility to the notion of Andorra as a state and required that the French coprince take action. Two solutions were devised: officially ordering French diplomats to acknowledge Andorra as a state and to continue managing the Andorran affairs along with the AEC and the *Mitre* or removing the French foreign office from the negotiations and replacing it with his own staff. The French coprince chose the second solution for it allowed him to keep silent about his position toward Andorra.

Andorra's domestic negotiation in early 1986 was the next step. The direct involvement of the French coprince in the negotiation made it possible to consider many solutions; these solutions took on a political character because the actors were now part of the decision-making process. Thus, the eviction of French diplomats made it considerably easier to build a memorandum shared by the three components of the Andorran power. To reassure the AEC about his intentions, the French coprince agreed to enlarge the negotiating process to include the AEC's delegates. Admittedly, the AEC still did not have the possibility of establishing official contact with the Commission. However, henceforth, the AEC received a minimal guarantee: the possibility of vetoing the agreement. In short, the AEC would never have accepted giving France a free hand in the negotiations and being represented by an agent it did not trust. In January 1986, the coprinces agreed upon the elaboration process of the memorandum for the Commission. They assigned the AEC the mission to act as the leader in this process. As such, the AEC was received by the *Mitre* in March 1986 and then by the French coprince in April 1986. At the conclusion of this last meeting a memorandum was accepted, stating the negotiating positions shared by the three components of Andorra.

Following the talks, the French coprince asked the AEC to seek agreement with Spain, prior to any negotiation with the Commission. Spain was now able to concentrate on the customs negotiations; earlier, Spain was involved in the EC decision process. Spain took a very tough stand on the Andorran issue. Talks should have focused exclusively on customs, but the Spanish negotiators brought up social matters at the first meeting in May 1986. The AEC delegation understood that Spain was attempting to get Andorra to change its social legislation to enable its workers to create trade unions. Andorran leaders could not meet such a condition for it would jeopardize Andorra's identity and independence. Nevertheless, Spain took this stand for one year, locking the EC–Andorra negotiation process. Finally, facing the Andorran leaders' determination and EC's reprobation, Spain withdrew its demand and the process started again in September 1987.

In February 1988, the three components of Andorra approved the memorandum drafted in April 1986. The Andorran memorandum was delivered to the Commission's president in Brussels on 15 July 1988. From the Commission's standpoint, Andorran affairs remained a minor concern, as it had been before Spain's accession. It was only in spring 1987 that direct contacts were established with the main parties in the negotiations. The AEC was only unofficially contacted by the Commission. An atmosphere of suspicion developed in the negotiation process. Unlike the French and the Spanish representatives, who met with the Commission in Paris and Madrid, the *Mitre*'s representative had to go to Brussels because the Commission did not want to be accused of having direct contact with AEC taking advantage of its visit to the Séo de Urgell. Following those consultations, the Commission drew up a draft agreement to be presented to the three components of Andorra in December 1987.

The final phase of the negotiation in Brussels, one and a half years later, was carried out in two rounds. By a twist of fate, the coprinces chose the head of the AEC to speak for the three components of Andorra. This was done because neither coprince was interested in playing this role. The first negotiation round took place on 13 and 14 April 1989. The objective of the agreement was to transfer a large proportion of Andorra's trade under the tightly regulated EC customs union regime and to keep the remaining fraction under the free-trade regime. The purpose of the negotiation was to decide which chapters of the customs tariff should be administered by the EC customs union regime and which by the free-trade regime and to discuss the adjustments necessary to comply with the customs union regime. Andorra acknowledged that it did not know enough about free trade and did not have an exact understanding of what it could reasonably get from its powerful counterpart. The Commission viewed the Andorran demands as quite excessive and was not willing to make substantial concessions because it was bound to negotiate within limits given in the draft agreement submitted to and accepted by the EC Council. Nor could the AEC make more concessions than the Commission, because it also had to negotiate within the limits set by the Andorran memorandum as it had been accepted by the Council of the Valleys.

Although there was no real animosity, the talks were carried out as a dialogue between deaf partners. On one side of the negotiation table sat the Commission that completely disregarded the Andorran requirements; on the other side sat the AEC that clung to its positions. The constraints on the proxy of the Council of the Valleys were not the only reasons for the AEC's rigid negotiating position. From the beginning of this first negotiation round, the AEC was very uncomfortable with the huge gap between its positions and those of the Commission. The AEC realized that it was not adequately prepared for this negotiation for it did not have a clear view of the parameters necessary to assess the main negotiation stakes. The fear of having to make too many concessions and being manipulated by the much more experienced EC negotiators brought the AEC to a standstill. Eventually, the two parties broke off negotiations.

In the months that followed, the AEC was able to draw some lessons from the failure of the first negotiation round. The AEC obtained permission to increase the number of official contacts with the Commission. Thus, Andorran leaders learned more about the Commission's methods and constraints. The second and last negotiation rounds took place on 13 and 14 December 1989, in Brussels, with the same delegations. The AEC had fewer requirements and the negotiation started. Several times clashing interests resulted in a deadlock. Tobacco was one of the most bitterly discussed issues, for the AEC's leader was the owner of a tobacco factory. The parties had a strong desire to bring the negotiation to a successful end; however, no one was ready to sacrifice his or her position to those of the other side. A final agreement was reached after more concessions from the AEC. During the first half of 1990, each party completed the internal ratification process. The agreement was signed in Brussels on 28 June 1990 by the three components of Andorra on one side and by the two components of the EC (the Council and the Commission) on the other side.

The AEC achieved a major, if unexpected, goal, an aim that was inconceivable 10 years before: to be present at an international negotiation table. In this sense the side effect of this negotiation has been nothing less than a crucial step toward the peaceful creation of a new state, internationally acknowledged in 1993.

5.5 Analysis

A number of situations and events demonstrate the power relations between the different protagonists of the negotiations. Particular events reveal the dynamics in the power structure and distribution. In the prenegotiation phase, France appears to have built a position of structural power. France was a compulsory intermediary for any relations between Andorra and the rest of the world. Its position was reinforced by the possibility of exerting economic coercion, which had been used in the past when tension arose between Andorra and France. Such coercion could be exercised in two ways: excise restrictions and freezes on exchanges. Such a position with all the attached advantages results in a boundary spanner role (Crozier 1964).

The *Mitre* disposed of a positional power that was qualified as negative by some authors (Handy 1985). It concerned the capacity of the *Mitre* to lock up the process by its position within the structure. Such power does not enable one to act, but rather paralyzes the actions of others. It is a power of inertia, structurally unavoidable. It should be noted that Spain, during the domestic negotiations that followed, exhibited a similar power, stemming in this case not from the structure but from the process, generated through the manipulation of strategic variables.

Andorra could have been reduced to nothing by its two powerful neighbors, but this was not the case. Andorra owes its millenary survival to extremely clever management given its location. Playing one country against the other, Andorra has succeeded over the years in minimizing its dependence on the two countries. Spain's entry into the EC did more than add another player to the game. It changed the very nature of the game. A survival-oriented strategy based on a three-party equilibrium lost its significance because the whole system was undergoing a change. The Andorran strategy would no longer be effective.

Spain, the last element of the structure, had a long-lasting dispute with France that was exacerbated during the negotiations over its admission into the EC. Confronted with the extremely assertive attitude of France over the question of Andorra, Spain joined a coalition with the Andorran Executive Council and the *Mitre* to counterbalance France.

This alliance modified the distribution of powers. However, such an alliance could only take place under exceptional circumstances, otherwise it would have challenged the existing relations of domination with Andorra. This coalition had a considerable influence on the Commission's perception of the problem and on its subsequent behavior. Despite its appreciable power, the Commission could not afford to displease three of the four parties.

In the negotiation phase, tactical action played an essential part within the process dynamics. Taking advantage of events became a major means of appropriation of new fragments of power. The first of these events was the initial silence of the French coprince, who refused to take a clear stand on his role as the head of the Andorran state. The Andorran Executive Council turned these uncertainties to its advantage and used it as a source of power (Crozier 1964).

The capacity to cope with uncertainty became a major element leading to a structural modification of the game: France was no longer the compulsory intermediary. The pseudo-coalition EC–AEC resulted in the eviction of France. This coalition was based on two connected interests: the AEC's aim to obtain the international acceptance of Andorra as a sovereign state and the EC's will to impose a contractual concept of relations among entities, which in turn presupposed the recognition of the Andorran party as well as the establishment of direct relations. Thus, the intentional action of the AEC resulted in a substantial change within the global structure of power.

Finally, taking advantage of the "legal slack" of power was done in conformity with the cultural characteristics of the actors. The local saying according to which what works in an unclear, rather complicated, or even suspicious way is "as Andorran businesses" closely illustrates such an attitude.

Spain's lock up of the memorandum is evidence of the exercise of a "negative power," which is the capacity to freeze the process without making any progress toward reaching an objective (Handy 1985). Such a position was not acceptable to the EC for it interrupted the negotiations. In addition, there was no intermediate solution because the workers' right to establish unions was a writer of law and this left no room for maneuver. After one year Spain withdrew its objection.

During the external negotiation the global power was modified considerably. If the AEC were to lean on a powerful third party – the Commission – the AEC would become rather helpless. One must admit that the situation was extremely imbalanced at the economic and technical levels. To obtain an accurate picture of the extent of the asymmetry, one should imagine a group of shopkeepers from the same town district joining the General Agreement on Tariffs and Trade (GATT) negotiations. Such a disproportion explains the uselessness of the deadlock introduced by the AEC. When the negotiations started again, the AEC's expectations were more realistic; an agreement was then possible.

Andorra's dependence on France and Spain, lack of alternatives, and high commitment to the possibility of achieving international recognition further strengthened the Commission's power. The latter could do without agreement, but Andorra could not. In this situation, Andorra was not able to mobilize the tactical means to substantially modify its power relations. In return, the Commission demonstrated its reward power with its ability to provide resources such as low custom duties and reduced taxes (French and Raven 1959; Pfeffer and Salancik 1978). From that very definition nothing could be opposed to the will of the Commission. The extent of the imbalance and the disproportion of strengths were such that at no time, even during the deadlock, was there any strong animosity among the parties, but some was clearly noticeable as a reaction to the veto strategy implemented by Spain. Here, power spoke and brought about an agreement. But power was also exercised within reasonable limits, though it did not elicit any sense of strong unfairness or frustration.

5.6 General Lessons

Several general conclusions can be drawn from the observations of these negotiations. First, in the case of extreme asymmetry, the weaker party improves its chances by putting its destiny into the hands of a third party, such as the EC, even if it acts only as an arbitrator or a mediator. Second, as demonstrated in the Andorran–French relations, the weaker party may elicit (if its weakness is extreme) enough disinterest from the other side to turn the conflict into a relation of indifference; this situation occurred during the main stage of the prenegotiations.[2] Third, as in the Andorra–EC negotiations, the stronger party in such a situation tends not to resort to the full extent of its power. It acts according to a logic that keeps it within narrower margins than the compared strengths of both parties would have assumed. There are several reasons for this:

- The gains that Andorra might have obtained corresponded to concessions that were considered insignificant by the Commission.
- A major concern for the Commission was the prevention of an anti-communitary wave from the Andorrans.
- Another concern of the Commission was to emphasize the durability of the new situation; by respecting the interests of all parties, a sustainable order could be established.
- A norm of management governed the actions of the Commission; it wanted to deal with communitary situations as a "wise father" would.

Fourth, this example helps to answer an important question: If power relations depend upon the very structure of the situation, will tactical action bring about any noticeable change? Andorra's exercise of its limited power led to advantages that were quite inconceivable given its power structure. The direct outcome of this tactical action was to turn what should have metaphorically been an "arranged marriage" into a "free choice marriage" – that is, a union in which both parties express personal assent. Thus, in its confrontation with France, Andorra obtained the power structure to enable it to voice its preference.

Finally, Andorra was limited in its ability to negotiate with the EC. In this situation, the Commission offered what it considered a fair deal, following the principles of Boulwarism by integrating the other party's interests, up to a limit, into the offer of what can be tolerable. At this point power talked. But here again power was not laid bare. Andorra went through a learning process that progressively lowered its level of aspiration concerning concessions from the Commission. This learning process, in the true school of realism, was established with the help of informal contacts between the two parties.

5.7   Pending Questions about Power

This case provides an investigation into power that is focused not only on the balanced relations between a strong party and a weak party, but also on a complex system of power distribution. It is a system characterized by a certain stability in which the actors attempt to modify the components or to transform the logic to shift the center of gravity. An organizational approach defined by a concrete system of action is, in this case, of particular relevance (Crozier and Friedberg 1980). The dynamics of the system are created by actors who develop strategies to maximize their gains by first establishing a more favorable power situation.

When the parties to a negotiation are in a position of extreme asymmetry, a number of specific strategies and tactics can be implemented. The weaker party seeks to change the structure by:

- Finding allies to build coalitions to modify the existing power system.
- Neutralizing the stronger party through a game of balance using another powerful party as a counterweight.
- Canceling oneself out of the conflict by trying to appear insignificant.
- Designating a party for intervention as a mediator or arbitrator.

The stronger party's strategy (that is, the organization of tactical action in the negotiation process) follows a different logic. In a cooperative setting, it should avoid going to the limits of its power in order not to give rise to contentious reactions and to preserve future relations. The more powerful party must meet standards of fairness, which should be widely accepted and taken as the border condition of its action. In a competitive situation some limits must be set. The main obstacle to power exercise is not the other party but the external audiences such as neighbors, outsiders, and public opinion. The action of the most powerful is limited by external norms of fairness and concern about its image and reputation.

It seems that the effectiveness of power can only be understood by considering the conditions of its exercise. Ultimately power can be defined as exercising a capacity within a total system of action – that is, a game structure. Several elements can influence the intensity of power that can be attained. Some stakes prompt a mobilization of resources that are unacceptable in other circumstances. The choice of grounds can also influence power actions because an actor may, for instance, occupy a strong position at the legal level and a weak position at the economic or military level. The final outcome of the game will then be conditioned by the capacity of an actor to impose one set of ground rules on others. Exerting power is subsumed into the category of selection of the ground rules.

The degree of conflict within a negotiation is another crucial element of power distribution. The power available to an actor in a cooperative setting can be notably different from the power available in a highly conflictual situation. Here again the situational context is a variable playing a major role in the organization of the game.

Power itself has an internal dynamics that makes it likely to vary over time. This characteristic tends to prevail when an element is introduced that makes one party more vulnerable than the other. There is a whole repertoire concerning the management of the time dimension of power for which the Andorran case provides illustrations.

Alinsky (1971) concludes that in a power relation it is not the power available to the actor that is important, but the power attributed to him by the other side, as is expressed in propositions 1 and 2 of the introductory chapter. Power is then equated with perception, and action would be based only on expectation. The Andorran case does not confirm this conclusion, for if the Andorrans were to have underestimated the power of the Commission, the latter would have reminded them of the harsh laws of reality. When perception is too far from reality and this gap is not operationally productive, then reality strikes back.

Power has been defined as quantifiable according to the following equation (Atkinson 1980):

Party's power = Expected costs to opponent for not complying

This definition is similar to the notion of power as an added value, as discussed in the introductory chapter. Taking into account the extreme difficulty of measuring a rating of power, such an attempt is not without merit, particularly its implied relation to actions. However, it fails because it assimilates power to a ratio of subjective costs. The Andorran case demonstrates the multiple actions that constitute power and shows that power cannot be equated to the foreseen costs of its implementation. If this were the case, the utility theory would be sufficient to deal with the question, and power would be returned to an equation with outcomes.

5.8   Theoretical Implications

The Andorran case enables one to advance a hypothesis concerning research on negotiation in a more general way. In particular, one can only speak about strict structural determinism if one postulates that there is no room for actors to maneuver. In this case, to equate power with outcome, as the Marxist approach does, turns negotiation theory into a deterministic theory by rejecting the core of any negotiation, the process itself. If power is not to be mistaken for its outcome, the dependence theory (Bacharach and Lawler 1981) may appear as tautological as Dahl's approach (1957). If it is assumed that the bargaining power of a party is grounded in the other party's dependence on resources (Keohane and Nye 1989), then power is identified with the strength of this dependence, a conclusion that is a relational tautology.

The existing system of perceived power initially structures the negotiation; the implementation of tactical actions aims at modifying this structure. Each move can be subjected to a power play. The outcome of the negotiation is the end result of the interaction between structure and process, interaction through which games of power manifest themselves.

The observations from this case provide more support to the Machiavelli problematique than to the Hobbes problematique. The Hobbesian approach to power emphasizes causality and develops a mechanistic vision of the action process, whereas Machiavelli's concept of power provides more space for the implementation of the actors' will through strategies of a pragmatic nature (Clegg 1989). Thus, the Machiavellian understanding of power better captures the essential characteristic of the negotiation situation and its dynamics – the importance of tactical action as power. Perceived power distribution is not the ultimate explanation of an outcome, but playing power is the game of negotiation. As has been shown, such a game is particularly relevant in the case of asymmetrical negotiations.

Notes

[1] The French constitution does not consider the possibility of the president being the head of two states simultaneously. This situation forced France to postpone recognition of Andorra as a state.

[2] Another possible alternative in such a situation is the Third World strategy of helplessness, which may give rise to a paternalistic attitude or the arousal of guilt.

References

Alinsky, S., 1971, *Rules for Radicals*, Random House, New York.

Atkinson, G., 1980, *The Effective Negotiation*, QUEST.

Bacharach, S., and Lawler, E., 1981, *Bargaining: Power, Tactics and Outcomes*, Jossey-Bass, San Francisco, CA.

Clegg, S., 1989, *Frameworks of Power*, Sage, London.

Crozier, M., 1964, *The Bureaucratic Phenomenon*, University of Chicago Press, Chicago.

Crozier, M., and Friedberg, E., 1980, *Actors and Systems*, University of Chicago Press, Chicago.

Dahl, R., 1957, The concept of power, *Behavioral Science,* **2**:201–215.

French, J.R.P., and Raven, B.H., 1959, The bases of social power, in D. Cartwright, ed., *Studies in Social Power*, University of Michigan Press, Ann Arbor, MI.

Handy C., 1985, *Understanding Organizations*, Penguin Business, London.

Kaplan, A., 1964, Power in perspective, in R.L. Khan and E. Boulding, ed., *Power and Conflict in Organizations*, Tavistock, London.

Keohane, R.O., and Nye, J.S., 1989, *Power and Interdependence*, 2nd edition, Scott Foresman, Boston, MA.

Pfeffer, J., and Salancik, G.R., 1978, *The External Control of Organizations: A Resource Dependency Perspective*, Harper and Row, New York.

Bibliography

Ayberk, U., 1978, *Le mécanisme de la prise de décision communautaire en matière de relations internationales* (The mechanism of community decision making on international relations), Thèse Bruxelles, Brussels, Belgium.

Barate, C., and Riera, G., 1980, Le dépassement des contradictions en Andorre: Un scénario de l'impossible? (Getting past the contradictions in Andorra: A scenario of the impossible?) *Revue du Droit Public,* pp. 367–407, Paris.

Bélinguier, B., 1970, *La condition juridique des Vallées d'Andorre*, Pèdone, Paris.

Berr, R., and Tremeau, J., 1981, *Le droit douanier* (Customs law), Librairie Générale de Droit et de Jurisprudence, Paris.

Fiter i Vilajoana, R., 1973, Legislacio administrativa andorrana (Consell General 1900–1973), Casal i Vall, Andorra.

Flaesch-Mougin, C., 1979, Les accords externes de la CEE: Essai d'une typologie (The external treaties of the EC: Attempt at a classification), Thèse Rennes, France 1976, Éditions de l'Université de Bruxelles, Brussels, Belgium.

Groux, J., and Manin, P., 1984, *Les Communautés Européennes dans l'ordre international, Collection "Perspectives européennes,"* Office des Publications Officielles des Communautés Européennes, Luxembourg.

Klaousen, P., 1989, *Les effets de l'integration communautaire sur le régime juridique des échanges commerciaux de l'Andorre,* Thèse Toulouse, Toulouse, France.

Monumenta Andorra, Casal i Vall, 7 volumes, Andorra.

Parellada i Farrero, 1978, *Informe sobre les taxes de consum a Andorra*, Centre d'Estudis de Planificacio, Andorra.

Pou i Serradell, V., 1986, *Negociations Andorra–Mercat comu Europeu* (Analisi i documentacio sobre les relations entre Andorra i la CEE), p. 96, Credit Andorra, Andorra.

Zemanek, K., 1981, *Le statut international d'Andorre*, Casa de la Vall, Andorra.

Interviews with Main Actors of the Process

Most of the data concerning the process were collected through interviews with high-ranking European Commission officials, French and Spanish diplomats, and political authorities of Andorra.

Cerqueda, F., Syndic général des Vallées d'Andorre, Andorre la Vieille, Andorra.

Deblé, L., Ministre Plénipotentiaire, Viguier de S.E. le co-Prince français, Andorre la Vieille, Andorra.

Diezler, H., Commission Européenne, Direction générale de l'Union Douanière, Brussels, Belgium.

Galainea, J., Représentation Permanente de l'Espagne auprès de la Communauté Européenne, Brussels, Belgium.

Godechot, Délégation Permanente de la France au Conseil de l'Atlantique Nord, ex-sous-Directeur Europe méridionale du ministère français des relations extérieures, Brussels, Belgium.

Imbert, A., Commission Européenne, Direction générale des Relations Extérieures–Méditerranée–Nord, Brussels, Belgium.

Joubert, Représentation Permanente de la France auprès de la Communauté Européenne, Brussels, Belgium.

Kuijper, Commission Européenne, Service Juridique, Brussels, Belgium.

Marques, M.N., Représentant Permanent de S.E. le co-Prince épiscopal, Séo de Urgell, Spain.

Riberaygua-Miquel, B., Ministre des Finances d'Andorre, Andorre la Vieille, Andorra.

Chapter 6

Nepal–India Water Resource Relations

Dipak Gyawali

The water resource relations between Nepal and India, two South Asian countries that share the Ganges River basin system, provide a study of resource conflict over environment and development between asymmetrically endowed nations. India is 40 times larger than Nepal in terms of population and 22 times larger in terms of area; it produces 400 times more electricity than Nepal, and its per capita gross national product (GNP) is almost twice as large as Nepal's (WRI 1990). Over the past eight decades Nepal–India water resource negotiations have featured the dynamics of interaction between a country rich with as yet unexploited resources (Nepal) and a country that has developed a hungry market since its earlier encounters with modernization (India). The relationship is perceived by both sides and by outside observers to be very asymmetrical; the attitudes and actions of the parties reflect this asymmetry between a "yam" and a "boulder."

This relationship has evolved slowly, overcoming ignorance and power limitations. On the one hand, landlocked Nepal, often described as being India-locked, does not have much power in conventional quantitative terms. It does, however, enjoy power as the upper riparian nation owning the sites where storage dams can be built. This power, based on legitimacy as a resource in international affairs (described as *satwik* power in this essay), allows Nepal the final veto in negotiations. On the other hand, India, the lower riparian nation, enjoys market power (described further below as *rajasik* power) that could overwhelm, subvert, capture, or use the resources and institutions of its weaker neighbor.

In the past 40 years, India has relied on a less subtle source of power as force (described as *tamasik* power) but without much success. Recently, however, the process of economic liberalization in South Asia has opened new opportunities for exercising market (*rajasik*) power by strong countries such as India. It remains to be seen how Nepal will enhance its *satwik* and *rajasik* powers with improved technical studies and efficient economic reform measures to assure itself a better deal in the development of its large water resource potential.

Nepal's water wealth is contained in the four main snow-fed tributaries of the Ganges – the Mahakali (called *Sarada* in India), the Karnali (called *Ghagra* in India), the Sapta Gandaki, and the Sapta Kosi – which originate from glaciers high in the Nepal Himalayas and join the Ganges in the flat subtropical plains of India. It is estimated that these rivers contribute 45% of the annual flow of the Ganges and 70% of its dry-season flow, making Nepali tributaries the lifeblood of the fertile Indian lowlands. However, the annual floods in these Himalayan tributaries during the wet monsoon season cause much destruction of life and property in the northern Gangetic plains.

Studies show that the Nepali tributaries of the Ganges flowing through high gradient Himalayan terrain are endowed with phenomenal economic potential. The 89 sites identified so far could provide about 30 gigawatts (GW) of power and 145,000 gigawatt-hours (GWh) of energy. Thirty sites have live storage capacity of about 61 billion cubic meters that could provide perennial irrigation and flood control benefits in the lowlands (Gyawali 1989). Nepal at present has a power demand of only about 300 megawatts (MW); in 20 years, at a 10% per annum growth rate, demand will still be below 2 GW. The bulk of the potential could be used to meet energy needs in north India, which suffers severe power shortages with demand growing over 1 GW per annum.

Nepal can use only a fraction of the reservoir-regulated waters for irrigation since it has limited arable land. A system of 30 reservoirs has been proposed in Nepal; this system would submerge about 145,000 hectares of mostly agricultural land in the lowland valleys (WN 1993). India, on the other hand, could use all and more of the regulated storage as it is water and not land limited. Because the Ganges up to Allahabad has already been declared India's national waterway, an increase in dry-season flow in the Nepali tributaries of the Ganges, through the construction of high dams in the hills, could lead to navigation benefits for not only Nepal but also the inner hinterlands of north India. These Nepali hydro sites would enhance the security of Indian cities, highways, and railways by converting wild monsoon inflow to controlled dry-season outflow.

Nepal is one of the world's poorest countries in terms of GNP and per capita income, and its weak economy cannot generate a demand for the electricity that can be produced from its large water resource endowment. In India, too, the regions of Bihar, Uttar Pradesh, and West Bengal adjacent to Nepal are very poor and underdeveloped. They are, however, the hinterland of large industrial cities between New Delhi in the west and Calcutta in the east that would be the primary users of Nepal's hydroelectricity.

The demand for intervention into the regime of the Nepali tributaries of the Ganges has arisen from modernization efforts of industrial cities in India and their agro-industry. In these regions, efforts to modernize must ensure cheap electricity for basic energy needs as well as for growing industries, year-round irrigation for two and even three crop harvests per annum in the fertile Ganges plains, and moderation of the monsoon flows to mitigate flood damage. The prioritization of these benefits is the subject of debate in India and makes Nepalis wary of Indian proposals.

6.1 Analysis of Power Relations

The conventional reductionist approach sees power as something that one has. Consequently, the effort to quantify what can be measured and neglect the rest is almost inevitable. Alternatively, it may be insightful to consider power in comprehensive ecological terms, with dynamic interlinkages in that context. In this perspective, one's power is dependent on the power of others and how they exercise it; change in status can occur simply because something has transpired elsewhere, affecting the interdependence of the parties (Keohane and Nye 1989:11–18).

Oriental societies have approached power in this way, as a dynamic interplay between elements within a specific context. In Hinduism, which is the principal religion in Nepal and northern India, power is conceived of in the form of Shakti, the Mother Goddess, in three manifestations.

Raw physical power, such as military might, is represented by Maha Kali, and the basic quality of this force is termed *tamasik* with the characteristic color of black. The power that comes from money and human hierarchies is represented by Maha Lakshmi; this industrious source of power is termed *rajasik* and is symbolized by the color red. The power of thought is represented by Maha Saraswati; this subtle power is called *satwik* and is denoted by the color white. While all three are ultimately manifestations of the One, life is an interplay of the three – one balancing or negating the others. Power relations between Nepal and India can be seen in terms of this symbolic metaphor portraying the sources of different types of action.

Military seizure of a territory with desirable resources is the ultimate expression of *tamasik* power. Recent world events, such as the Gulf War in 1991 and the war in Bosnia since 1992, are reminders that the exercise of *tamasik* power is not uncommon in this day and age. The temptation to use physical force, however, is tempered by the perception of one side's strength vis-à-vis the other side and constrained by the judgment of how such an action would affect one's manifold relationships with many partners around the globe. It has been hypothesized that a purely bilateral relationship increases the stronger party's temptation to exercise military power against the weaker party. This hypothesis proposes that the strong party is inhibited in a bilateral relationship that is tempered by ramifications of valuable multilateral linkages.

Nepal, sandwiched between China and India, was described by Prithvi Narayan Shah, who unified the small Himalayan principalities into a kingdom in 1769, as a "yam between two boulders." Despite the absorption of her neighbors Tibet by China and Sikkim by India, Nepal's military annexation by either of its two giant neighbors is improbable for many reasons.

Such an exercise of military (*tamasik*) power by either China or India would require an expensive military infrastructure along a 1,000-kilometer buffer zone in difficult terrain for questionable gains. Nepali water is too far from China's industrial centers to be considered a resource of value. Furthermore, an aggressive action by China, if it were not met by instant Indian retaliation, would deny China access to the Indian market to sell electricity or regulated water that flows south to India.

India also could not gain much from such an annexation. Unlike mining for oil, which can be done by military control for as long as it takes to extract the stock underground, water resources exploitation requires sustainable harvesting of a renewable bounty demanding a continuous socio-systemic involvement for successful operation. If feelings of Nepali nationalism were damaged through military intervention, unrest and sabotage might follow, making it difficult to build and operate hydraulic structures. This would be in addition to any hostile behavior on the part of China or the international community (such as international financial institutions, which would provide the intensive capital for building dams) that would find it difficult to condone such actions. Nepal perceives that its manifold multilateral relations would prevent the exercise of *tamasik* power by its neighbors, and so gains in power from them.

In this situation, power as the expression of blatant military force can be excluded as an element in the water resource negotiations. Nepal does not have military power, and India cannot consider using the military power it has. However, even with the use of military force excluded, India still enjoys a plethora of *rajasik* advantages over Nepal, allowing India to prevail over Nepal in this asymmetrical relationship.

A good account of market (*rajasik*) power is provided by Schmookler (1984) who, having defined power first in the standard behavioral terms as "the capacity to achieve one's will against the will of another," distinguishes between power's coercive capacity and its persuasive capacity. In its coercive capacity, it is "the ability to impose one's will regardless of the will of others," presumably in *tamasik* fashion, by having the means that allow one not to have to give in and to force the environment to do so. In its persuasive capacity, power "changes how others decide to exercise their choice." Without the use of raw force, this is done by restricting, through economic methods, the range of another's options or by pointing out the attractiveness of alternative packages.

Schmookler sees the market as a form of noncoercive power. It can be used to expand the options providing a larger variety of elements from which tradeoffs can be arranged. An expanded menu "changes how others decide to exercise their choice" without the use of force and often without the other party feeling that it has lost. This is because surrendering in one sensitive area can be balanced by gains in other areas, which can assuage actors at the domestic level.

In a distinguished lecture at a workshop on Cooperative Development of Indo–Nepal Water Resources in Patna, on 29 May 1992, India's former Foreign Secretary, Muchkund Dubey, said that India was able to gain concessions from Nepal on the controversial Tanakpur hydroelectric power plant on the Nepal–India border (described below) only by being generous on trade and transit issues with landlocked Nepal and by providing aid for other projects such as hospitals and roads. This linkage can be considered an exercise in *rajasik*, rather than *tamasik*, power.

The most potent source of power is *satwik* power. It is considered to be achieved by balancing the other two and then transcending them. Kautilya, who was a contemporary of Alexander the Great and who is revered as South Asia's Machiavelli for his ability to forge the Gupta empire from the ashes of Hellenic pillage, derived his formidable authority from *satwik* power (Kautilya 1960; Modelski 1964). Having negated the other two – he was not the commander of any army but an ascetic owning no wealth – he was able to command the loyalty of kings and generals. This was because he was upholding a principle larger than himself, which was the principle of political unity of a civilization facing external aggression.[1]

In this sense, Kautilya was perceived as someone speaking on behalf of an overarching legitimacy that could command the loyalty of infighting kings. The importance of direct communion with this type of legitimacy is also highlighted in occidental thinking when Thomas Aquinas spoke of the divine origin of power involving three factors: the manner of acquisition, the use to which it is put, and its very form. The last is always blameless and good in itself because it comes from God and thus is good, provided the other two factors do not affect this absolute goodness (Bigongiari 1953).

If military (*tamasik*) power is not exercised, it is often because of the power of the idea of the nation-state and inviolability of sovereign boundaries (*satwik* power). Those with the power to violate international borders do not do so because they are held in check by the power of the belief that such actions are incorrect. The importance of the *satwik* power of overarching legitimacy has been incorporated into the concepts of development, modernization, and market growth.

Provided these concepts are perceived as analogous and desirable by Third World countries, development as a phenomenon acquires an overarching legitimacy. The arguments presented by environmentalists against high dams and factories, valid though they may be on ecological grounds, find little sympathy with many in the Third World. This is primarily because such views are perceived as being anti-developmental. The need for "development" is often translated into moral pressure that can be brought to bear on a recalcitrant environmental activist.

Western technology, together with control over it, is a resource available to plains India but not to mountainous Nepal. India has many engineering institutes of international stature, but Nepal has only three engineering colleges. Nepal–India relations are thus characterized by significant asymmetry, if power is defined as knowledge and control over technology, a hybrid of *satwik* and *rajasik* forces.

The Nepali state was once powerful enough to defy British military power and retain its independence, unlike many Indian states that did not. This was partly because its inaccessible mountains were a military resource. It now finds itself less powerful simply because the other state has acquired market and technological power that can easily overcome these hurdles. Such developments change the context within which power in toto is exercised. Nepal's only power is that it is the upper riparian sovereign owning the hydro sites where the controlling structures can be built mostly to India's benefit. It can indefinitely stall negotiations. This negative power stems from the strength or inviolability of the idea of legitimate ownership and is an example of *satwik* power holding even *rajasik* power in check.

Given the extreme hydrological nature of Himalayan rivers, where the difference in dry- and wet-season discharge can be more than a hundredfold, high dams for flow regulation need to be fairly large. Such large-scale interventions in river regimes require financing well beyond Nepal's ability and often beyond India's too. The 10.8-GW Karnali multipurpose project alone is estimated to cost about US$5 billion at 1988 prices, which is about three times the GNP of Nepal. The result is that both Nepal and India have to turn to international financing institutions. This means the entry of a new set of actors with *rajasik* powers in the previously bilateral arena.

The entry of Western banks means the entry of international consultants they trust, who bring in their wake competing sets of international contractors and manufacturers. These actors are supported by their home governments, who thus become important actors at the macrolevel in Indo–Nepal water resources development. Furthermore, such potential financiers and their governments bring with them their own views of what development is and how it should be pursued – ideology energizing enterprise. Because their activities span the globe, concerns of a different nature find their way into conceptual frameworks of intervention exercises for river control.

An example is the recurring flood-induced loss of life and property in Bangladesh. Since donor agencies are asked to contribute to both flood relief and disaster mitigation in Bangladesh, it is not uncommon for them to look for and promote solutions in other areas of their involvement such as in Nepal with flood-controlling high dams in the Nepal Himalayas. This internationalization of what was previously a bilateral matter has led to advantages and disadvantages in the negotiating postures of both Nepal and India.

6.2   Nepali Perceptions

Nepal was a latecomer to development. It remained in feudal isolation under the Rana rulers, much as Japan did under the Tokugawa shogunate, until the mid–twentieth century. It thus maintained independence and prevented colonization by the British, but this was at the price of remaining quarantined from world industrial and intellectual attainments. As a result, the articulation of demand for modern amenities, such as those that can arise from hydrotechnical constructions, is still feeble; Nepal's understanding of the value of its resource has swung from pathetic underrating in the 1920s to zealous overvaluation in the 1990s. Its perception of the power of its downstream riparian neighbor has crystallized into a fear that India bulldozes decisions on water resources development in its favor.

The first recorded water resource negotiations between Nepal and its southern neighbor occurred between 1910 and 1920. British India needed to harness the Sarda (Mahakali) River, which formed the western boundary between Nepal and British India, to develop irrigation in the United Provinces (now Uttar Pradesh). Because Nepal lacked any understanding of the value of a site for water resource development, it agreed to the 1920 Sarda treaty, which gave the British 4,000 acres of the left bank in exchange for an equivalent forested area (Gyawali and Dixit 1991). Forest land was valuable to the Nepali rulers because it provided saleable timber and land that could subsequently be settled for farming. Land to build a dam's abutment was not so valued.

When the left bank became available for abutment construction on this border river (effectively making the Sarda in this stretch an Indian river), the British were able to build the Sarda Barrage and the right bank Sarda Canal to irrigate areas in India. The agreement allowed Nepal between 3% and 4% of the dry-season flow and no more than 9% of what

India withdrew during the wet season. This allotment was used by Nepal only half a century later through a World Bank loan for the Mahakali Irrigation Project. The negotiation documents of this period, available from the British Library in London, show that Nepal's lack of technical expertise regarding water resource engineering was a serious drawback to effective bargaining (Gyawali 1993).

The Sarda treaty is an example of Nepal's lower riparian neighbor making plans for water resource development on its own and approaching Nepal for the minimum needed for the construction. Over the years following the agreements, Nepalis have learned about Indian plans, their implications, and the value of Nepali consent to India's future plans. These realizations have led to an aggrieved feeling, post facto, of having been "cheated" in water treaties, a word used by the current king of Nepal shortly after ascending the throne in 1975 to describe the results of the negotiations so far.

Major water resource projects were conceived by the British in the Nepal Himalayas in the 1930s, just before the outbreak of World War II. These projects were meant to generate hydroelectricity and to provide irrigation and flood control in the northern Ganges plains. A high dam was considered at the Barahakshetra gorge on the Sapta Kosi, a major tributary of the Ganges known as "Bihar's river of sorrow" for having changed course in Bihar by 150 kilometers over the past 200 years. These benefits, however, would not be realized without Nepal's consent. The advent of World War II and the postwar withdrawal from India stopped further British initiatives. Nevertheless, the value of dams in Nepal for the downstream plains was, and is still, valid. A secret British memo of 1945 states that the flood control and irrigation benefits from storage dams in Nepal are so great that even giving a hydroelectric dam free to Nepal would still benefit the Indian plains.[2]

After Indian independence in 1947 and the overthrow of the Ranas in Nepal in 1951, the goals of modernization and development and the welfare state adopted by both nations imparted a new impetus to harnessing the Himalayan tributaries of the Ganges. Nepal concluded two agreements with India on the Gandak and the Kosi in the early 1950s; construction of the barrages and the final agreement proceeded in a clumsy manner until 1966, requiring 15 years. India has maintained full control over the headworks on Nepali territory and, at the operational level, the agreed-upon water releases to Nepal have not been timely. Nepali decision makers are not comfortable with Indian insistence on management (headworks) control, and India's refusal to allow independent assessment of downstream benefits has induced suspicions that Nepali acquiescence has been more beneficial to India than publicly stated.

Under such circumstances, the tactics that best suited the Nepalis, and which they adopted, was one of stalling. Since Nepal's demand for hydroelectric power or modern irrigation was already very low compared with that of India, they could afford to wait. The result was that no new agreements were entered into with India until 1991, although several feasibility studies of medium- and large-scale projects were conducted with Western expertise.

Introducing Western consultants was seen as a means of importing technology, obtaining an unbiased view, and preventing dependence on India. The strategy might have worked if not for the structural weaknesses of Nepal's old feudal order, which led the country to dependency on foreign aid and a new type of impoverishment wrought by vested interests within and without. An example of this was the Karnali (Chisapani) high dam multipurpose project.[3] A feasibility study was conducted in 1966 by Japan's Nippon Koei consultants. Because the project was deemed feasible, a request for initiating financing was made; however, the funding agencies, wishing a reconfirmation, opted for a second feasibility study, which was carried out in 1968 by the Snowy Mountain Hydroelectric Authority of Australia. By then Nepal had begun to realize the impossibility of funding such large power projects with soft loans and grants. In 1977, Norconsult (Norway) and Electrowatt (Swiss) conducted another feasibility study; in 1989, a consortium of US and Canadian consulting firms, called Himalayan Power Consultant, completed a fourth feasibility study financed through a World Bank loan. All four studies found the project technically and economically attractive; however, because of the growth of the Indian power system (for which the plant had to be optimized), the project's installed capacity grew during the course of the studies from 1.8 GW to 3.6 GW to finally 10.8 GW.

In all the studies, however, the macroeconomic impact assessment was not considered because it had been excluded while preparing the terms of reference for the studies. Based on such studies, which did not consider the financial feasibility and sociopolitical risk assessment for Nepal, the country has not been confident enough to negotiate with India. The talks for "fixing the parameters of the Karnali project," as agreed upon between the Nepali and Indian prime ministers in December 1991 (MWR 1991), ended in a deadlock over the apportioning of benefits.

The projects constructed in Nepal for its own needs have been very expensive. The Marsyangdi hydroelectric project – drawing on expatriate advice and World Bank lead funding – cost Nepal almost US$4,000 per kilowatt (kW) – about five times more expensive than a similar project in Bhutan under Indian aegis and about three times more expensive than projects in the Indian Himalayas. In August 1995, the World Bank withdrew support for the Arun-3 hydroelectric project, which was projected to cost US$5,000/kW.

In the many negotiations on Karnali and other major dam projects, Nepalis were upset that India has consistently either denied or downplayed irrigation and flood-control benefits. India also wanted to pay only for the cost of energy and not for the cost of peaking power, thus transferring the bulk of the costs to a Nepali export item (electricity) and letting other benefits (irrigation, flood control, etc.) that accrue from regulation of monsoon flows become free-rider gifts. Nepal wanted to link the cost of electricity sold to the cost of alternative thermal generation in India to maximize its profit. India, on the other hand, insisted on a "cost plus" formula whereby, once costs are known, some small percentage of incentive is added for Nepal (ToI 1991c). This would leave the power to grant benefits in Indian hands while reducing its own cost of energy. In this case it would be in Nepal's interest to build lower (or smaller) dams at lower costs relative to base electricity load. Nepal could also opt for run-of-river schemes that have only energy benefits and provide no regulated-flow benefits for irrigation or flood control in the Indian plains.[4]

Given the strong Indian interest in developing and benefiting from Nepal's water resource, as well as Nepal's unfavorable balance-of-payments position with India, the tactics of aloofness or stalling could not be sustained for long by Nepal. At the December 1991 meeting of the joint economic commission, after a new democratic regime came to power in Nepal, India did not show much interest in taking up landlocked Nepal's concerns of regularizing the trade and transit treaty after the 1989 "blockade" unless Nepal seriously considered India's concerns regarding water resources. It indicated (through market, or *rajasik*, pressures that tilted toward the military, or *tamasik*, force) that water resource development could not be pursued by Nepal isolated from other elements in the gamut of relations between the two countries. Nepali politicians, especially the newly elected members, were also under strong ideological (*satwik*) pressure to develop water resources as per the paradigm of development and modernization. They could not use the tactics of stalling indefinitely.

In December 1991, the newly elected democratic government of Nepal came to what it called an "understanding" with India on several water-related issues. Among them was one allowing India to construct an "afflux bund" embankment in Nepali territory to operate the barrage of the Tanakpur power project on the Mahakali (Sarda), mostly in Indian territory upstream of where the British had built the Sarda project in 1928. This "understanding" caused an uproar in the Nepali Parliament. The reason was that in April 1990, a people's movement in Nepal changed an absolute monarchy into a constitutional monarchy with a parliamentary democracy. In the process of drafting a new order, Nepal included Article 126(2) in its constitution, which requires that any agreement by a Nepali government with another government regarding the sharing of natural resources must be ratified by a two-thirds majority of Parliament or a simple majority if the matter is not deemed to be a "pervasive, serious, and long-term" issue. This was clearly done in view of past experiences regarding Indian pressure on successive governments to acquiesce to water resources agreements proposed by and perceived to be more favorable to India.

The opposition saw the government's move as an attempt to bypass Parliament on a vital issue. The matter was challenged in the Supreme Court, which decided in December 1992 that allowing India to build an afflux bund was not an "understanding" but a treaty that must be presented to Parliament. It left the matter of deciding whether the matter was "broad, grave or long-term" to Parliament, however.

Meanwhile, in September 1992, a special all-party committee of Parliament highlighted the weaknesses in the government's "understanding" with India on Tanakpur. It advised the government to seek clarifications with India and to try to increase the benefits for Nepal. In November 1992, during a state visit to Nepal by India's Prime Minister P.V. Narasimha Rao, the Indian government agreed to double the quantum of electricity to Nepal from Tanakpur free of charge from 10 million kWh to 20 million kWh, to provide 150 cusecs of irrigation waters in addition to the amount received from the downstream Sarda and other benefits.

After the Supreme Court verdict, the government formed a committee in January 1993 to evaluate the technical, legal, political, and diplomatic impacts on Nepal and to make recommendations. The committee concluded that the treaty as it stood after amendments and clarifications was beneficial to Nepal overall and that Nepal had received benefits commensurate with its contribution (ERC 1993). Based on this recommendation, the government proposed to ratify the treaty with a simple majority. The move was opposed by the Communist opposition and by elements within the ruling Nepali Congress Party disgruntled with their own prime minister. The matter was sent to another all-party special committee of Parliament, which also was not able to fix the criteria that would classify agreements as grave (requiring passage by a two-thirds majority) or not grave (requiring a simple majority).

This constitutional provision has been an effective response by Nepal to increase its bargaining (*satwik*) power by tying its hands with a constitutional principle. As mentioned by Terrell (1991), Nepal alone can make the decision not to build a major hydro-project but Nepal alone cannot decide to build one. Although it was obvious that India was not going to sign the new trade and transit treaty without Nepal's assurance that it would be allowed to complete the Tanakpur Barrage's afflux bund on 577 meters of Nepali territory (ToI 1991a), it is now equally obvious that water agreements signed by Nepal with India must have a large social consensus behind them. By forcing India to please the government in power as well as the opposition – and hence a large segment of the Nepali electorate – Nepal has maneuvered itself into a favorable bargaining stance. This provision of the constitution is a new feature in the history of Nepal–India water relations, and it is currently being tested.

State-to-state water resource relations are now complicated by the openness induced by newly won democracy in Nepal, as well as the increased flow of information in the region resulting from modernization and growth. The state is perceived less as a deliverer of the fruits of development and more as a power entity with interests that may not coincide with that of the domestic groups for which it claims to speak.[5] Microlevel domestic groups have sprung up that can and do manipulate the framework within which the nation and its bureaucracy exercises power. The entire environmental movement of recent times, with global and domestic horizontal linkages that often bypass national positions, is a testimony to this postulate.

In the Nepal–India context, environmental groups against dam building and the domestic groups for irrigation or power interests in Uttar Pradesh and Bihar can promote or subvert New Delhi's position vis-à-vis Kathmandu. For example, New Delhi has traditionally opposed navigation access to the sea for Nepal, while Nepal has considered this one of the possible benefits to accrue from the Kosi high dam. Bihar Chief Minister Laloo Prasad Yadav, together with Bihari intellectuals, in a clear departure from New Delhi's position, has expressed the view that Bihar would benefit from developing navigation on the Kosi since it is as landlocked as Nepal (Dahal 1992a, 1992b).

6.3   Indian Perceptions

Modern India inherited the British mantle in more ways than one. Its legitimate inheritance as the successor state consists of the industrial, transport, and communications infrastructure; the scientific and technical establishments; and the legal institutions. It is also the main heir in South Asia of the capitalist market civilization. Unfortunately, it has also inherited the British perceptions of security that have dominated its foreign policy and relations with neighbors since its independence from British colonial rule in 1947.

Security is a legitimate concern for any nation. Extending military significance into all matters, however, stems from a lack of confidence in other relations of interdependence, such as the regimes and commercial treaties the nation enters into. This results in water resource development in Nepal being perceived less as a commercial venture and more as a strategic one by India. Hassan (1991) describes the Bangladeshi understanding of how India's security concerns have translated into the use of water as a bargaining chip: Prime Minister Rajiv Gandhi is said to have linked Indian assistance in solving the country's flood problems to a Bangladeshi commitment to resolve tribal disturbances along the Chittagong hill tracts border with India. India's stance in many water issues stems from the fear that its smaller neighbors could make alliances with its hostile larger neighbors, making it dependent on resources controlled by others.

Modern India's first water resources agreement with Nepal was the Kosi Agreement in 1954. The original plan was to construct a high dam at a gorge in Nepal just before the river debouched onto the Tarai plains. Because Nepal had just undergone a change of regime, its technical expertise was not adequate, and it had not conducted an assessment of its potential, it had agreed to the Indian plan for the construction of the Kosi high dam. However, Indian security perceptions deemed that locating such a major structure deep inside Nepal would not be wise.

Internal Indian politics also played a part. Because of the limited resources available to New Delhi, the choice was between building the Kosi high dam for Bihar and Nepal or the Bhakhra Nangal Dam for the Punjab. Pratap Singh Kairon, the Chief Minister of the Punjab, was able to convince Jawaharlal Nehru that his state's needs were greater than Bihar's and Nepal's. Bihar had to make do with what existed: embankment technology instead of a high dam primarily for flood protection with a low barrage for irrigation diversion at the point where the Kosi leaves Nepal and enters Bihar.[6]

Another agreement on the Gandak, very similar to the Kosi Agreement, was entered into in 1959 with the advent of a new government in Nepal. As with the Kosi Agreement, the management of all irrigation structures associated with this project lies with India; this condition has led to complaints from the Nepali side that water releases or breach maintenance are never on time. The fact that India is willing to bear all the criticism and negative feelings from Nepalis by taking upon itself the burden of unilateral management stems from the larger Indian need, arising from security considerations, to have hydraulic structures under its control.

The question of control is a vexing one that must be addressed in the current negotiations for the high dam projects. India is unable to enter into any agreement with Nepal unless its feeling of insecurity is assuaged by Nepal, allowing it control over the structures and their operation. Nepal, on the other hand, sees this control as a threat to its sovereignty and is unwilling to surrender it. Indeed, if the northern Indian electricity grid, irrigation structures, and flood protection measures were to be beyond its control, one could expect a sense of insecurity on the part of India; but, given the past history of "encroached sovereignty" that Nepalis have experienced in Kosi and especially in Tanakpur on the Mahakali in recent years, Nepali fears are not unfounded.

India also opposes "trilateralization" or regionalization of what it considers bilateral water-sharing issues with its neighbors. Bangladesh shares an important basin with India and is affected by events upstream in India. In its water negotiations, India has upheld diametrically opposite doctrines with its upstream (Nepal) and downstream (Bangladesh) riparian neighbors. With the upstream riparian neighbors, it maintains the doctrine of natural flow that would allow it to stake claims on the entire dry-season (useful) flow of the Nepali tributaries (Gyawali 1989). With the downstream riparian neighbor, it has maintained the doctrine of absolute sovereignty, asserting its right to divert the dry-season flow of the Ganges at the Farakka Barrage toward Hooghly, the Indian distributary of the Ganges. This situation continues to create considerable bad blood between India and Bangladesh (Abbas 1982). India and Bangladesh signed a water-sharing treaty on 12 December 1996, and tested its provisions in the subsequent pre-monsoon dry season, but the treaty has been criticized for being guided more by political considerations than by concerns over optimal resource sharing (Dixit and Mirza 1997).

Whereas embarrassment at dealing simultaneously with two riparian countries upholding two contradictory doctrines partly explains Indian resistance to a trilateral policy, a more fundamental reason seems to be the loss of control over the negotiating process that would ensue. One could anticipate Bangladesh as a downstream "consumptive use" claimant on regulated waters from high dam-building exercises in Nepal, leading to a reduction in water availability for the irrigable command area in India. Moves from bilateral interdependence to trilateralism or multilateralism would represent a weakening of the control of the strongest party and an increase in options for the weaker ones. But Nepalis also wonder if – when India and Bangladesh eventually get together – the interests of two downstream riparians, like blood, will be thicker than water law doctrines.

India has recently embarked upon a new course of economic management. In step with the changes in Eastern Europe and the former Soviet Union, it is beginning to pursue a liberal economic policy wherein power development is seen in its commercial context of reliability, cost-effectiveness, and availability. This is unlike the past policy of Nehruvian socialism where electric power generation was taken to be the "commanding heights" of the economy that needed to be nationalized and kept under state control. The present policy of the government of India in this matter, together with its liberalization policy in trade and industry, is a reversal of past policies and allows even 100% equity ownership to foreigners with a tariff that allows a 16% per annum rate of return on the basis of a 68% average generation of the installed capacity (ToI 1992).

This action may be the result of worldwide trends, but it also reflects India's newfound sense of confidence in its legal, industrial, and commercial establishments. Over the past four decades the water resource negotiation policy toward Nepal has not led to any major breakthroughs in the development of large projects, but there are indications that India is prepared to change its strategy from a policy of control assured by the Indian government through bilateral agreements to policies of a less coercive nature, assured by private commercial agreements. For example, an agreement on electric power trade signed on 17 February 1996, by the Nepali Ministry of Water Resources and the Indian Ministry of Power, allows any governmental, semigovernmental, or private enterprise in Nepal or India to buy or sell electricity to the other's and in the process to determine their terms and conditions.

If such a strategy actually materializes, it may be described as a move from a military (*tamasik*) stance to an economic (*rajasik*) one, and will have occurred in part because of what India perceives to be Nepal's intransigence, in part because of the constitutional stumbling block, and in part because of the different levels of manipulation by domestic microlevel actors in India such as industry, provincial governments, and environmental activists. To achieve the objective of more commercial developments, some in India think that allowing Nepal to control the powerhouse and other structures is permissible provided supply risks are avoided through commercial penalties.[7]

The overarching legitimacy of the market, which derives from the developmental benefits that it assures to "hewers of wood and drawers of water," has allowed India to exert a kind of moral (*satwik*) pressure on Nepali leadership. The complaint that, by stalling, Nepal has behaved as "a dog in the manger," not developing its resources and not letting anyone else do it, has rankled politicians and business leaders in Nepal. Upon returning from India after talks with his Indian counterpart in December 1991, the Nepali prime minister used the above expression to describe the type of policy he would not pursue.[8] Such *satwik* pressure prevents Nepali politicians from countering otherwise. While international law forbids an upper riparian country such as Nepal to cause any harm to a lower riparian country, it does not oblige it to cause any benefits unless it is willing to do so.

If India pursues this policy of using noncoercive market power (as described by Schmookler 1984) to achieve what it could not by a more coercive use of state power (such as blockades during the 1989 trade and transit impasse), it would then be doing what Habeeb (1988) describes as conceding on principles and getting tough on questions of details such as price. It would also be redefining the problem to its advantage by shifting the debate from military (*tamasik*) control to commercial (*rajasik*) benefits. Nepal would then have lost its ability to stall because, with nationalism not being the issue in question, the commitment of its populace to sustain a fight with India will have been weakened and the possibility

of maintaining a coalition with international forces (Bangladesh and supporters of Nepal in Europe and America who are sympathetic to a small
nation in its fight with a big one) would have been lost.

By linking water resource development benefits with industry, trade,
and other developments, it will have adopted the ancient Chinese
stratagem "Toss Out a Brick to Attract Jade" – the give-and-take strategy of giving something less valuable to oneself but valuable to someone
else to obtain something valuable to oneself.[9] On the one hand, India
perceives Nepal's strength in its ability to stall indefinitely with the *satwik*
power of legitimacy of ownership. On the other hand, India's perception
of its own strength is both a realization of the limitations of *tamasik* power
and the rich potential of the *rajasik* forces of the market it commands.

6.4   Continuing Negotiations

The negotiations in the mid-1990s illustrate the complex situation of interdependence marked by both negative and positive exercise of power.
Because of strong personal animosities among the political leaders of the
different parties, the Special Committee of the Nepali Parliament could
not reach consensus on how to proceed on Tanakpur, or define what constitutes a "broad, grave or long-term" water-sharing issue according to
Article 126(2) of the Nepali Constitution. Parties exhibited early signs of
"Tanakpur fatigue." In December 1993, India's Water Resources Minister V.C. Shukla obtained an "action plan" for implementing the Tanakpur
Agreement from the Nepali government of Prime Minister Girija Prasad
Koirala even though the main treaty had not been approved by Parliament,
as required by the Supreme Court verdict of December 1992. Nepal then
granted a private Australian company a "hunting license" to build the approximately 750 MW West Seti hydroelectric storage project upstream of
the Karnali site and sell the electric power to India. The matter was never
presented to Parliament; there was no discussion concerning the benefits
of regulated flow that would accrue to India; and no political party or figure showed any interest in the matter, although this issue had implications
regarding Article 126(2) of Nepal's Constitution.

The Koirala government fell in July 1994, when members of Parliament from Koirala's own party boycotted the House and a bill elaborating
his government's policy was voted down. The Tanakpur Agreement with
India and the ensuing row contributed significantly to Koirala's downfall.

In mid-term general elections in November 1994, Koirala lost the majority in the house and the Communist United Marxist-Leninists (UML), who had vociferously opposed the Tanakpur Agreement, emerged as the single largest party in a hung Parliament. The UML then formed a minority government. Both the UML and and the RPP, a right-wing party, called for renegotiating the Tanakpur Agreement. India, now in a negative power position, refused. To resolve the impasse, in April 1995 the UML government, ostensibly after signals from India, put forth a "package deal" that increased the quality of electricity and water available to Nepal, but made Nepal acquiesce to constructing a massive (315-meter high, 6.48-GW) storage high dam of the Pancheshwar Project in the mountains upstream of the Tanakpur site on the Mahakali River. India had wanted the dam for more than two decades, but Nepal had not been interested because its requirements for water and power were smaller than India's. The UML government, however, was not able to do much with this package deal because of differences within its ranks over the deal's implications and complications over the controversial Arun-3 hydroelectric project, from which the World Bank withdrew its support in August 1995.

The minority UML government fell in September 1995, and a coalition of the Nepali Congress, the RPP, and a southern ethnic party formed a new government. By then, "Tanakpur fatigue" had overtaken all parties to some degree. On 26 January 1996, the day India's Foreign Minister Pranab Mukherjee arrived in Kathmandu, a meeting was called between representatives from the Nepali Congress, the UML, and the RPP, who signed a "National Consensus on the use of the Waters of the Mahakali River." This meeting took place outside Parliament and its committees and small parties were not represented; the "Consensus" furthered the earlier UML-proposed "package deal" on the Mahakali. Three days later, the foreign ministers of Nepal and India signed the "Treaty concerning the Integrated Development of the Mahakali River Including Sarda Barrage, Tanakpur Barrage and Pancheshwar Project." The prime ministers of Nepal and India re-initialed the treaty on 12 February, during Nepali Prime Minister Sher Bahadur Deuba's visit to India. The treaty provided more water and electricity to Nepal from the Tanakpur power plant but wrested from Nepal its consent to build the Pancheshwar high dam. The treaty also contained some water- and cost-sharing provisions, which became controversial as their implications were analyzed.

Public debate began to heat up prior to parliamentary ratification of
the new treaty. On 10 April 1996, the UML's Central Committee formed
a working group to study the treaty's implications. The Committee presented its report on 2 September 1996, highlighting 17 positive and 26
negative points regarding the treaty. Reactions to the report within the
UML (a main opposition party whose votes were required to achieve a
two-thirds majority in Parliament) were split: the Bolsheviks felt that the
treaty should be ratified first and the negative points taken care of when
the engineering report on the high dam project was being prepared; the
Mensheviks thought the treaty should not be ratified until all the negative
points had been cleared up with India. During August and September
1996, in what was widely seen as an effort to pressure the UML into
ratifying the Mahakali treaty, the British Minister of State for Parliamentary Affairs, Liam Fox, and the US Assistant Secretary of State for South
Asia, Robin Raphael, hinted during their visits to Nepal that failure to
ratify the Mahakali treaty would drive away private international investments in Nepal.

UML's Working Committee and Central Committee met almost continuously between 2 and 20 September to iron out the differences between
the Bolsheviks and the Mensheviks. Just before the parliamentary vote
for ratification, the UML's Central Committee agreed, with a single-vote
majority, to ratify the treaty. The party's Mensheviks called this an "artificial majority," and some of them abstained from voting in Parliament.
The Mahakali treaty was ratified on 20 September 1996 by a more than
two-thirds majority of the joint upper and lower houses of the Nepali
Parliament. However, before ratifying the treaty, the Parliament unanimously passed a significant stricture, binding on the Nepali government,
that defines certain clauses to mean 50% shared benefits for Nepal. Because India could interpret these clauses differently, the entire treaty came
under question. According to the treaty, within six months of ratification,
the detailed engineering report of the Pancheshwar high dam project was
to be completed jointly by Nepal and India. As of March 1999, this work
had not been done. Significant differences remain between Nepal, which
wants a 315-meter high dam producing 6.48 GW for peak power production, and India, which wants a 268-meter high dam producing only
2.0 GW in the first stage and another 2.0 GW at some future date. India
also wants the requirements of the Lower Sarda Canal to be considered
its prior water rights, while Nepal thinks that is not what the treaty or the
stricture says.

The coalition government also signed an agreement with India to study the mammoth Kosi high dam project and the prime minister proposed granting a "hunting license" to Enron Renewable Energy Corporation of Texas for the 10.8-GW Karnali project. The prime minister was opposed in this attempt by the cabinet minister for water resources, and the matter is at a stalemate.

The coalition government led by Prime Minister Sher Bahadur Deuba collapsed on 6 March 1997, when he failed to win a vote of confidence. A coalition of the right-wing RPP and the Communist UML came into power; neither party was in favor of the new treaty. This coalition too fell and a quick succession of others followed until the Parliament was dissolved by the king and fresh elections were declared for May 1999. A wholly new issue has emerged – that of the presence of Indian troops in Kalapani at the headwaters of the Mahakali on land that Nepal considers its own – and threatens to upstage the entire treaty with a fresh conflict. As these events illustrate, Nepalis are sometimes victims of their own hype and their belief that they could become rich by harnessing Himalayan waters and selling the electricity to India. Without adequate research on the costs and benefits and on the intense and complex bargaining required to realize these ambitions, Nepal could easily find itself unprepared to face the *rajasik* forces of the market, leading again to a post facto feeling of having received a raw deal.

6.5 Conclusion

Nepal–India negotiations on water resource development in the Ganges River basin system they jointly own present a case of negotiations under asymmetric conditions, in both aggregate power and issue-specific power. The former is understood as the totality of resources at a player's command, and India clearly perceives an overwhelming imbalance in its favor. The latter is understood as control over the interactional process, and Nepal, by owning the sites where hydroelectric plants can be built, has been endowed with veto power to stop a project from being developed.

Nepal has not always been successful in preventing projects. The forces of modernization have acquired a legitimacy in the minds of the masses, making development a major raison d'être of the modern state. Despite their uncertainty about the value of the resource, Nepali rulers have had to accept the philosophy of building hydraulic structures for the good of the masses. India has used this moral legitimacy of modern development, as well as the occasions when regimes have changed in Nepal, to conclude treaties for the building of dams, irrigation schemes, and power plants that have been perceived by Nepal to have benefited India overwhelmingly.

These treaties have not helped India settle the issue permanently in its favor. The developments on the Kosi, the Gandak, and the Mahakali at the Nepal–India border in the plains represent only a fraction of the benefits that would accrue if large storage dams were built deeper in Nepal in the mountain gorges. Because it is uncertain of the benefits that it would acquire, and because of the imprint of the historical legacy, Nepal has adopted the tactics of stalling in negotiations. Given the legitimacy of modernization, however, this strategy is essentially a negative one and cannot be carried out indefinitely.

The recent regime change in Nepal has resulted in a new, more democratic constitution, one feature of which is a provision binding any elected government to conclude pervasive, serious, and long-term resource-sharing agreements with foreign powers (especially India) only after approval by a two-thirds majority in Parliament. This provision was tested in both Parliament and the Supreme Court of Nepal. In this way, Nepal has increased its bargaining power by forcing India to make proposals that must be acceptable to a larger section of the Nepali public than just the ruling party.

The negotiation dynamics have now entered a new phase, the character of which can only be speculated at this stage. Both players are showing signs of structural failure in their internal dynamics. The stalemate has forced lower-level players to assert themselves. The Indian states of Bihar and Uttar Pradesh, which need the high dams in Nepal, have begun to question New Delhi's past strategy which has alienated Nepal, and to make direct contacts through academics and other leaders. Environmental activists in the flood plains concerned with the interests of the poor, who are opposed to high dams in Nepal for physical and economic security reasons, have begun building horizontal linkages with Nepali activists and are trying to influence thinking in Kathmandu directly without having to route their views through New Delhi.

A key factor in the course of the negotiations is the perception of overarching legitimacy in modulating the exercise of power. In the case of Nepal, linking the issue of water negotiations with the sensitive issue of aggrieved nationalism at Kalapani has provided legitimacy for the tactics of stalling and inclusion of third parties. In India, the issue of security has allowed justification of a tough bargaining stance, irrespective of the disastrous economic consequences of blocked capital, misspent labor, and lost time. Now, as both countries are faced with new challenges of cooperation, the overarching legitimacy will have to come from the imperatives of development and modernization within the framework of an open technical society, market pressures, and rambunctious democratic polity.

Notes

[1] Vidhyalankar's (1966) historical novel of Kautilyan times, as well as Mitra's (1978) scholarly treatment of Kautilya's *Arthashastra*, brings out the strong imprint of this ancient thinker's paradigm on South Asian minds.

[2] A demi-official letter from Sir Maurice Hallett, GCIE, KGSI, Governor United Provinces, to Sir Olaf Caroe, KCIE, CSI, Secretary to the Government of India, External Affairs Department, 18 February 1945.

[3] A former Nepali diplomat writes that Nepali intent to go ahead with the megaproject was stymied by donor competition between the United Nations Development Program (UNDP) and the World Bank and their interests in promoting consultants they had confidence in (Upadhya 1991, 1992).

[4] At the May 1992 Patna Workshop, India's water resources secretary reiterated that the Karnali project had no irrigation benefits, whereas the UP irrigation chief engineer mentioned incremental benefits of 13 million acre-feet.

[5] Institutionalized rent-seeking behavior in public utilities and construction agencies is a major factor diminishing the legitimacy of state-led institutions. See Bharti (1991) or Wade (1984).

[6] Information from keynote address by Bhognedra Jha, Communist Party of India member of Parliament for the past 25 years, at the Patna Workshop.

[7] This is former Indian Foreign Secretary Muchkund Dubey's views expressed at the Patna Workshop.

[8] Former Indian Prime Minister Chandra Shekhar had complained to Bijaya Kumar, a popular Nepali TV anchorman: "With your (Nepali) attitude, not only will you Nepalis continue to remain poor but you will force us Indians to be poor too" (Personal Communication).

[9] "Pao zhuan yin yu" – Throw brick attract jade: give your opponent something expendable now to gain something more valuable later (Von Senger 1991).

References

Abbas, A.T., BM, 1982, *The Ganges Water Dispute*, University Press, Dhaka, Bangladesh.

Adhikary, R.B., 1992, Tanakpur barrage dispute from a "riparian rights" perspective, *Deshanter*, 19 April, Kathmandu, Nepal.

Amatya, R.M., 1992, Interview, *Drishti Weekly*, 11 March (in Nepali), Kathmandu, Nepal.

Becker, C., 1965, *Progress and Power* (first published in 1936, Knopf), Vintage Books, New York.

Bharti, I., 1991, Fighting the irrigation mafia in Bihar, *Economic and Political Weekly*, **26**(38):2185–2187, Bombay, India.

Bhasin, A.S., ed., 1970, *Documents on Nepal's Relations with India and China 1949–1966*, Academic Books Ltd., New Delhi, India.

Bigongiari, D., ed., 1953, *The Political Ideas of St. Thomas Aquinas*, Hafner Publishing Company, New York.

Breslin, J.W., and Rubin, J.Z., ed., 1991, *Negotiation Theory and Practice: Program on Negotiations Book*, Harvard Law School, Cambridge, MA.

Chhetri, D.P., 1992, *Nepal India relations in the context of nationalism and the water resources question*, paper (in Nepali) presented to the seminar organized by the Nepal National Intellectuals' Organization ad hoc Committee, 28 February, Kathmandu, Nepal.

Dahal, R., 1992a, Biharis live in hope of Kosi high dam, *Deshanter Weekly*, 7 June, Kathmandu, Nepal.

Dahal, R., 1992b, Nepali–Bihari Bhai Bhai, *Himal*, **5**(4), Kathmandu, Nepal.

Dixit, M.M., 1992, This water has such humanism – This water has such nationalism (in Nepali), *Sameekshya*, 24 January, Kathmandu, Nepal.

Dixit, A., and Mirza, M.Q., 1997, Who's afraid of Farakka's Accord? *Himal*, **10**(1):January–February.

Douglas, M., ed., 1982, *Essays in the Sociology of Perception*, Routledge Kegan Paul, London.

Dutta, N., 1992, Water diplomacy: Sharing of river resources between India and Nepal creates a controversy, *Sunday*, 19–25 April, Calcutta, India.

ERC, 1993, *Evaluation and Recommendation Committee (Baral Committee) on the Tanakpur Barrage Treaty with India*, His Majesty's Government of Nepal, Kathmandu, Nepal.

Gyawali, D., 1989, *Water in Nepal: An Interdisciplinary Look at Resource Uncertainties, Evolving Problems and Future Prospects*, Occasional Paper No. 8, Environment and Policy Institute, East–West Center, Honolulu, HI.

Gyawali, D., 1991, Troubled politics of Himalayan waters, *Himal*, **4**(2), May/June, Kathmandu, Nepal.

Gyawali, D., 1992, Update: Troubled waters, *Himal*, **5**(2), March/April, Kathmandu, Nepal.

Gyawali, D., 1993, Tanakpur on the Thames, *Himal*, **6**(4), July/August, Kathmandu, Nepal.

Gyawali, D., and Dixit, A., 1991 Righting a British wrong, *Himal*, **4**(2), May/June, Kathmandu, Nepal.

Habeeb, W.M., 1988, *Power and Tactics in International Negotiations: How Weak Nations Bargain with Strong Nations*, Johns Hopkins University Press, Baltimore, MD.

Hassan, S., 1991, Playing politics with South Asian water, *Himal*, **4**(2), May/June, Kathmandu, Nepal.

Independent, 1992, Tanakpur barrage: Resident's letter throws light, *The Independent Weekly*, 27 May, Kathmandu, Nepal.

Kadri, S.I., 1990, *Ganga ko Abiral Bahane Do* (Let the Ganga flow unhindered), Ganga Mukti Andolan (Ganga Liberation Movement), Bhagalpur, Bihar.

Kautilya, 1960, *Arthashastra*, Mysore Publishing House, Mysore, India.

Keohane, R.O., and Nye, J.S., 1989, *Power and Interdependence*, 2nd edition, Scott Foresman, Boston, MA.

Lamichane, B., 1992, Construction of Tanakpur barrage: An analysis (in Nepali), *Sameekshya Weekly*, 13 March, Kathmandu, Nepal.

Mahara, K.B. (Member of Parliament), 1992, What are the facts about Tanakpur? (in Nepali), *Janadesh*, 10 March, Kathmandu, Nepal.

Mitra, S.K., 1978, Political and economic literature in sanskrit, in *The Cultural Heritage of India, 5, Languages and Literatures*, The Ramakrishna Mission Institute of Culture, Calcutta, India.

Modelski, G., 1964, Kautilya: Foreign policy and international system in the ancient Hindu world, *American Political Science Review*, **508**(3):549–560, September.

Muni, S.D., 1992, Pangs of power: fissures in the Nepali Congress Troika, *Frontline*, 27 March, New Delhi, India.

MWR, 1991, Notice of the Ministry of Water Resources, *Nepal Rajpatra* (Gazette) Part 4, **41**(36), 23 December, Ministry of Water Resources (MWR), Kathmandu, Nepal.

Paudel, B., 1992, Tanakpur dispute and facts, *Drishti Weekly*, 4 March, Kathmandu, Nepal.

Perrin, N., 1980, *Giving up the Gun: Japan's Reversion to the Sword, 1543–1897*, Shambhala, Boulder, CO.

Poudyal, B., 1992, New tricks of the power mafia, *Saptahik Bimarsha*, 8 May, Kathmandu, Nepal.

Pradham, R., 1991, Indo–Nepal panel breathes into life, *Times of India*, 7 August, New Delhi, India.

Pratipakshya, 1992, Nepal again loses an opportunity, *Pratipakshya Weekly* (left-oriented), Kathmandu, Nepal.

Rangarajan, L.N., 1992, *Kautilya: The Arthashastra*, Penguin Books, London and New York.

Sameekshya, 1991, Water resources agreement: Indian press refutes Girija's defense, *Sameekshya Weekly*, 5 June, Kathmandu, Nepal.

Schmookler, A.B., 1984, *The Parable of the Tribes: The Problem of Power in Social Evolution*, University of California Press, Berkeley, CA.

Sharma, J., 1992, Judiciary: Interim order issued, *The Independent*, 15 January, Kathmandu, India.

Shrestha, A.P., 1991, *Hydropower in Nepal: Issues and Concepts of Development*, Resources Nepal and Chharu Press, Kathmandu, Nepal.

Suresh, N., 1991, Water sharing with Nepal: End of 30-year stalemate, *Times of India*, 22 December, New Delhi, India.

Terrell, P.D., Jr., 1991, Karnali (Chisapani) in retrospect, *Himal*, 4(2), May/June, Kathmandu, Nepal.

Thompson, M., 1982, A three-dimensional model, in M. Douglas, ed., *Essays in Sociology of Perception*, Routledge Kegan Paul, London.

ToI, 1991a, Indo–Nepal talks: Water resources issue resolved, *Times of India*, 6 December, New Delhi, India.

ToI, 1991b, Indo–Nepal ties on a firm footing, *Times of India*, 7 December, New Delhi, India.

ToI, 1991c, Fruitful visit (editorial), *Times of India*, 10 December, New Delhi, India.

ToI, 1992, Aid to boost power sector in India, report datelined Washington, DC, by G. Adhikary, *Times of India*, 2 June, Patna, India.

TRN, 1992, Nepal has not ceded even an inch of land to India, *The Rising Nepal*, 1 March, Kathmandu, Nepal.

Upadhya, D.R., 1991, Indo–Nepal relations: Suddenly raised issue of two treaties (in Nepali), *Nepali Patna Weekly*, 27 December, Kathmandu, Nepal.

Upadhya, D.R., 1992, Bad advice from World Bank, *Himal*, 4(2), March/April, Kathmandu, Nepal.

Vidhyalankar, S., 1966, *Acharya Vishnuqupta Chanakya*, translated in Nepali, Binod Prasad Dhital, Kathmandu, Nepal.

Von Senger, H., 1991, *The Book of Stratagems: Tactics for Triumph and Survival*, edited and translated by M.B. Gubitz, Viking Penguin, New York.

Wade, R., 1984, The system of administrative and political corruption: Canal irrigation in South India, *Journal of Development Studies*, **18**(3):287–328.

WN, 1993, Report: Flood mitigation by multipurpose reservoirs, *Water Nepal (WN)*, **3**(2–3):81–82, Nepal Water Conservation Foundation, Kathmandu, Nepal.

WRI, 1990, *World Resources 1990–1991*, Oxford University Press, London.

Chapter 7

The Impact of Multiple Asymmetries on Arab–Israeli Negotiations

Saadia Touval

Studies of power have always been handicapped by the difficulties of defining the concept and forging it into an analytical tool. This work seeks to deal with these difficulties. The purpose of this chapter is to show that the conceptualization of power as a bilateral relationship can be misleading, unless analysis of aggregate power, perceived power, and action power takes all the actors surrounding the relationship into its calculations.

In this chapter, the possibilities of such analysis are exemplified through a discussion of three cases of Arab–Israeli negotiations in which there is a discrepancy between expectations derived from bilateral power relationships and the actual outcomes of the negotiations. In each case the weaker side gained more than the stronger did. To be sure, the phenomenon of the weak negotiating successfully with the strong has been discussed by several authors who have shown how the puzzling outcomes of such negotiations can be explained (see, for example, Habeeb 1988; Zartman 1971). The purpose of using the Arab–Israeli cases is to show

how the puzzle can be solved by highlighting a fundamental flaw in the conceptualization of power in negotiation that greatly diminishes its utility as an analytic tool for interpreting structures and outcomes of international negotiations.

This conceptualization is deficient because it implies a bilateral contest. But in the history of Arab–Israeli relations, the contest was seldom bilateral. It usually involved a third party mediating the negotiation, as well as additional actors who influenced the negotiations through a variety of means and channels. Although Arab–Israeli negotiations are a special case, the power interactions that take place in that process suggest that other negotiations as well, even when they are ostensibly bilateral, involve additional actors who exert power and influence the process.

This chapter opens with a brief discussion of the concept of power, as frequently applied in analyses of negotiations. Next, I present summaries of three cases of Arab–Israeli negotiations that demonstrate the deficiencies of bilateral conceptualizations of power. These summaries are followed by an examination of advantages and inadequacies of modeling Arab–Israeli negotiations as a triangular process. In the concluding section I offer some observations about the applicability of bilateral modeling of power in the study of negotiations in general.

7.1   Power in Negotiation

The term *negotiation* is employed here as "a process in which explicit proposals are put forward ostensibly for the purpose of reaching agreement on an exchange or on the realization of a common interest where conflicting interests are present" (Ikle 1964:3–4). Implied in this definition is an interdependence between the negotiating parties: Each needs the other's consent or cooperation to attain its goals. There is nothing, however, in this definition to restrict it to a bilateral relationship.

Viewing power as the action of one actor to induce another to do something that it would not have done otherwise appears especially suitable for explaining how a party to a negotiation can be persuaded to give its consent to proposed terms of an agreement that it had previously rejected. Such a conceptualization implies a bilateral interaction between *A* and *B*. The attraction of bilateral conceptualizations derives from their simplicity. Their appeal to students of negotiations has probably been reinforced by the persuasive logic of two-player games developed in game theory.

In such models, as in negotiation, players are interdependent; they need each other to achieve their respective goals. (For an early example, that has since become a classic, see Schelling 1960.) Power and influence (often used interchangeably) are assumed to derive from asymmetric interdependence, from a situation in which *A* needs *B* more than *B* needs *A*, making *B* the more powerful party. Interdependence between the parties may reflect need for certain goods that the other can supply or deny (Hirschman 1969; Keohane and Nye 1989:8–19). But *A* may also be dependent on *B* because *A*'s welfare depends on *B* refraining from military action that can harm *A*.

In the Arab–Israeli case, the need that the other could fill was often related to security – putting an end to the losses being imposed by the other's (actual or potential) military activity. But the parties recognized their interdependence also with respect to other needs that the other could supply, both tangible such as territory and intangible such as recognition and legitimacy.

The reference to needs and the conceptualization of power as deriving from the ability to supply or deny the other's needs imply that the parties have both resources and wants. Thus, the view that power is reflected in resources – military, economic, or political – is subsumed in this conceptualization. Possession of resources also encompasses means that enable a party to satisfy its needs in other ways, should its adversary withhold the supply of what is required for its satisfaction.

Arabs and Israelis, although interdependent, were not caught in such a web of "complex interdependence." Such a relationship, described by R.O. Keohane and J.S. Nye, is characterized by multiple channels of communication, the absence of hierarchy among issues, and the depreciation of the value of military force (Keohane and Nye 1989:24–29). On the contrary, since the Arab states and Israel were at war, concerns of national security dominated over all other considerations, and military threats played an important role in the bargaining.

In view of this we might expect the militarily stronger party always to prevail, eliciting from the weaker side an acceptance of the stronger side's proposals. Military strength and weakness do not imply necessarily a conceptualization of power as the possession of resources. The phrases fit behavioral conceptualizations as well, because they connote asymmetric interdependence: One party is more dependent on the other's refraining from coercive behavior than the other. This does not mean that the stronger would necessarily obtain all that it demands, and the weak

would get nothing. Even under the most advantageous circumstances,
the stronger party may prefer to yield on some issues, rather than bear
the costs of imposing its will to the fullest extent. An example is Japan's
ability, in negotiating the terms of its "unconditional surrender" at the end
of World War II, to secure a role for the Emperor. But power would be
meaningless unless we assume that the stronger – that is, the less dependent – will obtain more than the weaker – that is, the more dependent.

The preceding discussion of power as applied in studies of negotiations is not meant to be comprehensive, nor should it be interpreted as im-
plying that all studies of power in negotiation subscribe to this approach.
Its purpose is to describe a widely accepted view of the meaning of power
in negotiation and to show that bilateral structuring is closely associated
with such conceptualizations. It remains to be seen how applicable it is
to the analysis of Arab–Israeli negotiations.

7.2   Arab–Israeli Negotiations

A debate has developed in recent years among Israeli historians on
whether the Arab states really ruled out any possibility of peace with
Israel, as both Arab and Israeli public statements on the subject seemed
to indicate. The opening of Israeli archives of the early years of state-
hood have provided interesting evidence showing that, while maintaining
an intransigent public posture, Arab governments had engaged in secret
exploratory talks with Israeli representatives about possible terms of a
settlement (see Rabinovich 1991; Shlaim 1988). Nevertheless, it still
seems accurate to say that since Israel's establishment in 1948 and until
the 1970s, a perception prevailed on all sides that the conflict was zero
sum – namely, that the parties had not identified any common interests
worth negotiating over. This perception accounts for the fact that negotiations were only sporadic; when they did take place, their purpose was
to realize only the common interest of ending a costly war or of avoiding
some painful or risky consequences brought on by a war.

The outcomes of several Arab–Israeli negotiations can be interpreted
as corresponding to the approximate power balance – that is, the asymmetric mutual interdependence, that exists between the two adversaries.
But in a significant proportion of cases there was a remarkable incon-
gruity between the respective power of the two parties and their ability
to realize their preferences. This chapter does not allow for a discussion of all such cases, but a brief summary of three cases illustrates the

discrepancies between the two parties' resource power and the negotiation structures and outcomes. It also provides empirical referents for the theoretical discussion in the sections that follow.

7.3 The Egyptian–Israeli Armistice Negotiations, 1949

Egypt was the first of the Arab states participating in the 1948 war to conclude an armistice agreement with Israel (on 24 February 1949). The parties entered into the negotiations in compliance with a United Nations (UN) Security Council resolution adopted on 16 November 1948. A UN mediator, Ralph Bunche, played a key role in the negotiations, and is credited with their successful conclusion. (The discussion in this section is based on *Documents on the Foreign Policy of Israel* 1948–1949; *FRUS* 1977; Rabinovich 1991; Shlaim 1988; and Touval 1982.)

Israel was militarily the more powerful of the two protagonists. In October and December 1948 Israel launched two major offensives, forcing the Egyptian army to withdraw from most of the Negev, which it had occupied since May. Furthermore, a sizable Egyptian force was surrounded and besieged by the Israeli army at Faluja. Egypt was able, however, to hold on to the Gaza Strip. An Israeli push into Sinai and an attempt to occupy the Gaza Strip were cut short as a result of a British threat of military intervention unless Israel withdrew from Sinai and ceased military operations. The US added its own warnings, helping to persuade Prime Minister Ben-Gurion to comply.

Both parties wanted to end the war, weary of the heavy costs and burdens that it imposed. The opening of the armistice negotiations was delayed by Egyptian attempts to get Israel to withdraw to the line it held prior to its October offensive, in accordance with another Security Council resolution (on November 4) calling for such withdrawal. However, in view of Israel's continued military threat and the risk that the encircled Egyptian force at Faluja would be forced to surrender, Egypt finally agreed to begin the armistice talks.

The key issue in the negotiation was territorial – the delimitation of the armistice lines. This was important for two reasons: the tactical military advantage the armistice demarcation lines would confer in the event that fighting resumed and the influence that they would have (notwithstanding the parties' formal reservations on this point) on shaping the international boundary in the peace talks that were expected to follow.

The negotiations, mediated by Bunche, were held on the island of Rhodes. Israel's power, consisting mainly of its military advantage, forced Egypt to come to the table and implicitly to acknowledge Israel's existence through its signature of the armistice agreement. It also compelled Egypt to accept existing front lines as the basis for the territorial demarcation and to give up its demands for far-reaching Israeli withdrawals. Israel had to make three major concessions. First, early in the negotiations, Israel was prevailed upon to allow supplies to be delivered to the besieged Egyptians at Faluja. Second, Israel was unable to obtain the withdrawal of Egyptian forces from the Gaza Strip. Third, it had to yield to the Egyptian demand that the Nitsana/Auja al Hafir area be demilitarized, necessitating an Israeli withdrawal from positions there – a border post within Palestine (as it was during the British mandate) near the Egyptian border, which had been occupied by Israel in the December offensive.

During the negotiations, Egypt was, to some extent, at Israel's mercy. Israel possessed a military advantage; the Egyptian army was greatly weakened and demoralized, unable to protect Egypt's territorial integrity; and the Egyptian regime faced the risks of domestic political upheaval. Yet, despite its being the more powerful, Israel was unable to realize some important objectives and had to yield to certain Egyptian demands. How can this be explained?

The explanation lies in the power relationship between Israel and other actors that intervened in the situation. The most significant intervenors were Great Britain, the United States, and the UN mediator. They did not align in a coalition with Egypt; the structure resulting from their intervention was a multilateral one – a cluster of bilaterals with each pursuing its separate course.

Britain intervened because of its concern that Israeli advances would threaten Britain's ability to maintain military bases in the area. In the background of Britain's intervention was its quarrel with Egypt, which was demanding a revision of the 1936 Anglo–Egyptian treaty that had granted Britain the right to maintain bases in the Suez Canal area; Egypt wanted Britain out. When Israeli forces crossed the border into Egypt, Britain threatened military intervention to demonstrate its adherence to its obligation to defend Egypt, in accordance with the treaty that Egypt wanted annulled. Britain's intervention can also be linked to its opposition to the inclusion of the Negev in Israeli territory. The strained British–Israeli relationship, a legacy of the clash between Zionism and British policy in Palestine, would have precluded the possibility of moving the bases from the Suez Canal area into the Negev.

Israel was stronger than Egypt. Yet, despite showing its prowess and resolve by downing (in the course of the war with Egypt) five British airplanes, Israel did not feel strong enough to confront Britain militarily. Thus, the threat of British military intervention effectively neutralized Israel's military advantage vis-à-vis the Egyptians.

The United States viewed Britain as the main pillar of the Western alliance in the Middle East and supported the British position. Israel was already dependent on American diplomatic support. It was hoping that the United States would soon grant it de jure recognition (hitherto recognition had been de facto only) and was negotiating with the United States about a large government-backed loan. Thus, it was difficult for Israel to resist American diplomatic pressures to abstain from military action against the Egyptian-held Gaza Strip, and to accept proposals made by the UN mediator.

The mediator, Ralph Bunche, was a former State Department official and, although operating under the authority of the UN Security Council, was generally perceived as acting for the United States. Israel successfully resisted some of Bunche's proposals that would have required Israel to withdraw from large parts of the Negev, because no one was prepared to go to extremes to force Israel to withdraw from territories that had been allocated to it under the original UN partition plan, even though Israeli forces took possession of these areas in violation of a UN-ordered cease-fire. But when it came to relaxing the stranglehold over the encircled Egyptian forces in Faluja and accepting the demilitarization of Auja (and its becoming the seat of the UN Mixed Armistice Commission), Israel was forced to yield under the mediator's threat that if Israel's attitude produced a deadlock, he would raise before the Security Council the issue of Israel's noncompliance with the Council's November resolution requiring it to withdraw its forces. Concerned that this would weaken Israel's diplomatic position, specifically its quest for international recognition as a state and its prospects for admission to the UN, Israel yielded.

To summarize, the outcome of the negotiations not only reflected Egyptian–Israeli power relations, but was also the result of several power interactions. Egypt and Israel depended on each other's willingness to end the war. In addition, Egypt depended on Israel's refraining from military action. Egypt's position with respect to Britain was particularly weak: Egypt considered its sovereignty dependent on Britain withdrawing its troops from Egyptian soil, while depending on Britain to deter Israel. It depended on the United States to pressure Israel. Britain depended on Egypt's willingness to acknowledge the value of its military alliance with Britain; it depended on Israel for relaxing its military pressure on Egypt (without requiring Britain actually to join the fighting); it depended on the United States to pressure Israel and to support it in its dispute with Egypt. The United States depended on Britain for maintaining the West's military defenses of the Middle East; it depended on Israel for not undermining Britain's position in the region. Israel depended on the United States for helping its admission to the UN, for lending it development funds, and for not pressing Israel to withdraw its troops to the October cease-fire lines; it depended on the UN mediator for not raising the issue of Israel's noncompliance with the Security Council's November 4 call on Israel to withdraw its troops.

These interdependencies and the influences stemming from them were not of equal weight, yet they combined to produce the Egyptian–Israeli armistice agreement.

7.4   The Syrian–Israeli Disengagement Negotiations, 1974

The 1973 war ended after three weeks of fighting, as Israel, Egypt, and Syria complied with a Security Council order for a cease-fire. Thereafter, a prolonged process of negotiations followed, leading to several agreements stabilizing the situation along the front lines. These agreements were mediated by the United States, with Secretary of State Henry Kissinger playing a crucial role in the negotiations. Throughout this period Israel was clearly the more powerful party. Yet, the agreements included significant Israeli concessions. (This section is based on Kissinger 1982; and Touval 1982.)

Each disengagement negotiation holds some interesting insights about the nature and role of power, but I confine my detailed discussion to the Syrian–Israeli case because it best illustrates the inadequacy of the concept of bilateral power for explaining Arab–Israeli negotiations.

The Egyptian–Syrian attack on 6 October 1973 caught Israel by surprise. Despite an initial Syrian success in breaking through Israeli lines, the Syrian forces were quickly pushed back, and Israel expanded the territorial salient it had held on the Golan Heights since 1967. When the cease-fire came into effect, freezing front lines, Israeli forces were placed twenty-five miles from Damascus.

The disengagement negotiations were slow and difficult. The Syrian objective was to recover both the area it lost in 1973 and a portion of the area it lost in 1967. Besides the security reasons for wanting Israeli forces to be removed as far as possible from Damascus, there were political considerations that inspired Syrian objectives. Recovery of territory would have helped to justify the heavy losses suffered in the war. Furthermore, Syria believed that it was entitled to gain no less than Egypt, which had recovered a small portion of Sinai in the disengagement agreement it had concluded in January 1974. Israel viewed Syria as the most implacable of its enemies. From Israel's perspective, there were sound military reasons for holding on to the territory captured in the war, because it would provide Israel with an advantage when the next war erupted. Syria's main card in the bargaining that ensued was the group of 65 Israeli prisoners of war whom it had captured. Syria made the return of the Israeli prisoners conditional not only upon the return of the 380 Syrians that Israel held (which Israel was eager to do), but also upon an Israeli withdrawal from a significant portion of the territory it held, a concession that Israel was unwilling to grant.

The agreement, concluded on 31 May 1974, required Israel to relinquish all the territory it captured in the recent war. Israel also agreed to withdraw from a small stretch of territory that it held since 1967, including the town of Kuneitra, which prior to 1967 was the administrative center of the region. The agreement further required both sides to limit the size and quality of forces and equipment in areas close to the front and to accept a UN force to serve as buffer between them. Israel's demand that the agreement contain a mutual pledge to refrain from "all military or paramilitary actions against each other" was rejected by Syria, because it implied a Syrian commitment to prevent Palestinian raids from Syrian territory. But on this point, as well as others, Israel received some assurances from the United States (as did Syria for issues of concern to it). Finally, the agreement provided for an exchange of war prisoners, an issue about which the Israeli public was greatly concerned.

We are faced again with the question of why Israel, the stronger party, yielded on issues that it considered important, such as the extent of its withdrawals and the omission of the pledge to prevent Palestinian raids from Syrian territory.

Part of the reason is that the Israeli public was weary of war and wanted a disengagement agreement concluded. Besides the domestic reasons, there were formidable foreign policy reasons that influenced Israeli attitudes. There was a risk that if disengagement did not take place, the Syrians might engage in a war of attrition. "Normally" (if this is an appropriate term) this would require Israel to respond forcefully, but such a course appeared risky in view of the threat of Soviet military intervention – a threat that appeared more credible the closer Israel got to Damascus. Soviet support for Syria, thus, neutralized much of the bargaining advantage that Israel's military superiority appeared to confer on the Israeli side. Israel's ability to engage in military operations was further restrained by the United States, which did not want to risk being drawn into a confrontation with the Soviet Union. Furthermore, American mediation had a major impact. Through a combination of a few threats and major incentives (in the form of economic and military aid and political assurances), Kissinger was able to bring about Israeli concessions.

Why did the United States engage in mediation? Why did it put much effort into obtaining Israeli concessions? Several reasons led the United States to act the way it did. First, it wanted to stabilize the region and diminish the risk that an Israeli–Syrian war might push it into an unwanted confrontation with the Soviet Union. Second, the United States thought that by acting as mediator, it would improve its relations with Syria and perhaps weaken Soviet influence in that country. Third, the American economy, as well as America's stature as a great power, had been hurt by the Arab oil embargo. It was important for the United States that the Arab oil-producing states put an end to the embargo, and they agreed to do so on the understanding that the United States would bring about an Israeli withdrawal.[1] Finally, in the atmosphere prevailing in the 1970s, the United States came to believe that demonstrating its ability to deliver Israeli concessions was an effective means for persuading the Arab states to align with the United States and to distance themselves from the Soviet Union.

Thus assessing the asymmetries in Israel's and Syria's mutual interdependence and their bargaining power vis-à-vis each other, does not provide a sufficient explanation of the outcome of their negotiations. The key to an understanding of the outcome again requires looking at the complete picture of power interactions among the several principal actors involved. The intersecting interdependencies are indicative of the influences that were attempted. Israel and Syria were dependent on each other's consent to disengage forces and exchange prisoners of war. Israel further depended on Syria's willingness to curb transborder attacks by Palestinian groups. Syria depended on Israel's willingness to give up the area it seized in the 1973 war and to withdraw from part of the territory it occupied in 1967. Syria depended on the Soviet Union for military protection and deterrence against Israeli military pressure; it depended on the United States to obtain Israeli territorial concessions; and it depended on Saudi Arabia and other Arab oil-producing states to pressure the United States to extract concessions from Israel. The Soviet Union and the United States depended on each other to restrain their respective Syrian and Israeli clients, to avoid being dragged into a confrontation they did not desire. In addition, the Soviets depended on Syria for allowing the Soviet Union to maintain a military and political foothold in the Arab world and on the United States to allow it to participate in the Arab–Israeli peace process in a significant way, commensurate to its superpower status. The United States depended on the Soviet Union not to put obstacles in the way of Syria's cooperation with the American-led disengagement negotiations; it depended on Syria to distance itself from the Soviets and to allow the United States to reopen its embassy in Damascus; it depended on Israel to grant Syria, through American mediation, the territorial concessions that Syria required; and it depended on Saudi Arabia and other Arab oil-producing states to lift the oil embargo and refrain from publicly describing the mediation as stemming from the newly acquired Arab political clout. Saudi Arabia depended on Syria to refrain from criticizing the Saudi regime and its pro-Western foreign policy. It depended on the United States for political and military support and for obtaining concessions from Israel that would enable Saudi Arabia to justify its pro-American policies to the Arab world and on other Arab oil producers to defer to it on questions pertaining to the use of the oil weapon. It was the effect of these combined interdependencies and the power derived from them that shaped the Syrian–Israeli disengagement agreement.

7.5 The Egyptian–Israeli Peace Negotiations, 1977–1979

It is arguable which one, Israel or Egypt, was the stronger party in these negotiations. (This section draws on Carter 1982; Dayan 1981; Fahmy

1983; Quandt 1986; Sadat 1978; Touval 1982.) Israel was stronger militarily. But as the negotiations were conducted in a relatively stable and calm atmosphere, perhaps even one of growing mutual trust, Israel's military power played no role in the bargaining. As for the power flowing from other asymmetric dependencies, Israel was dependent on Egypt for much greater values than Egypt on Israel. They were mutually dependent on each other for peace, and it is true that Egypt not only granted peace, but received peace in return. However, Egypt's ability to grant or withhold peace had a much greater significance for Israel than Israel's ability to do the same held for Egypt. From Israel's perspective, peace with Egypt meant a break in the geographical encirclement by enemies to which it had been subjected for the entire extent of its land borders since 1948. More important, Israel stood to benefit because of the precedent that the peace treaty would create – putting an end to the long-standing Arab policy of refusing to come to terms with Israel's existence. Egypt was dependent on Israel's agreement for the restoration of Sinai to Egyptian sovereignty. Although this became politically important for the regime, its significance was of a different order than the significance of a peace treaty with a leading Arab state was for Israel. Therefore, given their mutual dependence, Egypt was in a stronger position than Israel.

Yet, Egypt made greater concessions to Israel than Israel made to Egypt. This was so with respect not only to the terms of the peace treaty, but also to the opening of the negotiations, with Anwar Sadat's dramatic visit to Jerusalem. It has been argued that Israel's concession was greater because Israel gave up real assets (strategic depth, military bases, oil fields), whereas Egypt gave only a written promise. If we consider, however, which side made a greater sacrifice in terms of its national ideology and national self-image, it was Egypt. In view of the policy that Egypt had pursued for the previous 30 years – that of rejecting the very existence of Israel – the conclusion of the 1979 peace treaty was clearly a major concession. Notwithstanding the importance that Egypt attached to regaining Sinai, the exchange of "land for peace" was unequal, because Egypt gave up a key principle of its ideology and foreign policy, while Israel relinquished important, but far from vital, strategic assets. Some sections of the Israeli public, including Yitzhak Shamir who later became prime minister, believed that Israeli concessions went too far because agreement to grant autonomy to the Palestinians in the West Bank and Gaza Strip and to negotiate over the ultimate status of these territories might weaken Israel's claim to the areas in question. But Prime Minister

Menachem Begin and the majority of Israelis thought that the sacrifice was worthwhile. Indeed, it was Begin who brought this proposal to Sadat when he visited him in Ismailiya in December 1977.

In the negotiations over the details of the peace treaty, Egypt made greater concessions than Israel. Egypt agreed that the peace treaty would be accompanied by a normalization of relations with Israel, and it also agreed to drop its insistence that the peace treaty establish an explicit link between Egyptian–Israeli peace and Israeli concessions to other Arab parties.

Why did Egypt grant this major concession? The answer to this question appears to lie in the bilateral realm of Egyptian–American relations rather than in the bilateral realm of Egyptian–Israeli relations. As the Egyptian leadership perceived the growing urgency of tackling domestic economic and social problems, its foreign policy priorities shifted. It became less important to continue to lead the Arab struggle against Israel and the West, and more important to create an atmosphere that would attract aid and investment. An improved relationship with the United States thus became imperative. But to have the possibility of massive American aid, it was necessary to conclude peace with Israel. Peace, rather than mere reduction of tension, was a condition imposed by the United States.

Events appeared to be moving gradually in this direction when an American attempt to place an emphasis on a comprehensive Arab–Israeli settlement (rather than to start with an Egyptian–Israeli one) alerted Sadat to the possibility that the restoration of Sinai and the future of Egyptian–American relations might be delivered hostage to Syria, the Palestinians, and the Soviet Union, each of which would have had de facto veto power over the proceedings. It was this danger that prompted President Sadat to seize the initiative and pay his dramatic visit to Jerusalem in November 1977. The visit and its repercussions in the Arab world had the desired impact, refocusing American attention on the Egyptian–Israeli peace process, and causing the United States to discontinue its efforts for a comprehensive settlement of the Arab–Israeli conflict in partnership with the Soviet Union.

Sadat's visit to Jerusalem was a major concession to Israel, signifying recognition and acceptance. It had a profound psychological impact in Israel – transforming Israeli perceptions of Egypt and strengthening those in Israel who argued that restoring Sinai to Egyptian sovereignty would not pose as great a risk to Israel's security as previously believed. Sadat made this gesture not because Egypt calculated its relative power

vis-à-vis Israel, and concluded that it must concede to the Israeli preference for direct negotiations. He went to Jerusalem because he wanted
to foil the American design for a negotiation structure ("the Geneva process") that he believed would not allow Egypt to achieve its goals.

To summarize, the concessions were granted not because Egypt perceived itself weak vis-à-vis Israel but rather because of their expected
impact on American–Egyptian relations. A similar argument can be
made about Israeli concessions: the Palestinian autonomy proposal and
the agreement to cede Sinai, to evacuate the settlers from Sinai, and to
suspend the construction of new settlements in other territories occupied
since 1967. It was not Egypt's bargaining power vis-à-vis Israel that determined these issues, but the expected impact of Israeli policies on these
matters upon American–Israeli relations. A telling indication for whom
the autonomy proposal was really intended is provided in Begin's handling of the issue: He first went to Washington to obtain President Jimmy
Carter's approval, and only after that did he submit the proposal to Sadat
and to the Israeli Cabinet.

Unlike the other two agreements, the negotiation of the Egyptian–
Israeli accords was essentially a triangular process, involving Egypt, Israel, and the United States. Other interested parties – Arab, European,
and Soviet – were excluded from it. Their exclusion was effected because the three principal parties did not perceive themselves as vulnerable to pressures for associating additional parties in the process. The
Soviet Union had little, if any, influence on Egypt or Israel, and the risk
of a Soviet–American confrontation over the Middle East had greatly re-
ceded. Europe deferred to the United States on this issue, albeit only
temporarily. The other Arab parties were excluded because they had little
leverage over Egypt, and because Sadat believed that they needed Egypt
more than Egypt needed them. Perhaps what is most important, both
Egypt and Israel were so heavily dependent on the United States, that
their dependence on other actors carried little weight in their calculations.

7.6   Mediators and Other Actors

As the discussion of the cases indicates, it would be difficult to explain
the outcomes of these negotiations within a framework defined by bilateral interdependencies and consequent power asymmetries. To conceptualize these negotiations as a bilateral system is an artifact simplifying
some analytical tasks but disregarding significant aspects of reality that

have important effects. Arab–Israeli negotiations were never insulated and self-contained. They were always part of a wider network of relationships, including power struggles, encompassing several regional actors as well as extra-regional states. Mediators, as well as other parties, influenced the negotiations, and it is necessary to take the impact of their power into account.

Why were additional parties so frequently involved in Arab–Israeli negotiations? The reason for this becomes obvious the moment we look beyond the Arab–Israeli dyad. The additional actors were involved because they believed that the Arab–Israeli conflict and Arab–Israeli negotiations affected their own important interests. Extra-regional powers were concerned because of the area's geostrategic significance and its oil resources. The regional powers were concerned because of their own power struggles and ideological commitments. Consequently, several additional actors were always involved in Arab–Israeli negotiations, trying to influence the conduct of the principal Arab–Israeli parties both directly and indirectly by exerting influence on mediators.

The extra-regional powers' desire for involvement in negotiations often converged with the desire of the Arab party that was negotiating with Israel to obtain external help for its positions. Usually such external help came through mediation. Both Arabs and Israelis were well aware that the participation of mediators in the negotiations tended to counterbalance the power of the stronger party. The involvement of mediators enabled the weaker side to obtain terms that were better than would have been possible had the negotiation been purely bilateral, allowing the relative power of the participants to have full impact. For this reason Israel, which often perceived itself stronger, preferred direct bilateral negotiations with the relevant Arab party and often tried to prevent the participation of mediators. Conversely, the Arab parties, which perceived themselves weaker, usually preferred that negotiations be conducted through a mediator. Yet Israel was usually unable to structure the negotiations according to its preference because the preference of the Arab party for a mediator that would neutralize Israel's strength worked in conjunction with the interest of the great powers to participate in the negotiations. (For a more detailed discussion see Touval 1987.)

Whereas many states played intermediary roles between Arabs and Israelis on many occasions, the most important mediator throughout the history of the conflict has been the United States. It was the United States that almost always helped structure the negotiations in a manner that assigned a key role to itself. Although the particular circumstances prompting the United States to shape the structure of the negotiation varied, the motive was essentially the same: the desire to ensure that it would be able to influence the politics in a region that it regarded strategically and economically important. America's assumption of the mediator's role usually meant that the influences of others – America's European allies as well as its Soviet rival – were minimized. Thus, the structuring of negotiations, as well as their conduct, was never a matter to be decided merely by the two states that were ostensibly the principal parties in the negotiation. It was not the power relations between the two adversaries that shaped the structure, but rather the power of the United States and the other intervenors.

How does the involvement of mediators affect the conceptualization of power? Although negotiations between the mediator and the parties locked in a conflict resemble other bilateral bargaining processes, they also differ from them in important respects. The essence of mediation is that it is a voluntary process. Parties are theoretically free to accept or reject mediators and to accept or reject their proposals for a settlement. Yet when a powerful state like the United States offers to mediate in a conflict, the adversaries often accept it not because they hope that the mediator will help them out of a predicament, but because they fear the consequences of spurning the powerful mediator's suggestion. (For a more detailed discussion see Touval and Zartman 1989.)

The intervention of the mediator transforms the negotiation system from a bilateral one into a trilateral, consisting of three interlocked bargaining sets: In addition to the negotiation between the two antagonists, we now have negotiations between the mediator and each of them. But this is not to imply that we should merely decompose the triangular structure, and conceptualize it as consisting of three bilateral negotiations. The power relations between a mediator and the two adversaries locked into a conflict with each other are somewhat different from those existing between any two negotiating parties.

The mediator's discussions with the parties resemble other negotiations because the mediator, like any negotiator, bargains with the other parties, using its resources as sticks and carrots. America's more powerful position vis-à-vis the Arab and Israeli parties stemmed in large measure from its infinitely greater resources. Beginning in 1967 Israel became heavily dependent on American economic and military aid. Its security also depended on the deterrence that the United States provided against

Soviet military intervention in support of its Arab clients. Furthermore, Israel always depended on American diplomatic assistance, especially in its dealings with the UN and other international organizations. Both Israel and the United States were fully aware of Israel's dependence upon the United States, an awareness that conferred considerable advantages upon the United States in negotiating with Israel. America's relationships with the Arab parties varied. Jordan, Lebanon, and for much of the time Egypt, were recipients of American aid, economic as well as military. On occasion Syria received American aid, but never in large amounts; however, the aid received and the potential of receiving additional aid placed it as well in a dependent position.

In addition to deriving power from its resources and global status, the United States acquired additional bargaining power with respect to the parties by simply being the mediator. As is often the case with triadic structures, they hold the potential for a coalition of two against one. In view of the conflict between the Arab and Israeli parties, the potential of a coalition between the United States and the adversary constantly worried both Arabs and Israelis, endowing the United States with additional bargaining power. For Arabs and Israelis the main concern was not their bargaining power relative to each other, but their respective complex relationships with the United States. Preserving, and if possible improving, relations with the United States usually took precedence over gaining concessions from the adversary.

The power of the mediator notwithstanding, each party to the conflict holds some cards that it can use to influence the mediator's conduct. It must be remembered that in international politics mediators intervene to promote their own self-interest. However, unlike some other forms of intervention, the promotion of one's interest through mediation is heavily dependent on the cooperation of the parties whose dispute is being mediated. Thus the mediator's use of its power is constrained by the need to maintain its continued acceptance by both parties. Furthermore, the realization of the mediator's objectives depends on the parties cooperating with the mediator and granting it the concessions that the mediator needs. Thus, after the 1973 war, America's ability to persuade the Arab oil producers to lift the oil embargo, and indeed its standing in the Arab world, depended on Israel granting the required concessions through the United States rather than any other channel.

It would, however, be misleading to depict Arab–Israeli negotiations as a triangular process, involving Israel, an Arab party, and a mediator.

Other actors also sought to exert influence on the negotiations. Their impacts must also be taken into account. The other interested parties' influence was applied both indirectly, by affecting the mediator's conduct, as well as directly on the Arab and Israeli parties.

The power of the other interested actors to affect American mediation of Arab–Israeli negotiations derived from US global and regional involvements, and consequent interdependencies. Until 1956, Britain was heavily involved in the Middle East and thus possessed both the motivation and ability to influence American diplomacy. From the mid-1950s, the military and political positions that the Soviet Union acquired in the area and its global rivalry with the United States, enabled it to influence American policy. American interest in Middle Eastern oil and need for regional allies enabled Saudi Arabia (and to a lesser extent other Arab states) to influence US mediation. The ability of such actors to influence US policies varied and fluctuated in accordance with America's power as compared with those of the various interested parties – that is, in accordance with the changing asymmetries of interdependence between the United States and those states.

The same intervenors exerted sometimes direct influence on the Arab and Israeli negotiators. Here, too, their leverage stemmed from asymmetric interdependencies – in this case between each of them and the Arab and Israeli parties. Their ability to influence the negotiation depended not only on the power relations between each of them and the Arab and Israeli parties. It also depended on the power relations – that is, asymmetries of interdependence among all those who sought to influence the process. Thus, for example, Saudi Arabia's ability to influence Syrian policy in 1974 depended not only on Syrian–Saudi interdependencies, but also on Saudi relations with Egypt, Iraq, Algeria, and other Arab actors that were interested in the issue.

In summary, the ability of the mediator to affect a settlement depended not merely on the bilateral bargaining between the mediator and the Arab and Israeli parties, but also on other actors in the system whose policies influenced the mediator's definition of its goals and capabilities and influenced Arab and Israeli attitudes toward the mediator. The outcome of the negotiations was not shaped by a trial of strength between the Arabs and Israelis, but it was the resultant of interactions between the two principal parties and other actors in the system, as well as the interactions among the potential intervenors.[2]

7.7 Parsimony versus Complexity

Attempts to explain how power shaped structures and outcomes of Arab–Israeli negotiations require that we confront the familiar dilemma of having to choose between parsimonious models and detailed descriptions of complex realities. As we have seen, explaining Arab–Israeli negotiations with the help of the widely accepted conceptualization of power as stemming from asymmetric bilateral interdependencies is fraught with deficiencies. The employment of such a model seems inappropriate because Arab–Israeli negotiations were shaped by the power of a number of additional actors, beyond the two parties whose negotiations are under examination.

Most likely, the inadequacy of the model is not confined only to interpreting Arab–Israeli negotiations. It probably also plagues the analysis of other negotiations that are not insulated from the impact of systemic forces. It is seen in Chapter 9 of this volume in the discussion of the Mali–Burkinabê negotiations and in Chapter 5 on the Andorra–European Community negotiations. Even some Soviet–American negotiations, which on the face of it should be least affected by the weaker members of the international system, cannot be adequately understood in terms of bilateral power relations. The outcomes of their negotiations on arms control and on regional conflicts were the result not only of Soviet–American power relations, but also of the power inputs through the actions of many other states that believed that their interests were at stake. Interactions between two actors usually do not capture the totality of a negotiation process, and the interdependencies between them do not explain the totality of power that impinges upon a negotiation. If this is so, then bilateral conceptualizations of power will often be misleading.

The study of power in negotiation requires that power within the relevant system be taken into account. Such systems usually consist of more than two actors. True, relationships within multilateral systems boil down to a series of bilateral relations. But to try to learn about the impact of power on negotiation by focusing attention on merely the bilateral interdependencies between the two principals, disregarding the impact of actions and relations in the system as a whole, is likely to lead to mistaken interpretations.

We invent models to simplify reality and to highlight the more important elements of a relationship. Binary models seem to hold a special attraction; perhaps they are grounded in nature, and perhaps they are culturally imposed perceptions (male–female, positive and negative electrical charges, good and evil). We are often willing to accept the cost that our models exact – the cost of certain misrepresentations of reality. But conceptualizing power in negotiation as a bilateral interaction can often lead us astray. When models seriously distort reality, and mislead us in our interpretations of phenomena, we should be prepared to improve them.

Until we find a simpler way to represent the totality of power relations that shape international negotiations, we may have to continue tracing multiple relationships, interactions, and linkages, and assessing the interconnections between several pairs of asymmetric dependencies. It is granted that such a method has disadvantages, not the least of them that it is extremely cumbersome. But if we want to understand how power causes things to happen in international negotiations, we may have no choice but take this long and difficult trek. The vista of reality that it opens should be a sufficient reward.

To the question, why and how do weaker parties in a bilateral relationship negotiate favorable results for themselves, the answer is that they reach out of their asymmetrical dyad to tap into other parties' relationships with the two principal parties and thus increase their own benefits. They even do this without taking actions of their own. They have "power," paradoxically, that they do not exercise.

Notes

[1] Kissinger in his memoirs denies that the United States succumbed to blackmail, but his discussion is nevertheless revealing of the delicate situation that the United States faced (Kissinger 1982, especially Chapter XIX).

[2] Hart (1976), in proposing a way to measure power in international relations, makes a similar point – namely, that outcomes reflect the power of several actors.

Acknowledgments

The author gratefully acknowledges the helpful comments offered by the editors, the conference participants, as well as by Emily Copeland, Lenore Martin, David Matz, and Steve Yetiv.

References

Carter, J., 1982, *Keeping Faith*, Bantam Books, New York.

Dayan, M., 1981, *Breakthrough*, Knopf, New York.

Fahmy, I., 1983, *Negotiating for Peace in the Middle East*, Johns Hopkins University Press, Baltimore, MD.

FRUS (Foreign Relations of the United States, 1949), 1977, **6**, United States Department of State, United States Government Printing Office, Washington, DC.

Habeeb, W.M., 1988, *Power and Tactics in International Negotiation: How Weak Nations Bargain with Strong Nations*, Johns Hopkins University Press, Baltimore, MD.

Hart, J., 1976, Three Approaches to the measurement of power in international relations, *International Organization*, **30**(2):289–305.

Hirschman, A.O., 1969, *National Power and the Structure of Foreign Trade*, University of California Press, Berkeley, CA.

Ikle, F.C., 1964, *How Nations Negotiate*, Praeger, New York.

Keohane, R.O., and Nye, J.S., 1989, *Power and Interdependence*, 2nd edition, Scott Foresman, Boston, MA.

Kissinger, H., 1982, *Years of Upheaval*, Little Brown and Co., Boston, MA.

Quandt, W.B., 1986, *Camp David*, The Brookings Institution, Washington, DC.

Rabinovich, I., 1991, *The Road Not Taken: Early Arab–Israeli Negotiations*, Oxford University Press, New York.

Rosenthal Y., ed., 1983, *Documents on the Foreign Policy of Israel, Armistice Negotiations with the Arab States, December 1948–July 1949*, **3**, Israel State Archives, Jerusalem.

Sadat, A., 1978, *In Search of Identity*, Fontana Collins, Glasgow, UK.

Schelling, T.C., 1960, *The Strategy of Conflict*, Harvard University Press, Cambridge, MA.

Shlaim, A., 1988, *Collusion Across the Jordan*, Columbia University Press, New York.

Touval, S., 1982, *The Peace Brokers*, Princeton University Press, Princeton, NJ.

Touval, S., 1987, Frameworks for Arab–Israeli negotiations: What difference do they make? *Negotiation Journal*, **3**(1):37–52, January.

Touval, S., and Zartman, I.W., 1989, Mediation in international conflicts, in K. Kressel, D.G. Pruitt, and associates, *Mediation Research*, Jossey-Bass Publishers, San Francisco, CA.

Zartman, I.W., 1971, *The Politics of Trade Negotiations between Africa and the European Community: The Weak Confront the Strong*, Princeton University Press, Princeton, NJ.

Chapter 8

Asymmetry in Multilateral Negotiation between North and South at UNCED

Gunnar Sjöstedt

This chapter explores the fundamental power relationships underpinning the 1992 United Nations Conference on Environment and Development (UNCED), held in Rio de Janeiro. More than 150 states took part in this process together with many international governmental organizations (IGOs) and the more than 1,400 nongovernmental organizations (NGOs) that were formally accredited by UNCED. It is fair to say that the UNCED process ended in relative failure. There are numerous plausible explanations for this disappointing outcome; the agenda was too large, the objectives were overly ambitious, and the issues were highly complex. However, the proposition put forward and assessed in this chapter is that the outcome of the UNCED process was significantly conditioned by the underlying distribution of power. This power asymmetry between the North and the South was perceived by both sides and significantly constrained what was possible to achieve in the negotiations. The stronger party – the North – was content not to push the environmental issues too far. The weaker party – the South – could not attain its goal of drawing attention to development issues.

The first section in this chapter provides a short description of the UNCED process, particularly the negotiations prior to the Rio meeting. In the sections that follow, the power asymmetry hypothesis is developed. Finally, the power relationship between the North and the South is characterized and evaluated according to the analytical framework developed in the introductory chapter.

8.1   The UNCED Process

In December 1989 the General Assembly of the United Nations formally decided to start preparations for the Conference on Environment and Development to be held in June 1992 (United Nations General Assembly 1991). The bulk of the preparatory work in the UNCED process was carried out during the five scheduled meetings of the Preparatory Committee (PrepCom): March 1990 (the organizational meeting), August 1990 (PrepCom I), March 1991 (PrepCom II), August 1991 (PrepCom III), and March 1992 (PrepCom IV) (Antrim and Chasek 1992; Chasek 1994; Gardner 1992; Kjellén 1992). The first meeting of the PrepCom (the organizational meeting) was essentially concerned with procedural and institutional matters. Two working groups were set up to deal with substantive matters on the vast UNCED agenda. The environmental area included a range of issues related primarily to the atmosphere, oceans, freshwater resources, forestry, desertification and land resources, wastes, biodiversity, and biotechnology. A number of so-called cross-sectoral issues, linking environment to development, were added including financial support, technology transfer, and education and information efforts. At PrepCom I the many environmental and related development issues on the UNCED agenda were introduced, and delegations made initial declarations. The Secretariat also presented its proposal for Agenda 21, which was designed to function as a coordinating plan of action during, as well as after, the UNCED process.

During PrepCom II participants continued their deliberations in working groups I and II on the basis of analytical papers prepared by the UNCED Secretariat. A number of concrete decisions were taken – for instance, that a nonbinding set of principles on deforestation should be worked out instead of a binding agreement. A third working group was created to deal with legal and institutional matters. PrepCom III partly changed the character of the UNCED process from issue analysis to problem-solving, at least in working groups I and II. In these bodies discussions increasingly focused on Agenda 21 and its ramifications for particular environmental issues. In contrast, working group III held its first substantive meeting during PrepCom III. Cross-sectoral issues were left to the plenary meeting.

It was not until PrepCom IV, only a few months before the Rio conference, that the exchange of concessions definitely predominated in the UNCED process. The form of the diplomatic process changed at this meeting. For instance, a number of informal contact groups were established in which selected key countries deliberated over outstanding issues. The number of meetings with the plenary and the formal working groups was kept to a minimum. Considerable progress was made in New York. Many of the texts related to Agenda 21 (some 750 pages of formal text) were finalized by PrepCom I. The anticipated Earth Charter had been downgraded to a more modest Rio Declaration whose text could unexpectedly be agreed upon without any brackets. However, at Prep-Com IV important and contentious issues were left unresolved – notably, climate change, deforestation, implementation mechanisms for Agenda 21, transfer of environmentally sound technology, and the ultimate question of financial support to enable developing countries to comply with environmental agreements that would supposedly be the result of the Rio meeting.

A special, and highly significant, feature of the UNCED process was its extensive connections to other negotiations and conferences. All multilateral processes of negotiation are likely to have such external linkages. In the case of UNCED however, they were exceptionally developed and also deliberately designed. It is noteworthy that in several of the most important environmental issue areas real negotiations for a treaty were conducted outside the UNCED context – for example, climate change negotiations took place in the Intergovernmental Negotiating Committee (INC).

8.2 North and South Perceptions

The North and the South were two coalitions in the UNCED process whose power relationship was characterized by asymmetry. This asymmetry assumption is based on realist and neorealist thinking that power is the relative capability of one actor to control, or constrain, the actions of another party and that the relative power of a state is roughly indicated by the total amount of military and economic resources it disposes (Knorr 1956; Morgenthau 1963). Accordingly, nations could be ranked by resource indicators such as gross national product or a similar aggregate measure such as total energy consumption (Ferris 1973). Without abandoning the basic realist ideas, some authors claim that the critical power base of a nation tends to be issue specific. For instance, in a negotiation on international shipping, a country's control over tonnage is likely to better reflect its power position than its gross national product (GNP). Some small states with a comparatively modest GNP but with very large commercial fleets (notably Norway) have often acted as a great power in international shipping diplomacy (Knudsen 1973).

The bilateral relationship between the North and the South in the UNCED process stipulated here represents a warranted simplification of reality. Industrialized and developing countries did not perform as monolithic blocs. There were, for instance, coalitions within the Group of 77 (G77) related to particular issues (e.g., Brazil, Indonesia, Malaysia, and others concerning forestry). China and several large Third World nations (e.g., Brazil and India) pursued autonomous national strategies on one or more issues. In spite of these special circumstances, however, Third World countries coordinated their negotiation activities through the G77 (Chasek 1994). At least until PrepCom IV, "editing diplomacy" with the purpose of ironing out the text of the various chapters of Agenda 21 started with the presentation of a position paper prepared by the members of the G77.[1]

Formally, the activities of industrialized countries in the negotiations were less coordinated than those of developing countries. For instance, in contrast to the members of the G77, industrialized countries did not work out common position papers.[2] The differences between the stand taken by, on the one hand, Green European nations such as the Netherlands and the Nordic countries and, on the other, hard-liners such as the United States, the United Kingdom, and Japan, were quite stark on several issues. However, industrialized countries coordinated their policies in the Organization for Economic Cooperation and Development (OECD) and other organizations informally – for instance, to persuade Third World countries to accept new international obligations with regard to the environment. Furthermore, they also had similar reactions to the main issues that the G77 struggled for in the UNCED process, notably its demand for massive transfers of money and technology from industrialized countries

Table 8.1.   Asymmetries indicators characterizing power relations between industrialized and developing countries: General power and issue-
specific power

	Industrialized countries (North)	Developing countries (South)
Indicator of general power: Share of world GNP	84%	16%
Indicator of issue-specific power: Share of world emissions of CO_2	70%	30%

Source: Young and Wolf, 1992.

to help developing countries implement environmental policies. The pattern of a North–South bloc confrontation was further pronounced by the
disappearance of the bloc of centrally planned economies led by the Soviet Union (Kjellén 1992).

Table 8.1 illustrates that, according to the standard realist measure of
GNP, the power relationship between the two main blocs in the UNCED
process was markedly asymmetrical; the power position of the North was
clearly much stronger than that of the South. The share of world emissions of carbon dioxide (CO_2) is used as an indicator for issue-specific
power. The key to issue-specific power is the control over disputed, crucial values in an issue area. In the sphere of international, environmental
politics these values are negative and are indicated by flows of emissions
causing environmental harm (Sjöstedt 1993). The rationale, following
from realist power conceptions, is that the more a country contributes to
pollution the more important it is that this nation is part of an agreement
to cut emissions. As industrialized countries are responsible for a considerably larger share of current critical emissions, it is the North rather
than the South that is likely to have an issue-specific power leverage in
international environmental negotiations. However, the gap between the
North and the South with respect to the emissions of pollutants is likely
to narrow and eventually become reversed in the future.

The realist power indicators displayed in *Table 8.1* signal that the
UNCED negotiations should have been dominated by industrialized
countries, as the North has usually prevailed in most, if not all, earlier
negotiations in the UN system and in the General Agreement on Tariffs and Trade (GATT) rounds (Winham 1986). However, realist power
indicators, be they general or issue-specific, do not describe or explain
power relationships in the UNCED process; they only offer *predictions*

of the theory of which they are an offspring. These hypotheses must be tempered by an analysis of how the North and the South actually performed in the negotiations, that is, the actions they were able to take. For this purpose the *process/outcome-impact approach* is employed. One premise of this approach is that an actor's relative contribution to the outcome indicates his or her relative power in the process. If the outcome reflects more of actor *A*'s interests than of actor *B*'s interests then one may assume that *A* has been more influential than *B* in the negotiation. Obviously it is difficult to evaluate precisely what extent two relatively diffuse coalitions such as the North and the South have contributed to the outcome of a negotiation with so many issues on the agenda as the UNCED process. Therefore, the evaluation of the outcome will depend on a so-called process assessment. The actors involved in the negotiation continuously take actions to affect the outcome in each step of the process, for instance, agenda-setting, concession-making, use of threats and promises, the search for formulas, and the bargaining over details. Accordingly, the way countries act in the negotiation indicates their relative influence.

Another premise is that the conditions for power and influence in a complex negotiation such as the UNCED change during the process. Thus, a state must usually act one way when it tries to steer agenda-setting and influence the strategy for problem-solving and another when it tries to elicit concessions from another party in the endgame. Different categories of activity are likely to require different abilities and resources: dissimilar *power bases*. It is possible to refine the description of varying conditions for power and influence across time, issues, and process developments. However, this analysis must be kept at a comparatively high level of generalization. Therefore, a distinction is made only between two stages of the UNCED process that seemingly represent different terms for the exercise of power. The first stage of *issue clarification* – that is, analysis and technical problem-solving or diagnosis and formulation (Keohane and Nye 1989:40–54, 198–202; Sjöstedt 1994a). The agenda is increasingly specified, the understanding of the issues on the agenda is built up, issues are made negotiable, and avenues leading to the solution of negotiation problems are prepared. This phase of the negotiation process evolves into the stage of *exchange of concessions*. The essence of negotiation activities now pertain to "choice" (Zartman 1986). "Editing diplomacy" begins to predominate; negotiations increasingly deal with the finalizing of texts. At this time, nations make and exchange offers and requests.

It is not possible to draw a precise line between the stages of issue clarification and exchange of concessions. Some concessions were exchanged at the start of the UNCED process when the General Assembly established a mandate for the forthcoming negotiations (United Nations General Assembly 1991). Issue clarification did not suddenly stop at a given point in time. However, the UNCED negotiation process underwent significant changes between PrepComs III and IV; it was not until the session in New York in early spring 1992 that "real bargaining" began (Kjellén 1992). Therefore, it is fair to approximate that the beginning of PrepCom IV represents the final transformation from the stage dominated by *issue clarification* to the new phase basically characterized by the *exchange of concessions* that continued until the termination of the Rio meeting.

In Section 8.4 on process analysis we search for indicators of asymmetrical power relations between the North and the South. A basic distinction is made between the process stages of *issue clarification* and *exchange of concessions*. However, before the process analysis is examined a rough assessment is made of the *outcome* of UNCED to clarify to what extent it reflected North and South interests.

8.3   An Outcome Assessment

It should be repeated that a nuanced evaluation of which party (the North or the South) was the winner of the UNCED process is not attainable here. The specific North and South positions have not been established with regard to all the issues on the UNCED agenda. However, a rough assessment can be made of the outcome of the UNCED process because as seen in a North–South perspective its outcome is clear.

Within the context of the North–South relationship, the UNCED agenda contained two sets of goals that were only partly interlinked in the process.[3] The large basket of environmental issues was primarily of concern to the North. The second basket contained the development issues on the UNCED agenda that were more significant to developing countries. "Additional financial resources" and "the transfer of environmentally sound technology" were the most important issues in the latter basket. The main link between environment and development was the tradeoff desired by the G77: large transfers of money and technology as compensation for minor commitments in the environmental area.

It may be argued that the environmental results attained or confirmed in Rio corresponded largely to what the North considered desirable and feasible. Some governments of the North (e.g., in Scandinavia) were not satisfied with the results of UNCED; they would have preferred more binding agreements in the environmental area as well as more economic assistance to developing countries to promote global environmental objectives. However, these comparatively radical ambitions were attained because of the divergences of interests and policy within the coalition of industrialized countries, not because of opposition from the South. Within the Northern bloc "the radicals," striving for far-reaching policy measures (e.g., more costly restrictions of emissions) tended to be small states with limited influence on the powerful parties such as the United States, the European Community (EC), and Japan, which took a moderate stance.

This is not to say that developing countries did not try to constrain the realization of radical environmental objectives desired by the North. One of the last outstanding issues at the Rio conference was an amendment proposal to the text concerning climate change put forward by Saudi Arabia and Kuwait; the objective was to dilute the text suggesting that the consumption of fossil fuels should be reduced in the future. Even more significant is that developing countries successfully vetoed the North's proposal to establish a formal text on forestry.

The South had some success with respect to issues on resource transfer. The financial and technological difficulties of developing countries to carry out environmental policy measures were acknowledged in the UNCED process. It was agreed that the influence of developing countries was to be somewhat increased in the governance system for the special fund established to finance the implementation of environmental treaties, the Global Environmental Fund (GEF). However, this modification was only marginal. The South's idea for a large Green fund to channel massive flows of critical resources from industrialized to developing countries was not accepted. Furthermore, contrary to the view of the G77, the majority of the OECD countries insisted that contributions to the GEF as well as other forms of financial assistance to help developing countries deal with environmental problems, should, in principle, be considered part of conventional development assistance.[4]

An overview of the outcome of UNCED indicates that industrialized countries had a higher degree of success in attaining their objectives than developing countries. Thus, the hypothesis about a significant power gap between North and South, based on the application of realist indicators, cannot be rejected on the basis of the outcome assessment undertaken in this study; the hypothesis is supported, albeit in a vague and diffuse way.

8.4   Process Analysis: The Stage of Issue Clarification

Interaction among the states during the stage of issue clarification in the UNCED process evoked some of the traditional conflict behavior of the South toward the North in the UN system: ideologically loaded interventions. From the start, the confrontational dialogue between developing and industrialized countries was encouraged by some of the conventional UN rules of procedure that were used in the UNCED process. Particularly noteworthy is the principle that discussions of texts should initially be based on position papers prepared by the G77. Thereby, consultations and negotiations in UNCED were conditioned to take on a North–South, bloc-to-bloc character. However, the bloc confrontation did not evolve into an ideological war similar to the struggle over the New International Economic Order (NIEO) in United Nations Commission on Trade and Development (UNCTAD) and other UN institutions during the 1970s (Rothstein 1979).

Actors who control agenda-setting and issue clarification attain a strong strategic leverage in the ensuing stages of the process: the exchange of concessions and the endgame. In the extreme case it may be possible to frame issues in a way that one particular negotiation solution is favored to such a high degree that the endgame only concerns relatively insignificant details. Therefore, in multilateral negotiations the stage of issue clarification is usually a hard struggle among a group of leading nations on such details as strategic perspectives, key concepts, and criteria for the accumulation of necessary background information. Weak nations have only a peripheral role to play. The prenegotiation of the Uruguay Round is a good illustration. Protracted, informal negotiations over the agenda and the definition of the so-called new trade issues primarily involving the main actors dragged on for several years before the Uruguay Round was formally launched. These prenegotiations had a clear North–South dimension but were also dominated by the powerful industrialized actors – notably the United States and the EC. Some 20 countries were very active in the prenegotiations that tried to define the issues and set the agenda. The GATT Secretariat was also a party to this "game of issue clarification" but acted only on instructions from national delegations. It is noteworthy that this pattern did not repeat itself in the preparatory work for the Rio meeting. In the UNCED process initiatives from states contributed to the clarification of issues to a much lesser extent than in the Uruguay Round, and the Secretariat of UNCED was much more important than that of GATT in this respect (Sjöstedt 1994b).

The confrontation between industrialized and developing countries emerged forcefully at the very start of the UNCED process. The origin of UNCED goes back to an initiative taken by a group of industrialized countries, inspired by the report of the Brundtland Commission, calling for a UN conference on the environment (World Commission on Environment and Development 1987). This proposal was largely opposed by developing countries. The inclusion in the UNCED agenda of the cross-sectoral issues, signaling demands for financial and technological assistance, was the price industrialized countries had to pay for the plan on a conference on the environment to be accepted by the UN General Assembly in December 1989 (Palme 1992; United Nations General Assembly 1991). This deal, codified in UN Resolution 44/228, gave direction to the UNCED process and established the basic elements of its agenda.

However, the mandate for UNCED given by the UN General Assembly was vague. During the first two sessions of PrepCom (the organizational session and PrepCom I) national delegations to UNCED strove for clarification of the agenda. Notably, delegations instructed the UNCED Secretariat on the gathering of information and the preparation of background papers and topical analysis (Chasek 1994; UNCED, A/CONF.151/PC13). Thereafter, state delegations became decreasingly assertive in this respect.

National delegations participating in a multilateral negotiation are usually serviced by some sort of international secretariat, especially when issues are manifold and complex (Haas et al. 1993). In UNCED this support was especially important. A striking feature of the UNCED process is that during most of the issue clarification stage (before PrepCom IV), no single country or any group of nations, neither from the North nor from the South, overtly took the initiative to frame the issues. In addition, powerful actors, including the United States and the EC, very conspicuously abstained from imposing their own understanding of the issues on the agenda. Thus, at this time, the interaction between the North and the South gave the impression of reflecting a kind of power symmetry; neither side directed the process of issue clarification. Instead crucial leadership was provided by the UNCED Secretariat (UNCED, A/CONF.151/PC/14; UNCED, A/CONF.151/PC 15). In fact, almost all negotiated texts had originally been proposed and prepared by the UNCED Secretariat. When, at the end of the stage of issue clarification, during PrepCom III, national delegations increased their rate of activity on matters of substance, these interventions were largely framed by proposals that had originally been prepared by the Secretariat. A particularly significant instrument of the Secretariat leadership was Agenda 21 (UNCED, A/CONF.151/PC/14). This proposal was introduced into the UNCED process at the beginning of PrepCom I in August 1990. It was soon acknowledged as a much-needed frame of reference for the negotiations. It established operational objectives for particular issue areas, such as climate change or fresh-water resources (UNCED, A/CONF.151/PC/100). Agenda 21 was also designed to serve as an overall strategy embracing the entire UNCED agenda. The concrete and detailed action plan of Agenda 21 was combined with the draft document that the Secretariat originally wanted to develop into an "Earth Charter" (Gardner 1992). Although this Earth Charter was eventually devalued into a more modest Rio Declaration, it retained an important supplementary role vis-à-vis Agenda 21 through the UNCED process; consisting of a set of overarching goals and princi-ples, it represented a preamble for Agenda 21. In particular, the would-be Earth Charter strengthened the internal cohesion and consistency of Agenda 21.

From the viewpoint of negotiation, the great value of Agenda 21 was that it offered a common language in which negotiation accomplishments could be expressed regardless of the issue area and that it represented a standard against which offers and requests by negotiating parties could be evaluated. A third task of Agenda 21 was to give guidance and le-gitimacy to the Secretariat's own work to clarify issues and to build up a pool of common knowledge for the UNCED process (UNCED, A/CONF, 151/PC/100).

The Secretariat was a comparably small body with relatively modest resources at its disposal that was set up to service the UNCED process. The internal organization of the Secretariat partly explains its effective-ness with regard to issue clarification. The Secretary General, the Cana-dian Maurice Strong, was a charismatic leader with worldwide contacts

in government and business circles. The highly competent staff of the
Secretariat, largely hand-picked by Strong, functioned as an efficient and
flexible task force. Through a network of working parties the Secretariat
could systematically draw knowledge and information from other international organizations – notably UN agencies (United Nations Environment
Programme, United Nations Development Program, World Meteorolog-
ical Organization, World Health Organization, or Food and Agriculture
Organization) whose spheres of responsibility covered the issue areas of
environment or development (Sjöstedt 1994a).

The Secretariat seemingly dominated issue clarification in UNCED.
Before PrepCom IV nearly all texts discussed at the sessions of the
Preparatory Committee originated in papers that had been prepared by
the staff of the Secretariat. However, did the leadership exercised by the
Secretariat reflect the true power relationships underpinning the UNCED
process? It seems that some parties, including the United States and the
EC, who could have made proposals on ways the issues should be further
developed, voluntarily abstained from doing so. They were seemingly
satisfied with closely monitoring the presentations on issue clarification
in the discussions taking place in the plenary and the working groups. It
was not until issues had been clarified and "editing diplomacy" was under way that nations began to take positions and become more assertive
(Chasek 1994).

8.5   Process Analysis: The Stage of Exchange of Concessions

With respect to some issues – for instance, the problem of financial resources – the UNCED process began to turn from issue clarification to the
exchange of concessions during PrepCom III in August 1991. However,
it was not until PrepCom IV, some six months later, that the exchange of
concessions prevailed completely in the process (Kjellén 1992).

The qualitative change of process characteristics occurring during
PrepCom IV manifested itself in the overall pattern of state interaction.[5]
A number of procedural rules, which had strongly influenced the UNCED
process through PrepCom III, were changed when PrepCom IV had been
under way for a couple of weeks. For instance, the G77 yielded from its
earlier position that only two meetings should be held simultaneously. As
a result, the number of plenary sessions was kept at a minimum to permit
nations to concentrate on unresolved issues in informal contact groups

focusing on a particular topic. For the first time the G77 also agreed to negotiate in English without simultaneous translation. International organizations, including the UNCED Secretariat, were now definitely pushed out of the process. The Chair of the main negotiating bodies in collaboration with the leading nations took over process control. A more pragmatic, flexible, and problem-solving atmosphere now prevailed. One explanation for this radical transformation is that the main actors of the UNCED process partly reframed their policy objectives. Thus, one basic aim was to avoid losses – to see that the UNCED process would not end in total failure in Rio.

As regards the leadership over the UNCED negotiations, the most important and visible change at PrepCom IV was the increased assertiveness of national delegations. For the first time in the UNCED process, governments started to act offensively and persistently to promote or protect their respective national interests. This is one reason why the UNCED negotiations were further split into issue-specific negotiation games.

It is within the context of this complex and diffuse configuration of diverging and converging state interests that the North–South confrontation must be analyzed. Also this bloc-to-bloc struggle was partly issue conditioned. For instance, in the area of "deforestation" developing countries tried to take over the initiative during PrepCom IV. In the second part of PrepCom IV, Malaysia, on behalf of the G77, tabled a long row of amendments to the proposed text on deforestation. Chasek reports that Malaysia proposed no less than 256 changes in the text (Chasek 1994). Still more significant, Malaysia and the G77 tried to impose a tradeoff between South concessions in the area of deforestation and North concessions with regard to, for instance, the trade regime under the GATT, the Earth Charter, biological diversity, and climate warming. However, the most significant North–South disputes pertained to two issues which for decades had represented the critical context for the political struggle between industrialized and developing countries: additional financial support and the concessional transfer of technology.[6] These were the issues in which the coalition of developing countries most assertively acted as a *demandeur*. Therefore, an important observation is that developing countries made some progress on these critical issues at PrepCom IV. For one thing, the G77 managed to keep financial support and technology transfer on the agenda as salient issues through both PrepCom IV and the Rio meeting. Hence, Third World arguments could not be brushed aside. It is indicative that a Mexican substituted for the Canadian Chair of the informal negotiating group on finance during PrepCom IV (Chasek 1994).

These developments might be taken as indications that the power relationship between North and South was becoming somewhat more symmetrical toward the end of the UNCED negotiations. The influence of the South was, however, to a great extent artificial. Northern countries were the offensive parties with regard to most environmental questions, constantly pushing the South toward larger concessions, in other words greater commitments. At the same time, the North did not make any real concessions with regard to the issues where Southern countries tried to be offensive, notably their requests for financial and technological assistance. It is true that Southern countries managed to keep these cross-sectoral issues alive in the PrepCom negotiations. Developing countries also had some tactical victories. In some areas, such as deforestation, Third World countries challenged the North with noteworthy assertiveness. However, with a few exceptions (e.g., finance and technology transfer) the general pattern was that the North was on the offensive striving for the South's acceptance of texts that the North had already accepted.

8.6   Conclusion

The realist model of *structural power* indicates that in the UNCED process interstate power relations were clearly asymmetrical; that the North was top dog and the South the underdog. When *issue-specific power* indicators are employed, the prediction about North hegemony must be marginally modified. A rough assessment of the general features of the *outcome* of the UNCED process further supports the asymmetry hypothesis: industrialized countries achieved more of their special interests than developing countries.

A different test of the asymmetry hypothesis concerns how the North and the South actually fared in the UNCED process. The basic analytical question raised was whether the performance of the two parties in the process tallies with the hypothesis that the UNCED negotiations were strongly dominated by Northern countries as a group. The underlying assumption was that the two sides tried to promote their own interests as well as they could. Like the outcome assessment, the *process analysis* was carried out at a high level of generalization. The aim was merely to identify a few leading characteristics of the performance of the North and the South that supposedly reflects the relative influence of each party in the negotiation process. For this evaluation a simple framework of analysis was employed. A distinction was made between the two process stages of *issue clarification* and the *exchange of concessions*. A second type of differentiation relates to the *kinds of action* a country resorts to in order to promote its interests: *significant initiatives* affecting issue definitions or process, *veto attempts* to block or delay the process, or *significant offers/requests*. *Norm-building* is a somewhat more diffuse and indirect way to influence process and outcome. It means that a normative consensus is established relating to how certain issues should be conceived of or how certain choices should be made. For instance, the concept of sustainable development can be regarded as a norm for the way environmental and development issues should be interrelated.

8.6.1 Significant initiatives

The experience from earlier multiparty negotiations with an extensive, as well as a complex, agenda indicates that because of its lack of resources (analytical, financial, and so on) the South should have been particularly weak in the stage of *issue clarification*. For instance, in trade and other economic negotiations, agenda-setting and issue clarification have often largely taken place in restricted groups to which Third World countries have had little access. At first sight, the stage of issue clarification in UNCED gives another impression. The South was actively involved throughout the stage of issue clarification, which took place during the meetings of the Preparatory Committee preceding PrepCom IV. In fact, position papers prepared and "tabled" by the G77 were continuously at the center of the discussions related to issue clarification. However, these submissions did not represent genuine initiatives on the part of the G77. They were largely commentaries on the Secretariat papers that represented the most important input into issue clarification activities. Furthermore, the central role of the G77 can seemingly be explained by the strategy of the North, first, to abstain from significant initiatives at the PrepCom meeting and, second, to respect traditional UN rules letting the G77 introduce the discussion of Secretariat papers.[7]

8.6.2 Initiatives

National delegations became generally more assertive and began to take more initiatives when negotiations decisively shifted from *issue clarification* to the *exchange of concessions* during PrepCom IV in March 1992.

As a result of this development the process became less transparent than the PrepCom meetings concerned with issue clarification. A few process features are discernible, however. Different groups of Southern countries took visible initiatives in some areas (e.g., desertification and forests). These attempts of significant initiatives were, however, largely unsuccessful. It was largely initiatives of Northern countries that contributed to increase the degree of state control over the process.

8.6.3   Vetoes

The procedural rule, generally used in the UN system, that the debate on Secretariat papers should be introduced by position papers prepared by the G77, clearly influenced the process of negotiation before Prep-Com IV. The rationale for this rule is that in the UN system final decisions are taken by roll calls and that the G77 controls an absolute majority of the votes. This potential veto power recurrently manifested itself at the negotiation table. When the representative of the G77 refused to accept an element of the text under discussion (e.g., a certain Chapter of Agenda 21), negotiations were liable to become deadlocked, at least temporarily. Other delegations had to take the position and arguments of the G77 under consideration. However, the G77 was usually not strong enough to halt the process, only to delay it.

There are other indications that the veto power of the South was considerably restrained. It was, for instance, dependent on the goodwill of industrialized countries because in reality decisions were taken by consensus in UNCED and not by roll calls. This conditionality was demonstrated at PrepCom IV when the process privileges of the G77, derived from standard UN procedural rules, were abolished to speed up negotiations to meet the deadline set by the Rio conference. However, the veto power of Third World countries affected not only the process of the UNCED negotiations but also the outcome. The population issue is one example; it was evidently kept out of the UNCED process due to the fierce resistance of certain Third World countries in the early stages of agenda-setting. Seemingly, a coalition of Third World countries managed to downgrade the ambitions in UNCED with regard to the deforestation issue. At the Rio conference two Arab oil-producing countries (Saudi Arabia and Kuwait) blocked a consensus decision on the Framework Convention on Climate Change until they eventually agreed to the decision.

The evaluation of this outcome must take into consideration that a su-perpower such as the United States was relatively unsuccessful in using its veto power in the UNCED issue area of climate change. Recall that Washington's threat not to sign the Framework Convention on Climate Change did not prevent the conclusion of the UNCED process (Gardner 1992). Thus, it may be argued that there was relative symmetry between the North and the South with regard to veto power. However, on the issue of climate change the United States was not in opposition to the coalition of Third World countries; rather they were allies. The main opposition arose from the other industrialized countries. It should be recalled that the main approach of the G77 in UNCED was to threaten to veto an agree-ment concerning the many environmental issues on the agenda unless the North made significant concessions with regard to additional financial as-sistance and technology transfer. This strategy, however, failed. Northern countries were conciliatory toward the South when the agenda was set, but unyielding when it was time to make a settlement.

8.6.4   Tradeoffs

Deals in international negotiations are often struck on the basis of com-promises or tradeoffs; there is an exchange of concessions between the parties. In fact, the initiation of UNCED was based on a tradeoff between the North and the South; the North accepted the inclusion of development issues on the UNCED agenda to get the South to agree to broad negotia-tions on global environmental problems. The significance of this North-ern concession, however, should not be exaggerated since the Brundtland Commission, which paved the way for UNCED, emphasized the con-cept of sustainable development: the need to integrate environmental and development considerations. All things considered, the trade of conces-sions between North and South was clearly asymmetrical. As in most other global negotiations on tangible values, developing countries had lit-tle to offer in the UNCED negotiations except their acceptance of new disciplines in the area of environmental politics desired by the North.

8.6.5   Norms

In multilateral regime-building processes concerning trade or other eco-nomic matters, Third World countries have often tried to compensate for their lack of capacity to trade in tangible concessions (e.g., market shares) by successfully pleading for "special and preferential" treatment. This norm-building strategy reappeared in UNCED in the form of some of the cross-sectoral issues, and notably financial and technological assistance. Although the South attained small tangible results with regard to these issues, they managed to establish the principle that Third World countries were justified to receive economic assistance from industrialized countries to implement environmental policies. However, this relative success must be balanced against the tremendous output of the UNCED process in terms of norms, supported by the North, demanding strengthened international action in the many environmental issue areas covered by Agenda 21 and the Rio Declaration. These were relatively new issues on the agenda of international politics and therefore norm-building achievements were highly important. The key topics of the norm-building offensive of the South – financial assistance and technology transfer – were old issues that had been at the forefront of the North–South confrontation for decades. Thus, in contrast to industrialized nations, developing countries did not break any new ground with the help of norm-building activities.

There are numerous cases of negotiations in which the nation with the largest resources did not prevail. For instance, Iceland has avoided losing cod wars with Britain; Norway has been the equal of Germany and France in shipping negotiations; and South Korea has offered strong opposition to the United States when voluntary export restraints have been discussed. One explanation is that resource measures such as gross domestic product (GDP) are too crude to predict who will win an interstate encounter. Many factors that are not obviously tapped by the GDP measure help to give one nation influence over another. Examples of such factors are the extent to which national decision makers can direct their attention to the issues concerned, the skills of decision makers and negotiators, and purely incidental factors.

However, North–South negotiations in the UNCED context do not represent one of these deviant cases where the strong cannot use their strength and where the weak are stronger than they seem to be. The process analysis demonstrates that different stages of multiparty negotiation (e.g., agenda-setting, issue clarification, or exchange of concessions) did not reverse the power relationship between industrialized and developing countries. The North consistently dominated UNCED in all of these stages, although for somewhat different reasons. For instance, in the stages of agenda-setting and issue clarification the North could draw from superior analytical capability. In the game of exchange of concessions, the South was clearly at a disadvantage because it controlled less tangible resources (money and technology) than the North. Hence, in the case of UNCED many of the specific and varied circumstances that give a nation power in the individual situation seem to vary with the crude realist power indicators.

Notes

[1] This procedure was observed at the PrepCom meetings.

[2] Smaller groups of industrialized countries coordinated their strategies and prepared joint position papers – for instance, the members of the EC and the Nordic countries.

[3] According to the directives for UNCED issued by the UN General Assembly, these two sets of goals were to be interlinked; this was, in fact, the whole concept of sustainable development.

[4] The assessment of the outcome of the UNCED process rests on an analysis of the final text of Agenda 21 and the Rio Declaration (see Gardner 1992; Susskind 1994).

[5] The account of the activities during PrepCom IV is based on an overview of the documentation produced during the session and draws heavily on Bernstein et al. (1992), Chasek (1994), and Kjellén (1992).

[6] The term *additional* was used because developing countries demanded financial support outside the normal aid programs.

[7] One probable explanation for the behavior of industrialized countries was that the UNCED Secretariat had attained the support of key Northern countries by means of informal intersessional consultations.

References

Antrim, L., and Chasek, P., 1992, The UNCED negotiating process, *Ocean and Coastal Management*, **18**(1).

Bernstein, J., Chasek, P., and Goree, L., 1992, A summary of the proceedings of the fourth session of the UNCED preparatory committee, *Earth Summit Bulletin*, **1**(27), 20 April.

Chasek, P., 1994, The story of the UNCED process, in B. Spector, G. Sjöstedt, and I.W. Zartman, eds., *Negotiating International Regimes: Lessons Learned from the United Nations Conference on Environment and Development*, Graham and Trotman, London.

Ferris, W., 1973, *The Power Capabilities of Nation-States*, Lexington Press, Lexington, MA.

Gardner, R., 1992, *Negotiating Survival: Four Priorities after Rio*, Council on Foreign Relations Press, New York.

Haas, P., Keohane, R., and Levy, M., 1993, *Institutions for the Earth: Sources of Effective International Protection*, MIT Press, Cambridge, MA.

Keohane, R.O., and Nye, J.S., 1989, *Power and Interdependence*, 2nd edition, Scott Foresman, Boston, MA.

Kjellén B., 1992, The UNCED Process: Lessons to be drawn for the future, in G. Sjöstedt and U. Svedin, eds., *International Environmental Negotiations: Process, Issues and Contexts*, Swedish Council for Planning and Coordination of Research, Swedish Institute of International Affairs, Stockholm, Sweden.

Knorr, K., 1956, *The War Potential of Nations*, Princeton University Press, Princeton, NJ.

Knudsen, O., 1973, *Politics of International Shipping: Conflict and Interaction in a Transnational Issue Area*, Lexington Press, Lexington, MA.

Morgenthau, H., 1963, *Politics Among Nations: The Struggle for Power and Peace*, Knopf, New York.

Palme, T., 1992, Rio-konferensen, FN:s konferens om miljö och utveckling i Rio de Janeiro i juni 1992 (The Rio Conference: UN Conference on Environment and Development, Rio de Janeiro, 1 June 1992), *UD Informerar*, **5**, Utrikesdepartementet, Stockholm, Sweden.

Rothstein, R., 1979, *Global Bargaining: UNCTAD and the Quest for a New International Economic Order*, Princeton University Press, Princeton, NJ.

Sjöstedt, G., ed., 1993, *International Environmental Negotiation*, Sage Publications, Beverly Hills, CA.

Sjöstedt, G., 1994a, Issue clarification and the role of consensual knowledge in the UNCED process, in B. Spector, G. Sjöstedt, and I.W. Zartman, eds., *Negotiating International Regimes: Lessons Learned from the United Nations Conference on Environment and Development*, Graham and Trotman, London.

Sjöstedt, G., 1994b, Negotiating the Uruguay round of the general agreement on tariffs and trade, in I.W. Zartman, ed., *International Multilateral Negotiation: Approaches to the Management of Complexity*, Jossey-Bass, San Francisco, CA.

Susskind, L., 1994, Regime-building accomplishments, in B. Spector, G. Sjöstedt, and I.W. Zartman, eds., *Negotiating International Regimes: Lessons Learned from the United Nations Conference on Environment and Development*, Graham and Trotman, London.

UNCED, A/CONF, 151/PC/13.

UNCED, A/CONF, 151/PC/14.

UNCED, A/CONF, 151/PC/15.

UNCED, A/CONF, 151/PC/100.

United Nations General Assembly, 1991, Resolution 44/228, New York.

Winham, G., 1986, *International Trade and the Tokyo Round Negotiation*, Princeton University Press, Princeton, NJ.

World Commission on Environment and Development, 1987, *Our Common Future*, Oxford University Press, Oxford, UK.

Young, P., and Wolf, A., 1992, Global warming negotiations: Does fairness matter? *The Brookings Review*, Spring.

Zartman, I.W., ed., 1978, *The Negotiation Process: Theories and Applications*, Sage Publications, Beverly Hills, CA.

Zartman, I.W., 1986, Practitioners' theories of international negotiation, *Negotiation Journal*, **2**(3):299–310.

Zartman, I.W., ed., 1987, *Positive Sum: Improving North–South Negotiations*, Transaction Books, New Brunswick, NJ.

Part III

Cases of Near Symmetry

There is no perfect symmetry in nature, but some cases are less asymmetrical than others. The following two cases illustrate examples of near symmetry in various ways and at various levels of power. In the first case, power was at a low level by any measure, and both parties – Mali and Burkina Faso – were equally weak. Both sides vigorously attempted to overcome the stalemate resulting from this equality, and both tried to restore the equality when the other made efforts to upset it. To do this, Mali and Burkina Faso went to war over the borderlands and then sought allies to impose their peace. The border ended up, appropriately, in the middle of the claims.

The second case lies at the other end of the power spectrum. In this case, two superpowers – the United States and China – were locked in a war for land and honor, a gigantic geopolitical struggle of the island continent against the heartland continent for a beachhead on the fringes. One party was a new nation in a status quo role; the other, a millennial nation with a revolutionary role. One was seeking to maintain the world order; the other, to have its security and equality recognized and protected. One, the distant power, had nuclear weapons and the (somewhat reluctant) world coalition behind it; the other, the proximate power, had its immense population and the (somewhat reluctant) revolutionary coalition at its disposal. The battle raged up and down the Korean Peninsula for a year, then settled in the middle, near where it had started. Given their proven equality in military power, both sides then attempted to find a small diplomatic edge, seeking an advantage in honor that they could not gain in territory so that they could claim that the costly war had not been in vain. It took two more years to negotiate a peace. The border ended up, appropriately, in the middle of the Peninsula, near where the fighting started.

The difference between these cases and those presented in Part II is not that these were symmetrical and the others were asymmetrical; it is that these cases, unlike the others, were not clearly and recognizedly asymmetrical. In the first group of cases, each party knew where it stood with regard to the resources and perceived power of the other; each took action and played its role according to these clear perceptions. In the group in Part III, the inequality between parties was not clear and uncontested; thus roles were not clear, and enormous efforts were expended in contesting, reversing, and restoring the power relation. Negotiations in these latter cases dragged on – for six months and two years. Negotiations in some of the asymmetrical cases were lengthy as well, although for different reasons. Much of the time in the symmetrical cases was spent toying with the power balance, lest negotiations transform an agreement into a power imbalance; in the asymmetrical cases, there were delays in calling negotiations, lest negotiations transform the power imbalance into an agreement.

Another difference is that, not coincidentally, the nearly symmetrical cases are all instances of wartime negotiations for a cease-fire. They all began with a battlefield stalemate – quite authoritative evidence of power equality – and they all proceeded under threat of revived hostilities – a quite compelling impetus to reach an agreement. These conditions made the delays in the symmetrical cases qualitatively much longer than those in the asymmetrical cases, as the status quo in the latter cases was pressing but not compelling. In fact the nearly symmetrical cases involved two parallel types of power and means of decision making that tracked each: the politicians and the military. When the power balance seemed in danger of being tilted at the negotiating table, or when attempts in that direction were being made, the military theater was revived and the stalemate was reaffirmed.

A third common characteristic is highlighted in the cases and in the summary of lessons: the importance of external actors in ostensibly bilateral confrontations. Whether by coincidence or not, more so than in the asymmetrical cases, negotiations in cases of near symmetry took place between two principals surrounded by an eager crowd of spectators, who did not hesitate to climb in the ring when it suited them.[1] The differences in the crowds are well illustrated by the two cases. In the West African case external intervenors came from "above," that is, from neighboring and distant states with greater power than the contestants. Like parents and police in a brawl involving neighborhood kids, intervenors stepped in when the confrontation became too much and reestablished order. They acted with informal authority. The intervention was direct in the outcome in West Africa. In the Korean case external intervenors came from "below," that is, from allies and neutrals around the world whose role was legitimized by the fact that both contestants were fighting for honor in the eyes of others, as well as for tangible territory. Like a crowd of fans and kibitzers at a boxing match judged by points in the absence of a knockout, these intervenors brought support and made suggestions but had no authority.[2]

Finally, the nature of the outcomes in this set of cases differs from those in the previous set; again these differences are not coincidental. To begin with, all of the parties in the first set of cases were in a relationship with one another, and their negotiations were aimed at improving or regulating details within that relationship. As already noted, they operated under the heavy constraints of ongoing cooperation and the mutual vulnerabilities of interdependence. The United Nations Conference on Environment and Development (UNCED) negotiations provide the limiting case: here, the relationship between North and South, both in general and on the issues of development and environment, was contentious and unavowed but was present nonetheless. By contrast, in the symmetrical cases either there was no relationship among the contenders or the relationship was quite different in nature from those in the asymmetrical case. This is a delicate distinction, perhaps, but an important one. In West Africa, the two parties only had real relationships with the external intervenors (hence their authority), not with each other, despite their common membership in regional organizations and even their shared border. In the Korean case, any relationship between the contestants was one of conflict, a notion that stretches the idea of relationship out of form. If anything, the outcome negotiated between the equals in the presence of intervening outsiders set up the beginnings of a relationship. China and the United States had a slightly better understanding of each other as a result of the negotiations and began to enter into contractual relations from which relationships eventually grow. In addition, the outcomes in the symmetrical cases regularized the slightly modified status quo, after a military test and reaffirmation of the power equality (mediated to varying degrees by external intervenors). In a curious twist, stronger parties gave up more to come to an agreement with weaker parties in the asymmetrical cases than in the nearly symmetrical cases.

Notes

[1] Were it not for the case involving Andorra, it might be suggested that participating spectators are a characteristic of symmetrical negotiations. Yet the case of Andorra is inherently, not characteristically, different, since it took place within a multi-state community and involved a nonsovereign actor. The issue of external actors is discussed further in the conclusion to this book.

[2] Related interventions came from internal crowds, the domestic public opinion of China and the United States, variously interpreted – given differences in freedom of expression in the two countries – by the rulers. These interventions were similar in nature to those from the external crowd and at least as important.

Chapter 9

Compensating for Weak Symmetry in the Mali–Burkina Faso Conflict, 1985–1986

Jean-Emmanuel Pondi

The inhabitants of Mali and Burkina Faso woke up to a tragic Christmas morning in 1985. For the second time in their common history, their countries were at war. The cause of the conflict developed from a 25-year-old dispute over the mineral-rich Agacher border that constitutes the boundary between the two countries.

Boundaries in Africa, having been drawn arbitrarily at an 1884–1885 Berlin conference by European colonial powers and inherited by the sovereign states of Africa in the 1960s, have always been a source of conflicts that have from time to time threatened the emerging interstate order of the continent (Asiwaju 1985; Touval 1972; Widstrand 1969; Zartman 1966). For example, territorial disputes have erupted between Morocco and Algeria, Ethiopia and Somalia, Somalia and Kenya, Uganda and Tanzania, Togo and Ghana, and Nigeria and Cameroon. Attempting to investigate how these conflicts between generally very poor and newly

independent international entities are resolved holds the key to understanding both the conditions of establishing greater peace and security in
a continent of more than 600 million inhabitants and, more broadly, the
conditions for resolving conflict among the weak.

Do the terms *power* and *negotiation* refer to the same concepts in
Africa and the West? Is it plausible to use the notion of asymmetrical or
symmetrical power relations in a conflictual relationship involving two
weak and poor actors? In other words, can specificities be identified in the
power relations of poor states, which make up the majority in the world
community? These and related questions are examined in the pages that
follow.

Before proceeding any further, a discussion of power as understood
in the context of this analysis is in order. In this chapter, the most important source of power is the ability of the protagonists to have access to,
and generate the diplomatic and military support of, influential African
countries as well as shadow partners from outside the continent. In other
words, it is a country's ability to bring in important allies that enables it
to isolate and ultimately defeat the opposite party. Given the extremely
weak economic and military capabilities of African countries, their ability to move other African countries rests largely on their decision-making
elites' capacity to build successful continental and intercontinental diplomatic and military coalitions that are willing to intervene for them in conflicts with other African states. Diplomatic dexterity and a willingness to
avoid rocking the boat of Franco–African relations appear to be some of
the skills needed by the African leadership to secure a certain degree of
power in French-speaking Africa.

Thus, most African leaders have historically been inclined to con-
ceive of power as an *exogenous*, rather than an *endogenous*, phenomenon.
African decision makers seem to view power as an entity that lies outside
the realm of their technological capabilities (hence their willingness to
spend 10–14% of their national budgets on weapons) and that can be secured through bilateral or multilateral agreements pertaining to military
assistance and cooperation. In both cases, power is added to a country's
national capabilities through outside devices, rather than generated from
within through an increase in, and exploitation of, a population's productive resources and know-how.

Consequently, and perhaps paradoxically, the *powerful* African country appears to be one whose vulnerability to an outside military alliance
and technological know-how has been most completely established. A

different way of stating this situation is to suggest that the extent of a state's power in the African scene seems inversely related to its degree of autonomy in the security and military fields. Far from being unique to Africa, this situation is evident in most dependent subsystems of the world (Middle East with North America, as discussed in Chapter 7).

Except for the size of their respective countries, which differs significantly, Mali and Burkina Faso have similar socioeconomic and military statistics.[1] With a per capita gross national product (GNP) of less than US$220 both nations have consistently been included in the World Bank list of least developed countries. In addition to having been independent since 1960, the two states share a 1,297-kilometer border according to Mali and a 1,380-kilometer border according to Burkina Faso, of which 1,022 kilometers in Mali's view and almost 900 kilometers in Burkina Faso's assessment have been satisfactorily delimited by mutual agreement between the two parties.

From a long-term perspective, the Christmas War of 1985 provided painful evidence that territorial disputes were still an explosive issue in African international relations despite all the previous efforts of the Organization of African Unity (OAU). As early as 1964 the OAU complemented its charter with the Cairo Protocol, which sanctified the principle of the intangibility of African frontiers inherited from colonization. On 23 June 1964, the Niamey Protocol was drawn up to deal specifically with the issue of the border conflict between Upper Volta (which was renamed Burkina Faso in 1984) and Niger. Following another military dispute which pitted Mali against Upper Volta in December 1974, the OAU's Mediation Commission met on 6 and 7 January 1975, and set up military and legal subcommissions to attempt to settle the conflict (Somé 1987:339–369). These efforts resulted in a cease-fire agreement announced on 10 July 1975. Thus, there is a history of territorial disputes between Mali, Niger, and Burkina Faso – three countries that share a border area also known as the tripoint.

More immediately, the conflict of the 1980s apparently started when the Burkinabê Committees for the Defense of the Revolution (CDR) attempted to carry out a population census in the highly contested Agacher area between 10 and 20 December 1985. On 21 December, the authorities of Bamako, the Malian capital, publicly denounced what they termed "a characterized aggression" from Burkina Faso (*Année Stratégique 1987* 1988:217). As tension mounted, President Chadli Benjedid of Algeria, a good friend of both protagonists, tried to mediate by phoning both heads of state. Also sensing the danger, President Thomas Sankara of Burkina Faso sent messages to several African heads of state and to President François Mitterrand of France. On 22 December, Burkina Faso withdrew its troops from the contested region.

On 24 December, taking an opposite stand, Malian artillery bombed the frontier village of Ouahigouya. The following day, the Burkinabê government called for a general mobilization. The next three days witnessed intense combat which, according to many observers, inflicted relatively heavy damages and casualties on both sides. Some analysts have suggested that each country lost approximately 300 men (Doucet 1986:4).

As is often the case under these circumstances, the perspectives held by the protagonists on the events and their assessment of the negotiations that led to their resolution differ somewhat. Before providing an account and analysis of the negotiation process that led to the resolution of the present conflict, the next two sections examine the perspectives held by the two protagonists involved.

9.1   Malian Perceptions

For both parties, the central problem was to ascertain the frontier that existed at the moment of independence. This task was not easy. In the opinion of Mali leaders, it was necessary to go back to the "last date on which the French colonial authorities participated in the exercise of jurisdiction for administrative organization" (*International Court of Justice Reports of Judgments 1986* 1987:20).[2] In simpler terms, one should go back to the last time the French colonial governors appointed administrative personnel and specified their territorial powers. This should then be taken as proof of territorial organization. The authorities in Bamako fixed that date at 30 January 1959 for the Sudanese Republic (as Mali was known then) and 28 February 1959 for Upper Volta.

In the opinion of the Mali government, the delimitation of the tripoint in litigation (the Agacher area) also involved Niger in addition to the two other protagonists. Consequently, a lasting solution could only be found by including Niger in the discussions.

The government of Mali has always referred to a number of maps of the area that reinforced its contention that the Agacher region was an integral part of the Sudanese Republic during the colonial era. Among the most significant was the 1:200,000 scale map of West Africa that was originally published by the French National Geographical Institute (IGN) between 1958 and 1960 (*International Court of Justice Reports of Judgments 1986* 1987:34). Drawn by a neutral third party, the IGN map was used by the French during the end of the colonial period to appoint different administrative authorities in the area. From the standpoint of the Bamako authorities, its configuration, which included Agacher, accurately identified the boundaries of the Sudan at the time of independence.

In reality, according to the International Court of Justice, "not a single map available to the Chamber can reliably be said to reflect the intentions of the colonial administration concerning the disputed frontier" (*International Court of Justice Reports of Judgments 1986* 1987:34). Moreover, even the basic text of 4 September 1947, which specifically organized French territorial administration in French West Africa, made no mention of a map and talked only in general terms of the boundaries now in dispute.

In terms of negotiation in the course of this conflict, Mali apparently stood on much firmer ground than Burkina Faso. From a Malian perspective, Bamako had managed to enlist the support of strong and influential allies in Africa and abroad, and was in a position to use a number of formal and informal networks to strengthen and further its options at the negotiating table.

President Félix Houphouët-Boigny of the Ivory Coast (whose pivotal role in the resolution of the conflict is analyzed more thoroughly later) placed all his weight, influence, and political experience on the side of Mali because the basic policy orientation of Burkina Faso's radical government was quite different from that of its neighbor, the Ivory Coast. Of course this bias was displayed in such a manner as to allow the Ivory Coast, a major mediator, to exert significant influence on Burkina Faso.

Senegal, an important diplomatic power on the continent, lent its *savoir faire* to the resolution of the crisis, but also sided with Mali, its neighbor. At the time of the conflict, President Abdou Diouf of Senegal also occupied the Chair of the OAU. Furthermore, the Accord of Non-Aggression Mutual Assistance and Defense (ANAD), the nonaggression and collective defense pact of French-speaking West Africa, was headed by Secretary General Jean Gomis, a citizen of Senegal. Created on 9 June 1977, the ANAD comprised six member states – Burkina Faso, the Ivory

Coast, Mali, Mauritania, Niger, and Senegal – with Togo acting as an observer (Bakary 1988:98; Traoré 1979).

A good relationship with France, the former colonial power, was another valuable though more discreet positive card in the hand of Mali in the Christmas War. Even though it has been rightly observed that this particular armed conflict was the first in postcolonial Africa to have been resolved without open interference from outside the continent, the influence of France was felt in numerous ways. For example, Malian President Moussa Traoré had just returned from the 12th Franco–African summit meeting held in Bujumbura, Burundi, on December 6. Burkinabê President Thomas Sankara not only refused to attend that gathering, but chose to invite Muammar Qaddafi, of Libya, for an official visit to Ouagadougou (the capital of Burkina Faso) at that time. Given the rather tense relations that existed between Libya and France, Niger, Mali, and the Ivory Coast, the Sankara gesture was clearly intended to be, and was indeed interpreted as, an act of defiance toward Paris and its African allies (Lemarchand 1988:106). Whether a coincidence or not, the Christmas War broke out only two weeks after President Traoré's return from the Bujumbura summit.

Some additional factors improved the relationship between Mali and France. After 22 years in "the monetary wilderness," during which the Bamako authorities experimented with the independent Malian franc, Mali decided in June 1984 to rejoin the ranks of the Communauté Financière Africaine (CFA) franc zone, a monetary unit created in the mid-1940s and closely linked to the French franc. Belonging to the CFA franc zone means conceding a considerable role to the French treasury in the management of the member country's economic and financial affairs (Martin 1983).

The authorities of Mali were aware that in Africa, where most countries are poor, power translates into the ability of a country to build up a strong diplomatic and military coalition with countries both within and outside the continent. Mali had achieved just that in December 1985. Also, the government of Bamako knew that both the political discourse and the acquaintances of the Burkina Faso regime considerably annoyed important African countries, as well as France and the United States. Given these factors, it was, therefore, not a coincidence that Mali struck first having calculated that both diplomatically and in terms of military assistance it could win the Christmas War.

9.2 Burkinabê Perceptions

Contrary to the position of Mali, which fixed 1959 as the starting date for assessing the territorial configuration of the contested area, Burkina Faso held that the initial date for this assessment should be the time of accession to independence of both states: 20 June 1960 for Mali and 5 August 1960 for Burkina Faso. In addition, the Burkinabê authorities maintained that the International Court of Justice was fully qualified to delimit the territorial configuration of the Niger–Mali–Burkina Faso tripoint, even without the participation of Niger, which was not a party to the 1985 dispute.

Among the many maps produced by the authorities in Ouagadougou, one is particularly worth mentioning. It was the 1:500,000 scale map of the colonies of French West Africa drawn in 1925, compiled by the Geographical Service of French West Africa at Dakar and printed in Paris by Blondel and La Rougery. Relying on administrative circular 93 CM2, 4 February 1930, Burkina Faso claimed that, until 1960, the colonial authorities consistently referred to the La Rougery map, which was the largest map of the region. It did not indicate, however, that Agacher was or was not in the French Sudan (*International Court of Justice Reports of Judgments 1986* 1987:33).

With respect to the negotiations that took place before, during, and after the outbreak of the Christmas War, Burkina Faso, globally speaking, appeared to stand on shakier ground than Mali. Its main ally, Libya, was a controversial entity in the African diplomatic arena of the 1980s (Pondi 1988:139–149). At that time, many African states were absolutely convinced that Colonel Qaddafi was determined to carry out an Islamic jihad against them to create "the Greater Islamic Republic of Libya." The new expanded entity would include parts of Cameroon, Chad, Niger, and Nigeria.

Beginning in 1980, the activities of the Libyan leader in Chad (among other places) became once again a major source of concern for most other African leaders. That an Islamic legion made up of Arab and African "volunteers" trained in and by Libya could so brazenly violate Chadian sovereignty shocked most OAU members. This situation reinforced their worst fears concerning the aggressive colonel (Pondi 1988:139–149). Equally unsettling was that assassination squads were said to have been sent by Qaddafi to liquidate the political leaders in Chad who opposed Libya's intervention (Cooley 1981:74–93). Moreover, in complete violation of OAU norms and values, in 1984 and 1985, Qaddafi directly and openly called on the peoples of Burundi, Niger, Rwanda, and Zaire "to rise up and topple their respective dictators" (*Africa Contemporary Records 1984–1985* 1985:A128). Understandably, such subversive calls exacerbated the tension between Libya and the countries singled out by the North African leader.

As if these actions were not enough, the relations between Libya and the United States (and France) were also at a very low point. Only a year later, in 1986, Washington launched an air raid on Tripoli and Benghazi with the intention of eliminating Qaddafi. Thus, Burkina Faso's alliance with Libya no doubt had a negative impact on Ouagadougou's negotiating powers at the time of the conflict resolution of the Christmas War.

From the point of view of Burkina Faso, however, Mali represented the prototype of African countries that "sold out" to their former colonial masters and, in this case, were only too ready to further "French neo-colonial interests" in Africa. Sankara's anti-French crusade was not, in the view of the Burkinabê leader, a personal vendetta. It was intended to restore African dignity in international relations (Andriamirado 1988).

It is probable that with these factors in mind the Burkinabê head of state took bold steps during the 1984–1985 period. Although French aid to Burkina Faso represented no less than 43% of all foreign aid received by that country, on 5 August 1985 President Sankara did not hesitate to declare that, "for the relations with France to improve, France must learn to deal with African countries on a new basis" (*Année Politique et Economique Africaine* 1985:22). It is likely that this is the reason the Burkinabê leader abstained from participating in the 12th Franco–African summit in Bujumbura in 1985. Furthermore, in his September 1985 speech before the United Nations in New York, Sankara condemned, in no uncertain terms, both the United States' invasion of Grenada and the Soviet Union's unsolicited presence in Afghanistan. That speech was as warmly received by the youth of Africa and the Third World as it was criticized by the continent's more conservative leadership and Northern observers.

Within the West African region, bilateral relations were at a low ebb in 1984–1985. In the eyes of the Ouagadougou authorities, the prosperous citizens of the Ivory Coast were perceived as being even greater tools of French neocolonialism than the less prosperous Malians. But in a conciliatory move, Sankara thought of using the occasion of the 25th anniversary of the creation of the Council of the *Entente* (which groups Benin, Burkina Faso, the Ivory Coast, and Niger) to travel to Abidjan and to meet personally with Houphouët-Boigny for the first time. The trip was arranged for 28 May 1985, but a plot to kill Sankara in the Ivory Coast was supposedly uncovered by Burkina Faso security. The authorities in the Ivory Coast vehemently denied that any assassination had been planned against Sankara. Houphouët-Boigny, often referred to as "the wise man of Africa," sent Balla Keita, his minister of National Education and Scientific Research, to Ouagadougou. His trip was not successful in that it did not end the mutually deep suspicion that existed between the two leaders.

Burkina Faso's assessment of its power basis in relation to Mali seemed to be derived more from an ethical and moral standpoint than from a military and diplomatic evaluation. In 1985, while Sankara and his team in Burkina Faso were making efforts to curb corruption, embezzlement of public money, and political dictatorship, authorities in Mali had accepted these activities as common practice. This difference in objectives and ethics explains the moralizing tone often adopted by Burkina Faso when dealing with Mali and the Ivory Coast.

Although Sankara had become a political hero for the often-disillusioned youth of Africa who saw him as the only righteous political figure of Black Africa (Andriamirado 1988), the support of the weak and powerless disenchanted masses did not translate into strong international, economic, diplomatic, and military coalitions capable of rendering a fearless African regime. Paradoxically, in the African diplomatic arena of the 1980s, Sankara's moral crusade for greater democracy from below, for more African dignity in the world, far from enhancing his status, was likely to weaken support for him both within African official circles and outside the continent. This is precisely what happened to Burkina Faso, a country whose leadership was convinced of the righteousness of its moralizing crusade. However, an international coalition did not materialize in Ouagadougou on these crucial themes, and this is what counted the most.

Although Burkina Faso and Mali were in low symmetrical power positions based on internal criteria, according to the definition of power discussed earlier, Burkina Faso had one major weakness that Mali did not. This weakness was not evident in evaluating differences in the objective indicators of strength, such as number of army divisions and per capita GNP. Rather, it was the inability of the Ouagadougou authorities to have access to and generate support from influential countries in Africa and shadow partners outside the continent that made Burkina Faso weaker than Mali, despite the perceived socioeconomic symmetry. It is probably for this reason that the Burkinabês chose not to begin hostilities. This inability may also explain why they sent a letter to President Mitterrand of France when they felt that war might break out.

9.3   The Power Differential

Having reviewed the different perspectives of the two main protagonists and the nature of the alliances they were able (or unable) to build up, at least three observations can be made of the power relation of Mali and Burkina Faso.

First, one should consider the role of the shadow partner, in this case France, to understand why an alliance with such a partner can significantly tilt the balance in favor of its beneficiary. In 1960, most French-speaking African countries signed formal treaties of military assistance with France, which stipulated that Paris would come to the aid of the signatory states whenever they felt threatened (Martin 1983:39–66). Between the time that the treaties were signed and the Mali–Burkina Faso war, France intervened in Gabon in 1964; Chad in 1960–1963, 1968–1975, 1977–1980, and 1983; Mauritania in 1977–1978; Zaire in 1977 and 1978; and the Central African Republic in 1979 (Martin 1983:39–66). Although French military units had never intervened in Mali or Burkina Faso, 1,100 French soldiers were permanently stationed in Senegal and 450 in the Ivory Coast (to mention only the West African region that primarily concerns us).

In the basic symmetry in power relations between Mali (an ally of France) and Burkina Faso (a country that contested French options in Africa), it is necessary to add a variable that accounts for influences from outside Africa. At this stage of development in the continent, any realistic attempt to calculate power relations in negotiations between African states must include the potential assistance from their Northern allies.

Second, as already noted, the moralizing discourse of the Burkina Faso authorities did not fit well either into African official circles – where, more often than not, corruption and complicity with Europeans reigned supreme – or into West European circles, which were still preoccupied with the situation in the Soviet Union. French–African relations were still managed according to the old tenets of political and economic submission by the African authorities, irrespective of the way they governed their countries. Burkina Faso's attempt to challenge this order did not play in its favor on either side of the Mediterranean Sea.

Third, one element of the perceived power relations that was very specific to the African cultural context later worked against Sankara at the negotiating table: the age factor. In the African tradition, it was quite unacceptable for a young man such as Sankara (35) to offer lessons on morality and decency in the art of governing not only to Malian President Moussa Traoré (in his mid-50s), but also to the dean of African presidents, Félix Houphouët-Boigny of the Ivory Coast (well into his 80s). This "impertinent" attitude was consciously or unconsciously condemned by most West African presidents on a continent that has always displayed great reverence for age, which is equated with wisdom before which the young must bow (Bascom 1972:445–465). Given the low institutionalization of the negotiation process in Africa, the human factor (with all its conscious and unconscious cultural biases) assumes a most prominent role in reaching the final outcome.

As noted in the introduction, the armed conflict broke out on Christmas Day and heavy fighting continued for three days. But what was the evolutionary path of the crisis? Who were the actors that intervened in the negotiation? Why did they do so? And what did they do?

9.4   The Negotiation Process

On 21 December 1985, when Mali publicly denounced what it termed the "characterized aggression" of Burkina Faso (namely, the attempt by Burkinabê armed forces to conduct a census in a contested area), it became obvious that a major crisis was developing. The spontaneous efforts of President Chadli Benjedid of Algeria did not succeed in preventing the outbreak of the military confrontation.

As hostilities deepened, many "peacemakers" volunteered their services to help resolve the situation. The first was Libya, whose foreign minister, after trips to both capital cities, thought himself in a position to announce a cease-fire as early as 27 December (*Année Stratégique 1987* 1988:218). As it turned out, this was premature.

The second negotiating initiative came from President Houphouët-Boigny, who was eager to take decisive action on a much larger scale than what had been done up to this point. On the eve of the Libyan announcement, which was dismissed by the Bamako authorities as "a farce" (*Année Stratégique 1987* 1988:218), the Ivory Coast began working closely with the OAU. Shortly after that, the Pan-African organization published a communiqué announcing a new cease-fire, together with a list of the African mediators who would be involved in the settlement of the dispute. These mediators were Benin, Ivory Coast, Niger, Senegal, and Togo. From that time on, it appeared that the juridical framework of ANAD would serve as the most appropriate venue for resolving the Mali–Burkina Faso conflict. But fighting continued on the battlefield, and none of the cease-fires were respected by the belligerents.

The third attempt at negotiating a halt to the hostilities was undertaken once again by Libya, which succeeded in enlisting Nigeria, the main power in the region (but not a member of ANAD), to supervise the cease-fire. Fighting stopped on December 29. To many observers, this occurrence was pure coincidence, and it was feared that the situation would probably worsen.

Taking advantage of this respite, ANAD diplomacy went into full gear and engineered the fourth and (in their terms) "real cease-fire," which was concluded in the form of a communiqué signed by Presidents Traoré and Sankara and released in Abidjan on 30 December 1985, after having been previously flown to Bamako and Ouagadougou (Doucet 1986:4).

Why did the ANAD proposition succeed where the Nigeria–Libyan arrangement failed? One of the main differences between the two proposals resided in the composition of the observation forces that would monitor the withdrawal of troops from the war zone. In the cease-fire negotiated through Nigeria and Libya, the surveillance would be carried out by troops originating in these two countries, an unacceptable proposition to the Ivory Coast and Niger, both at odds with Libya and suspicious of the ultimate intentions of the huge Nigerian army patrolling their borders.

The ANAD proposal, however, stipulated that monitoring be done by officers from ANAD states, as well as Benin, under the leadership of the Ivory Coast (Doucet 1986:4). Finding themselves with no real military means to impose their will on the battlefield and being in almost total diplomatic isolation, the authorities of Burkina Faso understood late on 30 December that agreeing to the terms of the ANAD cease-fire was their best option out of the conflict.

When the ANAD negotiations and capital-hopping were completed, the Ivory Coast Ministers of Foreign Affairs, Siméon Ake, and Defense, Jean Konan Banny, pointed out that it was their mission – which included ANAD Secretary General Gomis – that brought about the cease-fire. The ANAD communiqué of December 30 also announced that an extraordinary meeting of that institution would be held in Yamoussoukro, Ivory Coast, in mid-January 1986.

With armed hostilities put to rest, postwar diplomacy could begin. President Houphouët-Boigny was the chief organizer of the Yamoussoukro meeting. The summit was convened on 17 and 18 January 1986. Presidents Gnassigbe Eyadema of Togo, Seyni Kountché of Niger, Maouya Ould Taya of Mauritania, and Mathieu Kérékou of Benin were invited.

The official reconciliation took place on 17 January on the tarmac of the Yamoussoukro airport where the two former belligerents warmly embraced each other in a manner typical of African brotherly reconciliations. A meeting followed that touching moment in the afternoon. The meeting was to be an occasion for the airing of dirty laundry within the family, and as such, one can infer that it was probably a less joyful occasion than that which occurred in the morning.

This crucial meeting took place in President Houphouët-Boigny's hotel suite in Yamoussoukro. Its most striking characteristic was the total exclusion of anyone who was not a head of state. Contrary to the usual diplomatic protocol, the various ministers of foreign affairs, army chiefs-of-staff, and even the Secretary General of ANAD, who had actively helped organize the meeting, were excluded from the meeting. Originally scheduled to last three hours, the discussions went on for twice the scheduled time.

To the extent that all parties convened came to the Yamoussoukro summit, and that an official reconciliation was successfully arranged, it can be said that the Ivory Coast meeting was indeed a success. But the crisis was not entirely resolved. The Burkinabê Minister of External Relations and Cooperation, Basile Guisson, warned that "we have made agreements on peace before, which have broken down into war" (Doucet 1986:5). The cabinet member from Burkina Faso also added that "as long as Mali does not accept that the Burkina Faso of today is different from the Upper Volta of yesterday, peace in the subregion will be compromised."

In the next section a more thorough analysis of the different phases of the negotiating process is presented. It provides some insights into the motivations of the different negotiators taking part in this process of conflict resolution.

The negotiations fall into three stages: preventive diplomacy (before the war), active diplomacy (during the war), and conciliatory diplomacy (after the war).

9.4.1   The preventive diplomacy phase (21–24 December 1985)

Algeria and Libya, two North African countries, dominated this stage, and each attempted in its own way to prevent the conflict from reaching a military phase. Whereas Algeria was generally perceived in Africa as a credible diplomatic go-between, the reputation of Libya was substantially less flattering.

Predictably, the involvement of Libya, a diplomatic outcast in the Africa of the 1980s, only succeeded in irritating both the leaders of Mali and the Ivory Coast. In addition, it had been observed that Tripoli authorities tended to boast about things that had not been completely achieved (Pondi 1988:145); this characteristic manifested itself and only succeeded in prompting the Ivory Coast to enter the diplomatic arena to ensure that the Libyans not take an any active role in the negotiations.

The failure of Algeria was due primarily to its known bias toward Burkina Faso, a "progressive" African country. Algiers was anxious not to let France and other Western powers use an excuse to crush the young Burkinabê revolution. As for Tripoli, any opportunity to spread its Islamic jihad spirit through good offices was worth pursuing. The outbreak of the war on Christmas provided ample evidence that the preventive efforts of the two North African states ended in failure. From that day on, other diplomatic approaches were necessary.

9.4.2   The active diplomacy phase (25–29 December 1985)

This phase was relatively more complex than the preceding one. It revealed that the OAU's juridical doctrine of total equality of member states was increasingly becoming a hollow claim, an unconvincing exercise in wishful thinking. During this phase, it became increasingly clear that the Ivory Coast and Senegal were the main countries that, besides the conflicting parties, held the keys to the resolution of the Mali–Burkina Faso conflict.

A middle-income country by World Bank standards, the Ivory Coast has always exerted a considerable influence within the camp of the OAU moderates, which includes such West African countries as Mali, Senegal, and Togo. Perhaps more important has been the ability of Abidjan to command the attention of Burkina Faso, which had more than 2 million of its citizens gainfully employed in the Ivory Coast at the time of the conflict. There is little doubt that a decision made by the Ivory Coast to repatriate Burkinabê workers could have provoked an acute socioeconomic crisis and created major problems for the Ouagadougou authorities. In addition, in terms of external trade, the first destination of Burkina Faso's exports was the Ivory Coast (*Année Politique et Economique Africaine* 1985:27); in 1984, Taiwan, France, and West Germany ranked second, third, and fourth, respectively. Thus, the Ivory Coast had both the means and the will to take actions to influence the behavior of Burkina Faso.

In the past, Senegal had always enjoyed a high diplomatic and cultural standing in sub-Saharan African, in general, and with francophone countries, in particular. As the only real democracy in Black Africa since the late 1970s, Dakar has also been able to exert considerable influence in the Western world, particularly in France. Senegal has been the initiator of all subregional economic organizations and, in 1985, held the prestigious Chair of the OAU. The involvement of Senegal in this conflict would place Dakar in the heavyweight category of African diplomacy and produce possible economic dividends in a poverty-stricken country in the form of more investments in a politically stable haven.

The Mali–Burkina Faso conflict thus demonstrated the weight within Africa of two factors (economic influence and the ability to build diplomatic networks) as fundamental ingredients in the capacity to lead diplomatic negotiations. It clearly showed that in sub-Saharan Africa, too, relative economic power translated into relative diplomatic, political, and military power.

The second lesson to be drawn from this stage of active diplomacy during the Mali–Burkina Faso confrontation was the symbolic importance of the linguistic divide, apparently used as a basis for the delimitation of spheres of influence on the continent. President Houphouët-Boigny of the Ivory Coast and his peers from the ANAD did everything in their power to prevent Nigeria, the anglophone economic, military, and demographic giant of Africa, from playing any decisive role in the final settlement of this crisis, pitting two francophone countries against each other. Although Nigeria held the Chair of the 16-member Economic Community of West African States (ECOWAS) in 1985 (which included in its membership all the protagonists and subregional mediators in the conflict), care was taken by the French-speaking African countries not to involve Lagos in the talks. This attitude did not please the Nigerians who, through their foreign minister, Bolaji Akinyemi, declared that "Nigeria does not support the ANAD which is a francophone organization" (Akinyemi 1986:27).

As the most important country in West Africa, and despite the attitude of the ANAD states, Nigeria still felt it was its duty to mediate, but diplomatically; Lagos agreed to concede to the Ivory Coast's wishes that it not become involved. Had the countries in conflict been English-speaking, it seems highly unlikely that the Ivory Coast would have played the role it did in the dispute and even more improbable that it would have contested the right of Nigeria to assume leadership in the conflict resolution, as events in Liberia and Sierra Leone during the next decade would show.

Only a few countries on the continent seem to have the ability to resolve a regional crisis in Africa. The notion of subregional African powers sketched by Edem Kodjo, the former OAU Secretary General, in a critically acclaimed book seems to have become a reality (Kodjo 1985). More important perhaps is the economic competition for control of the important consumer market of the West African subregion that lies behind the linguistic divide between the Ivory Coast and Nigeria (Zartman 1983).

During the phase of active diplomacy, the ANAD countries succeeded in gaining control of the negotiating process at the expense of the countries of North Africa (Algeria and Libya) and of anglophone Africa (Nigeria). The last phase of the process, conciliatory diplomacy, was marked by other striking characteristics.

9.4.3   The conciliatory diplomacy phase
(30 December 1985–18 January 1986)

An extreme centralization of decision-making powers into the hands of African heads of state is the main feature of this stage. This was most evident during the Yamoussoukro summit where, as seen earlier, all the advisers of the Presidents were kept out of the negotiating room. This extreme centralization of power is one of the most distinguishing traits of African diplomacy at the highest level. Here the President becomes his own counselor.

When, as is the case of sub-Saharan Africa, the extreme personalization of power is combined with a very low level of institutionalization (Huntington 1968), the process of negotiation tends to become a fragile exercise that does not obey set rules, but that often has its outcome subjected to the moods of Africa's ultimate decision makers: the heads of state. The problem of conducting structured negotiations in Africa is compounded by the lack of trained professional negotiators on the continent (Kremenyuk 1991:400). Hence, the results obtained under such highly unstructured circumstances can be challenged at any time by whomever replaces the head of state who agreed to them.

An example could help to illustrate the point. Just after the end of the Biafran War that pitted eastern Nigeria against the rest of the federation between 1967 and 1970, Presidents Gowon of Nigeria and Ahidjo of Cameroon signed the Maroua Agreements, which delimited the borders between the two countries. At the time, Cameroon had played an instrumental role in the final victory of the federal government of Nigeria's army over the rebellious troops of Biafra by categorically refusing to allow any military assistance to the seceding side, as France and other powers were asking. The leaders that replaced Gowon alleged that, in an attempt to be grateful for Cameroon's support, the former Nigerian head of state conceded too much territory to the Yaoundé regime. The Maroua Agreements were therefore never ratified by the Nigerian Parliament and, as a consequence, never implemented.

9.5   Conclusion

The study of the Mali–Burkina Faso War suggests at least four concluding remarks. First, African countries tend to prefer informal collective mediation to the highly structured negotiating setting that is often seen in Europe and North America. The OAU charter of May 1963 formally created a commission of mediation, conciliation, and arbitration in article 19. Although several conflicts have occurred on the continent since its institutionalization, the commission has almost never been used. Instead, nearly all disputes have been successfully resolved through ad hoc committees made up of OAU heads of state. A marked tendency to resort to face-to-face contacts, a preference to use the services of mutually trusted mediators, and a legendary disregard for formal, rigidly structured negotiations seem to characterize the overall style of African collective negotiation.

Second, the importance of African culture – some aspects of which conflict with Western negotiation techniques – must be assessed. The impact of culture in negotiations is much more complex than has often been suggested. For the sake of clarity, one must distinguish the rural from the urban African culture. In traditional and rural Africa, negotiations (at the marketplace and to a certain extent at home, marriages for instance) are part of everyday life. From a political standpoint, the traditional way of ruling a chiefdom is for its head to surround himself with the council of elders. That body is a forum of negotiation par excellence (Crowder 1972).

In modern and urban Africa, post-independent leaders and city dwellers have attempted to combine the old with the new, with mixed results. Referring to a mythical past, many African political leaders have sought to confiscate the entire decision-making apparatus for themselves (Schatzberg 1988). In the urban setting, the unfortunate juxtaposition of old traditions (of which the culture of submission is a prominent feature) and supposedly new and modern organizations (evidenced by an authoritarian decision-making style in the polity) have reduced the likelihood of including competent negotiators with important margins of maneuver. Many among the ultimate holders of power in Africa are reluctant to delegate decision making to anyone other than themselves. Negotiation with designated teams can hardly take place under these circumstances.

Third, in terms of power relations and the negotiation process, the importance of shadow partners cannot be overemphasized, for their necessity is dictated by the basic economic and military vulnerability and weakness of African states. But even if generally poor, not all African countries exhibit the same level of dependency toward Northern countries. It is important to distinguish between influential states that are relatively autonomous militarily and diplomatically, such as Egypt, Nigeria, or South Africa, and those whose strength is almost entirely derived from a close link with powers from outside Africa, such as the Ivory Coast and Senegal. Both categories of African states exert an undeniable diplomatic influence on their region.

Hence, the African diplomatic arena is no longer homogeneous in terms of the conflict resolution capability of its units, the member states of the OAU. A hierarchical structure has emerged since the oil-supply shocks of the 1970s, which enriched a handful of countries and impoverished the vast majority. It follows that, as elsewhere, some selected countries of the continent are central to the resolution of conflicts within and outside their subregion, a tendency that supports the creation of an institution that most African countries have always resisted: an OAU security council for the resolution of conflicts. During the OAU Cairo summit in 1993, the Secretary General proposed the creation of a mechanism for conflict resolution in Africa, which was adopted. The mechanism has since been useful in dealing with a number of conflicts.

Finally, it is clear that perceived power symmetry in Africa can often be altered by an element of "borrowed power" provided by a shadow partner or partners. Therefore, the ability to form viable and reliable coalitions becomes the key to winning a local confrontation between two equally poor, weak, and vulnerable states. The perception of power in this context is subordinated to a country's ability to directly or indirectly mobilize allies with important economic, military, and diplomatic capabilities. In negotiation terms, interestingly enough, this reality has transformed the African diplomatic arena, by creating two very distinct sets of actors: the influential actors mentioned above who can directly mobilize continental or intercontinental allies and the large number of actors who are forced to use the members of the former category to secure the support of eventual allies.

Thus, the most common type of negotiation in Africa is the LL type, in which both parties realistically have a low perception of their powers and an equally low perception of the other's powers. But, if such is the case, then hostilities should not break out in the first place (Paul 1994). This chapter has attempted to show that it is the additional support of the shadow partner or partners that tilts the perception of power and boosts the chances of success for one of the two parties in conflict negotiations. Thus, an LL-type confrontation and negotiation can be transformed into an $L(x.L)$ situation, x being the boosting factor or multiplying effect represented by the addition of the shadow partner or partners. Hence, x helps to transform L into H. Thus $L(x.L)$ becomes LH, yielding an asymmetrical power relationship. The highly polarized world of 1945–1989 with its emphasis on ideological warfare constituted an ideal arena for the formation of coalitions. Any Third World conflict, in general, and African conflict, in particular (even of a purely continental nature as in the case of border litigations), could potentially be translated into an international, coalition-generating situation. The end of the Cold War could establish an era of increasingly autonomous conflicts whose resolution could be conducted at the regional level through negotiation.

Given the worsening economic crisis on the African continent, it seems necessary, now more than ever, to reinforce the internal conflict resolution capabilities of Pan-African and subregional institutions (OAU, ECOWAS, Central African Customs Union, and so on). With the participants to the 1991 Kampala Conference on Peace, Security, Stability, and Cooperation in Africa, it seems urgent to acknowledge that the link between security, stability, and development demands "a common African agenda based on a unity of purpose and a collective political consensus derived from a firm conviction that Africa cannot make any significant progress on any other front without creating collectively a lasting solution to its problems of security and stability" (Obasanjo 1991:8). In a world of asymmetries of the weak, where power-borrowers try to tip symmetries in their favor, it is important that diplomatic skills be used preventively, to keep the wars of the poor from ever erupting.

Notes

[1] Mali occupies an area of 1,240,192 square kilometers and Burkina-Faso only 274,200 square kilometers. In 1985, the per capita gross national product of Mali stood at US$180, while that of Burkina Faso barely reached US$210. Furthermore, 90% of the 9 million Malians and 7 million Burkinabês work in the primary or rural sector of the economy of their respective countries. Finally, the armies of Mali and Burkina Faso number 7,300 and 8,700 volunteers, respectively (*New African Yearbook 1985–1986* 1986:23 and 118).

[2] Following an agreement concluded on 16 September 1983, Mali and Burkina Faso addressed a joint letter to the International Court of Justice (ICJ) at the Hague on 20 October 1983, requesting that an examination of their long-standing border dispute be made by the Court in accordance to article 26 paragraph 2 of the ICJ statutes. The Court, chaired by Judge Mohamed Bedjaoui, asked the following question: "What is the configuration of the border line between Upper Volta [now Burkina Faso] and Mali in the contested area, the triangle delimited by the points of Koro, Djibo and Béli?" The Court arrived at a judgment in equity on 22 December 1986 and that is why there were no winners or losers in the case. The configuration of the frontier line was different from the pretensions of both parties and espoused the halfway mark with respect to the propositions of Mali and Burkina Faso (see *International Court of Justice Reports of Judgements 1986* 1987).

References

Africa Contemporary Records 1984–1985, 1985, Africa Research Limited, Exeter, UK.

Akinyemi, B., 1986, Interview, *Jeune Afrique*, **1308**, 29 January.

Andriamirado, S., 1988, *Sankara le Rebelle*, J.A. Livres, Paris.

Année Politique et Économique Africaine, 1985, Vol. 5, Societé Africaine d'Édition, Dakar, Senegal.

Année Stratégique 1987, 1988, Fondation pour les Etudes de Défense, Paris.

Année Stratégique 1990, 1990, Iris, Paris.

Asiwaju, A.I., ed., 1985, *Partitioned Africans: Ethnic Relations Across Africa's International Boundaries 1884–1984*, St. Martin's Press, New York.

Bakary, C., 1988, *Le Problème de Sécurité Collective en Afrique: Le cas de l'Afrique Occidentale* (The Problem of Collective Security in Africa: The Case of Western Africa), Yaoundé Thèse de Doctorat de 3è Cycle, IRIC.

Bascom, W., 1972, The urban African and his world, in M.A. Klein and G.W. Johnson, eds., *Perspectives on the African Past*, Little Brown and Company, Boston, MA.

Cooley, J.K., 1981, The Libyan menace, *Foreign Policy*, **42** Spring:74–93.

Crowder, M., ed., 1972, *The Cambridge History of Africa, From 1943 To 1963*, Volume 8, Cambridge University Press, Cambridge, UK.

Doucet, L., 1986, Mali–Burkina: Border flare up, *West Africa*, **3566**, 6 January.

Huntington, S.P., 1968, *Political Order in Changing Societies*, Yale University Press, New Haven, CT.

International Court of Justice Reports of Judgments 1986, 1987, The Hague, The Netherlands.

Kampala Documents: Towards a Conference on Security, Stability, Development and Cooperation in Africa, 1991, African Leadership Forum Publication, Kampala, Uganda.

Kodjo, E., 1985, *Et Demain L'Afrique*, Stock, Paris.

Kremenyuk, V.A., ed., 1991, *International Negotiation: Analyses, Approaches, Issues*, Jossey-Bass Publishers, San Francisco, CA.

Lemarchand, R., 1988, The case of Chad, in R. Lemarchand, ed., *The Green and the Black: Qaddafi's Policies in Africa*, Indiana University Press, Bloomington, IN.

Martin, G., 1983, Les fondements historiques et politiques de la politique africaine de la France: Du colonialisme au néo-colonialisme (The historical and political foundations of France's Africa policy: From colonialism to neo-colonialism), *Genève–Afrique*, **21**(2).

New African Yearbook 1985–1986, 1986, I.C. Magazine Ltd., London.

Obasanjo, O., 1991, *The Kampala Document*, African Leadership Forum, New York.

Paul, T.V., 1994, *Asymmetric Conflicts: User Initiation by Weaker Powers*, Cambridge University Press, New York.

Pondi, J.-E., 1988, Qaddafi and the Organization of African Unity, in R. Lemarchand, ed., *The Green and the Black: Qaddafi's Policies in Africa*, Indiana University Press, Bloomington, IN.

Schatzberg, M.G., 1988, *The Dialects of Oppression in Zaire*, Indiana University Press, Bloomington, IN.

Somé, G., 1987, Un exemple de conflict frontalier: La différence entre la Haute-Volta et le Mali (An example of border conflict: The difference between Upper Volta and Mali), *Année Africaine*, Volume 23, Pédone, Paris.

Touval, S., 1972, *Boundary Politics of Independent Africa*, Harvard University Press, Cambridge, MA.

Traoré, D., 1979, *La CEAO: Réalités et Perspectives* (The CEAO: Facts and Perspectives), IRIC, Mémoire de Maîtrise, Yaoundé, Cameroon.

Widstrand, C., ed., 1969, *African Boundary Problems*, Scandinavian Institute of African Studies, Uppsala, Sweden.

Zartman, I.W., 1966, *International Relations in the New Africa*, Prentice-Hall, Englewood Cliffs, NJ.

Zartman, I.W., 1983, ed., *The Political Economy of Nigeria*, Praeger, New York.

Chapter 10

Seeking Honor under Strong Symmetry in the Korean War Armistice Negotiations

Xibo Fan

The Korean War started as a civil war and ended with the international intervention of the United States and the People's Republic of China (PRC). The objectives of the intervenors in supporting one of the parties in the civil war were to safeguard the intervenors' own interests (ideological superiority or national security). The two intervenors possessed high power in the war, and perceived and exhibited that high power in the process of the armistice negotiations. During the three years of war (from 25 June 1950 to 27 July 1953), the main campaigns took place only in the first year; the negotiations lasted two more years as a conflict over the principles of a cease-fire. Both sides exercised their power to force the other side to accept cease-fire terms under which their own interests were safeguarded.

The armistice negotiations were about the following: (1) the demarcation line and the demilitarized zone; (2) implementation and enforcement of the armistice; (3) repatriation of the prisoners of war (POWs); and

(4) recommendation to concerned governments for a political conference on the unification of Korea.

This chapter tests the hypothesis that a competitive negotiation in which both parties possess and perceive high power will explore more alternatives among different senses of justice but will be less effective in reaching agreement because both sides try to exploit gains as much as possible to maintain their power reputations.

10.1   The Korean War

At the end of World War II, a demarcation line along the 38th parallel was arbitrarily drawn for the armed forces of the Soviet Union and United States when they occupied the Korean Peninsula to receive the surrender of Japanese armed forces.[1] The Soviet army controlled the northern part of the peninsula and the US army the south. In August and September of 1948 two governments were established in these two parts, the Democratic People's Republic of Korea (North Korea–DPRK), and the Republic of Korea (South Korea–ROK). The United Nations (UN) General Assembly on 12 December 1948 recommended that the occupying powers withdraw their forces from Korea as early as practicable (UNGA, R195/III). Hence, on 25 December 1948, the Soviets announced their withdrawal from Korea, and in July 1949, the United States announced that the US armed forces had completed their withdrawal at the end of June (Appleman 1961:5).

The establishment of the Communist People's Republic of China on 1 October 1949 was regarded by the United States as the loss of China because the United States supported the Kuomintung (KMT, the Chinese Nationalist Party), the rival of the Chinese Communist Party (CCP), during the Chinese Civil War from 1945 to 1949. Therefore, when the PRC government claimed China's seat as a permanent member in the UN Security Council, the Soviet Union backed the PRC and the US government continued to support the representatives of the KMT government, which had been defeated in the Chinese Civil War and escaped from Nanjing to Taipei on Taiwan. Consequently, the Soviet representative to the UN, Jacob Malik, announced on 13 January 1950 that the USSR would not participate in or recognize any UN Security Council action so long as the KMT representative illegally occupied China's UN membership. The Korean War further reinforced the hostility and distrust between China and the United States.

10.2 Outbreak of Civil War

On 25 June 1950, North Korea attacked the South across the 38th parallel. On 28 June, DPRK troops captured Seoul, the capital of South Korea. Before the attack, according to the Soviet archives, the North Korean leader Kim Il Sung had made more than 50 appeals to Joseph Stalin seeking the Soviet Union's support for his unification plan (Sneider 1993). The Chinese leader Mao Zedong was informed of Kim's intention but he was not certain how and when the attack would start. Moreover, Mao questioned the possibility of success in the war and warned Stalin and Kim that the United States might intervene (Hao and Zhai 1990:96–97). However, based on the optimistic assumption that the United States would not involve itself in the war, Stalin approved Kim's plan.

The United States did intervene, at extremely high speed. On the day the war broke out, 25 June 1950, the US mission urged the UN Security Council to pass a resolution (UN S/1501) stating that the North Korean attack "constitutes a breach of the peace; calling for the immediate cessation of hostilities; and calling upon the authorities of North Korea to withdraw forthwith their armed forces to the thirty-eighth parallel" (UNSC 473/V:7–8, 13–14). On 27 June, the UN Security Council passed another resolution that stated:

> Having noted that urgent military measures are required to restore international peace and security, it is recommended that the members of the United Nations furnish such assistance to the Republic of Korea as may be necessary to repel the armed attack and to restore international peace and security in the area. [UNSC 474/V:4]

On the same day, President Truman ordered US navy and air forces to support the ROK and ordered the US Seventh Fleet to "neutralize" the Taiwan Strait.[2] On 30 June, President Truman ordered US ground forces to Korea. They entered battle in less than a week; and on 7 July, US General of the Army Douglas MacArthur was appointed supreme commander of the UN Command in Korea.

The initial US intervention was not successful. Within two months, the DPRK troops occupied almost the whole of the Korea. At the end of August, US and ROK forces defended the Pusan Perimeter on the southeast corner of the peninsula waiting for a surprise operation.

On 15 September, UN forces landed at Inchon near Seoul and the 38th parallel. Cut off from their rear supplies, the DPRK Pusan offensive collapsed and their troops were forced to withdraw. Seoul was recaptured by the UN force on 28 September. On 1 October, South Korean troops crossed the 38th parallel in pursuit of the retreating North Korean army. Immediately on the following day, 2 October, Chinese Foreign Minister Zhou En-Lai informed Indian Ambassador Panikkar in Beijing that, if US troops entered North Korea, China would intervene in the Korean War.[3] Unfortunately, on 7 October, US troops began crossing the 38th parallel. On the same day, the UN General Assembly authorized UN forces to pursue the enemy across the 38th parallel.[4]

Three pieces of evidence indicate that the Chinese were unaware of the decision to attack, according to Hao and Zhai (1990:100–101). First, in May 1950, the CCP Central Committee decided to demobilize 1.4 million of the People's Liberation Army (PLA) forces; second, the Chinese embassy in North Korea had not yet been set up when the war broke out; third, only one army (the 42nd Army of the Fourth Field Army) was stationed along the Chinese–Korean–Russian border area when the war started.

When the US government ordered the US Seventh Fleet to "neutralize" the Taiwan Strait and later the UN declared that the objective of the UN joint forces was to unify Korea, Chinese leaders perceived these actions as the worst threat from the United States directly against China. On 7 July, Mao ordered four armies to Manchuria to form the Northeast Frontier Defense Army (NFDA) and appointed General Deng Hua as commander.

When the fighting at Pusan Perimeter clearly showed a stalemate, Zhou En-Lai, the Chinese Premier as well as Foreign Minister, consulted the PLA General Staff headquarters to find out the possible scenarios of the next UN operations. The answer was that MacArthur might conduct a landing operation at a place near the waist of the Korean Peninsula. Mao and Zhou passed this message to Kim Il Sung (Chai and Zhao 1989:67). He ignored the warning.

According to Zhou En-Lai, China had hoped the UN forces would stop at the 38th parallel and then settle the Korean issue through negotiations. However, when South Korean troops crossed the 38th parallel on 1 October, despite strong warnings from the PRC government, China entered the war (Chai and Zhao 1989:73). After making the decision to intervene in the Korean War Mao Zedong sent a telegram to Stalin on 2 October 1950, in which he explained the planned Chinese operations in Korea and asked the Soviet Union to provide air force support (*New York Times*, 26 February 1992). When US forces crossed the 38th parallel on 7 October, the CCP Politburo made the final decision to intervene on 8 October. General Peng Dehui was appointed as the Commander for the Chinese People's Volunteers (CPV) with General Deng Hua as his deputy. On the same day Zhou En-Lai went to Moscow to negotiate with Stalin for military aid, and Chinese Ambassador Ni Zhiliang informed Kim Il Sung that the Chinese would fight in Korea (Chai and Zhao 1989:82–85). Stalin shifted from optimism to pessimism, fearing that a joint Sino–USSR intervention would invoke a world war; therefore, he did not support the CCP's decision.

Without Soviet air support, the Chinese army delayed its operations. It was not until 19 October, when Pyongyang, capital of North Korea, was captured by UN forces that the first troops of the CPV secretly entered Korea from northeast China – four armies of 260,000 men. General Peng told Kim Il Sung that the total number of troops to be deployed in Korea was about 600,000 (Chai and Zhao 1989:98). On 26 October, Chinese troops attacked ROK units at the Yalu River and then advanced south of the Sino–Korean border (the first CPV campaign). After 13 days of fighting, the CPV suddenly withdrew from the theater, deliberately creating an impression that only a small army of Chinese troops entered Korea.

Still holding to the belief that the Chinese government would not commit itself to the Korean War, General MacArthur announced on 24 November a "win-the-war" offensive but his plan was defeated by the CPV. Coordinating with the North Korean People's Army, on 26 November the CPV attacked both fronts of the UN forces (the second CPV campaign). MacArthur reported to the UN and the US government: "an entirely new war!" (Senate, p. 3495). UN forces were in full retreat, and Pyongyang was recaptured by the Chinese army on 4 December. According to the plan of General Peng, the Chinese troops would not fight across the 38th parallel at this moment, but would rest and then cross the parallel in the following spring of 1951 (Chai and Zhao 1989:114–116). While the CPV and UN forces were in hot fighting in Korea, the Chinese delegate Wu Xiu-Quan arrived at UN Headquarters in New York on 27 November and accused the United States of aggression in China's Taiwan Island, which was then blocked by the United States from discussion in the UN Political Committee. On 30 November, Truman mentioned the possibility of using nuclear weapons in Korea and China (*New York Times*, 1 December 1950).

Frightened by the prospect of an atomic war, British Prime Minister Clement Attlee urged Truman not to use A-bombs. He also recommended that the United States allow the PRC membership in the UN and negotiate a cease-fire with the Chinese. The United States and United Kingdom reached an agreement that stated that A-bombs would not be used without consulting each other, but the United States rejected Attlee's negotiation suggestion.

While UN forces were in hurried retreat, India and 12 other neutral nations drafted a proposal for a cease-fire on 7 December 1950. The Chinese government interpreted it as a trick for UN forces to gain time because the so-called "neutral" nations included the Philippines, which had already sent armed forces to fight in Korea under the UN command. The Chinese government further challenged the 13 nations by questioning why they had not suggested a cease-fire when UN forces crossed the 38th parallel. Facing the 13-nation proposal which demanded that China unilaterally stop the war, Mao changed the plan and ordered the CPV to fight another campaign across the 38th parallel.

On 1 January 1951, Chinese and North Korean forces launched an all-out offensive against the UN (the third campaign). On 4 January, Seoul was again captured, this time by the Chinese. Since this campaign was only a response to the 13-nation cease-fire proposal and because the longer rear supply line was becoming increasingly vulnerable, the CPV did not pursue the quickly retreating UN troops but instead halted the offensive to rest. The UN commanders perceived that the intention of the CPV offensive was to destroy the Eighth Army. Therefore, they ordered UN troops to withdraw from the theater without hard resistance. MacArthur urged the US government to open war against China, to use the KMT troops to fight the CPV, to drop atomic bombs in China, and to bombard the industrial cities of China. He considered evacuating the Eighth Army to Japan if the CPV pushed further south. President Truman, however, insisted that the war be limited to Korea.

While retreating, General Matthew Ridgway kept his Eighth Army in contact with the CPV until the CPV offensive was exhausted, and on 21 January issued orders for a counteroffensive. The CPV turned to the offensive (the fourth CPV campaign) but was forced to withdraw north of the Han River. On 14 March, UN forces recaptured Seoul for the second time at a price of high casualties. The US government asked MacArthur not to pass the 38th parallel without permission and hoped to find a chance to settle the conflict through negotiations (FRUS VII 1951, pt. 1:251).

Being eager to escalate the war, MacArthur repeatedly challenged Truman's limited-war policy. Knowing that President Truman tried to deliver a peace announcement, MacArthur deliberately issued on 24 March a communique in which he proclaimed that:

> the enemy [China] must ... by now [be] painfully aware that a decision of the United Nations to depart from its tolerant effort to contain the war to the area of Korea through expansion of our military operations to his [Chinese] coastal areas and interior bases would doom Red China to the risk of imminent military collapse. ... Within the area of my authority as a military commander, however, it should be needless to say, I stand ready at any time to confer in the field with the Commander-in-Chief of the enemy forces in an earnest effort to find any military means whereby the realization of the political objectives of the United Nations in Korea, to which no nation may justly take exceptions, might be accomplished without further bloodshed. [FRUS VII 1951, pt. 1:265–266]

MacArthur completely sabotaged Truman's peace initiative. On 5 April, Minority Leader Joe Martin released MacArthur's letter to him, in which MacArthur stated that the Korean War had "no substitute for victory" and suggested using KMT forces to attack the mainland of China (FRUS VII 1951, pt. 1:298). Pushed into a corner, President Truman relieved MacArthur on 11 April. General Ridgway replaced him as Supreme Commander of UN forces, and James Van Fleet became the commander of the Eighth Army.

On 22 April, the CPV launched its fifth offensive and UN forces withdrew to the prepared positions north of Seoul. After the second phase of the offensive on 16 May, the CPV's energy was exhausted. On 21 May, UN Command launched a counteroffensive that succeeded in driving the enemy north of the 38th parallel. UN forces captured Chorwon and Kumhwa in the Iron Triangle on 13 June. After the dismissal of General MacArthur, UN forces built a firm defensive line under the command of Ridgway.

From the middle of 1951, the situation in the Korean War went into a stalemate. When UN forces recaptured Seoul and established a solid defensive front, there was a psychological opportunity to begin the armistice negotiation.

10.3   US Perceptions

After World War II and at the beginning of the Cold War, the United States focused its efforts on containing the expansion of Communism in Europe. Asia was not as important as Europe. To generate a new policy for postwar global politics, the State Department Policy Planning Staff, led by Paul H. Nitze, worked out a new global strategy initiative in National Security Council Proposal 68 at the end of 1949. According to NSC 68, the United States ought to lead the free world in containing Communism in every corner of the world. The outbreak of the Korean War provided an opportunity for the US government to implement NSC 68 strategies and to open an additional theater of containment against the Soviet Union in Asia. The US government used the Korean War to generate the perception that all the Communists were expansionist.

The original objective of the US military intervention was to repel the Communists; this objective was reached when US troops advanced to the 38th parallel. From then on, the US side lost its political control over the military operations. Although the United States accused China and the Soviet Union of supporting the invasion, most military and government leaders did not believe China and the USSR would dare to intervene. The United States wanted to win both the war on the battlefield and the propaganda contest of blaming China and the USSR. Especially after MacArthur's brilliant Inchon landing operation, no one in the Joint Chiefs of Staff (JCS) or the government dared to challenge his war plan in Korea. As a result, General MacArthur's plan for the theater of the Korea War "commanded" both President Truman's political decision in Washington and the UN's resolutions on Korea. MacArthur pursued a total victory strategy by occupying all of Korea, and even further suggested expanding the war to the territory of China. These unlimited war actions resulted in an unexpected reaction from China.

10.4   Chinese Perceptions

In contemporary history, China had been invaded by Great Britain, Portugal, France, Germany, Russia, America, and Japan. Many Chinese people suffered from these aggressions, losing lives and resources. The memory was fresh. China was the first country to care about the war on the Korean Peninsula because almost all its invaders came from this flank.

Western countries had always considered the DPRK's attack against the ROK to be a joint conspiracy of the Communist governments of North Korea, China, and the Soviet Union. However, China thought the war was a civil war of Korea, and so believed that all foreign forces should withdraw from Korea and that the Korean people themselves should decide the outcome.

When the Korean War started, the US government accused China of supporting the aggression by sending troops to Korea. Actually, these troops were Korean soldiers. In World War II, Koreans resisted the Japanese aggressor in northeast China, then took part in the civil war in China; these settlers returned to Korea before the Korean War started.

In September and October, PRC Foreign Minister Zhou En-Lai repeatedly warned that if US troops entered North Korea, China would intervene in the war. Western countries believed that these warnings were merely diplomatic blackmail and therefore not credible. However, the rational interpretation of these warnings is that: (1) China silently agreed to the UN resolution of 25 June 1950, or at least did not reject the UN action in South Korea, based on the assumption that the UN believed that North and South Korea were two independent countries, because the UN is an organization for international affairs; and (2) China agreed that South Korean armed forces had total authority to fight in the north, just as the North Korean army had total authority to fight in the south, based on the belief that the Korean War was a civil war.

China did not believe North Korea would win the war if the United States intervened. However, waging a war for national unification was the domestic affair of the Korean people, and China could not but watch it cautiously. When the UN passed its resolution to intervene in the Korean War, Chinese leaders immediately ordered their armed forces to northeast China, organizing a "Northeast Front Defense Army." China had prepared for the worst situation and repeatedly signaled the United States not to pass the 38th parallel.

The United States and China were allies in World War II, but the United States was on the opposite (KMT) side against the Chinese Communists during the Chinese Civil War (1946–1949). In the 1950s, the Chinese people were concentrating on their domestic economic buildup and the unification of China, and were unwilling to divert their own strength to the affairs of others. But when UN forces crossed the 38th parallel on 7 October, lessons from history told the Chinese people that they could not ignore the forces that were marching toward the Sino–Korean border with a belligerent attitude. The US Seventh Fleet was patrolling in the Taiwan Strait under orders from the US President. China believed that US military action in Taiwan was an aggression against China's territory. There was no way to convince China that UN forces would stop while MacArthur was suggesting that UN air forces should bomb the industrial base in northeast China, as part of a strategy of aiming the war at all Communist governments.

The most crucial event that led the Chinese to fight against the Americans was the US military action in the Taiwan Strait and on Taiwan. These actions directly led to the perception that the eventual target of US action was China. In addition, the "war to contain Communism" had a very flexible explanation. Chinese leaders got the impression that a war with the United States was inevitable. As long as the United States planned to invade Chinese territory, the Chinese had the discretion to contend with US military forces anywhere. Korea was the optimal place and the early 1950s were an optimal time for the Chinese to fight the inevitable war against the United States.

The decision for China to intervene in the Korean War was made only after these factors were taken into account. If the United States occupied the whole Korean Peninsula, the industrial base in northeast China (Manchuria) would be under direct threat of US "imperialists" (Mao to Stalin, *New York Times*, 26 February 1992). The United States could wage a war directly against China at any moment if it planned to do so. The aim of the intervention was to stop the belligerent military operation against China.

When Truman ordered US armed forces to intervene in the war, the Americans had a strong perception that the USSR was the source of support for the DPRK's invasion. Unexpectedly, the enemy whom the United States faced was China instead of the Soviet Union. To the contrary, the USSR almost always proposed peace resolutions rather than fighting in that war. When the US government accepted the fact of China's intervention, it changed its objective from total victory to an honorable negotiated settlement. After President Truman released MacArthur, Washington restored its political control over the military operations in the Korean War theater. The Korean War became a war for a cease-fire with honor.

Originally, the Chinese side had perceived a strong US intention to wage war against China. According to Mao's 1950 telegram (*New York Times*, 27 February 1992):

> Since Chinese troops will fight American troops in Korea (even though they will be using the title Volunteer Army), we must be prepared for the United States to declare and enter a state of war with China. We must be prepared that the United States may, at a minimum, use its Air Force to bomb many major cities and industrial centers in China, and use its Navy to assault the coastal region.

During the war, however, the United States did not declare the war against China, did not bomb industrial centers, and did not attack coastal cities. The restricted reaction of the US government gradually changed this Chinese perception of the United States' intentions.

Although political leaders on both sides changed their views about the war in Korea, the military commanders still believed that it could only be settled through fighting. Only after the casualties suffered in gaining a tiny piece of territory became too heavy to bear did the perception of both the public and military leaders change; both civilian and military leaders preferred a cease-fire to a complete victory.

10.5   The Korean War Armistice Negotiations

The US government tried several diplomatic channels to search for a scent and to identify the intentions of China. Unfortunately, these efforts received no reaction from the Chinese side. US Secretary of State Dean Acheson (1971:119) asked George Kennan to try another channel by meeting with Soviet UN delegate Malik on 31 May 1951 and inquiring about the possibility of negotiating a cease-fire in the Korean War. Kennan proposed two points: a cease-fire and withdrawal of all forces from the 38th parallel; and a gradual withdrawal of foreign forces from Korea. The government of China credulously accepted Kennan's message as the US government's offer for cease-fire and decided to open the armistice negotiation based on this offer.

On 23 June, Malik proposed a truce in the Korean War in a UN radio broadcast, suggesting a cease-fire at the 38th parallel. Despite initial suspicions about Soviet intentions, the United States confirmed the sincerity of the proposal with Soviet Deputy Foreign Minister Andrei Gromyko late on 27 June (Blair 1989:927–928).

On 29 June, Truman ordered Ridgway to broadcast an announcement to CPV and DPRK commanders:

Message to the Commander in Chief, Communist Forces in Korea.
As Commander in Chief of the United Nations Command I have
been instructed to communicate to you the following:

I am informed that you may wish a meeting to discuss an armistice
providing for the cessation of hostilities and all acts of armed
force in Korea, with adequate guarantees for maintenance of such
armistice.

Upon receipt of word from you that such a meeting is desired I
shall be prepared to name my representative. I would also at that
time suggest a date at which he could meet with your representative. I propose that such a meeting could take place aboard a
Danish hospital ship (*Jutlandia*) in Wonsan Harbor. [FRUS VII
1951, pt. 1:583–587]

Peng Dehui and Kim Il Sung replied on 1 July with the following:

General Ridgway, Commander-in-Chief of the UN forces:

Your statement of June 30 this year concerning peace talks has
been received. We are authorized to inform you that we agree to
meet your representative for conducting talks concerning cessation
of military action and establishment of peace. We propose that the
place of meeting be in the area of Kaesong on the 38th Parallel. If
you agree, our representatives are prepared to meet your representatives between 10 and 15 July 1951. [FRUS VII 1951:612–613]

For the United States, the armistice negotiations were only alternative means to seek an honorable conclusion to the war. Therefore the UN
side, throughout the negotiations, presented its positions based on a set of
clearly defined criteria to seek honor by blaming Communists, by humiliating the rival governments, and by charging the opponent with injustice.
The UN positions were guided by the following goals:

1. A line of demarcation consistent with the UN objective of repelling
   aggression, based upon military realities and affording defensive positions for the opposing forces.
2. Other provisions offering maximum reasonable assurance against a
   renewal of the aggression.
3. Appropriate arrangements for an exchange of prisoners of war.
4. Avoidance of political issues not properly related to armistice negotiations. [Special Report by the Unified Command to United Nations,
   UN documents, A/2228, 18 October 1952:7].

All the positions were adapted to these goals with one single objective topping all other items: a cease-fire with honor, which later became a burden to the UN. In addition, the UN side decided that the fighting would continue throughout the process of negotiations (FRUS VII 1951, pt. 1:612–613). The UN would exercise military pressure against the North to reach favorable terms in negotiating agreements.

The Chinese and the North Koreans went to the negotiation table with straightforward solutions for a quick cease-fire because they believed that Kennan's suggestion was the US position, which almost satisfied the objectives of the North side. Because they lacked international negotiating experience, the CPV and DPRK team at the beginning was not fully prepared for the tricks of the US negotiators in the coming bargaining. However, when negotiators on the North side learned these tricks, they started to play tricks of their own, both at the negotiation table and on the battlefield. The original positions of the North side were as follows (Chai and Zhao 1989:141):

1. Simultaneous cease-fires by all sides.
2. Ratify the 38th parallel as the demarcation line, set up a 20-kilometer demilitarized zone (DMZ), and discuss the issue of POW exchange.
3. Withdraw all foreign forces from Korea as soon as possible.

The CPV command adopted a division of labor strategy that "those who fight fight attentively, those who negotiate negotiate patiently" (Chai and Zhao 1989:128).

10.5.1 Negotiation 1: The agenda

The opening meeting of the Korean War Armistice Negotiations was held at Kaesong on 10 July 1951. The UN team was led by US Admiral C. Turner Joy, and the North side was led by General Nam Il (DPRK Chief of Staff) and General Deng Hua (CPV Deputy Commander). With the delegates from both sides going to the negotiation table with different objectives, the negotiation on agenda became the first topic. When the UN side simply proposed a nine-point agenda without addressing solutions, the Chinese side perceived the changes in the US willingness to negotiate a cease-fire based on Kennan's proposal. The withdrawal of all foreign forces was impossible because the UN side insisted that this was a political issue and refused to discuss it in the military armistice negotiations. Therefore, the North side reformulated its positions into a five-point agenda and put a counterproposal on the negotiating table (Chai and Zhao 1989:141). The first day of the negotiations ended with no agreements.

Kaesong, which was under the control of CPV, was behind the lines on the North side. When the UN negotiators arrived, they were subjected to the CPV's security guards, making it appear that the UN team came with hat in hand to surrender. This put the UN team under psychological pressure. While the North allowed its journalists to take pictures, the UN press was barred from the negotiation location. To acquire equality, Ridgway ordered the UN team to boycott the meeting unless the North agreed to open a neutral region for negotiations and to provide equal access for journalists from both sides (FRUS VII, pt. 1:671). Believing that opening the negotiations to the press and neutrality of the meeting place were indeed essential factors for fair negotiations, Chinese Foreign Minister Zhou En-Lai instructed the negotiating team to establish a neutral region where both sides shared the duty of security; otherwise the CPV would have to bear the burden of security for the enemy's team. Therefore the North agreed on 14 July to open a five-mile-radius neutral zone covering Kaesong and to allow the UN side to bring in journalists.

On 15 July, when negotiations resumed at Kaesong, differences remained on the issue of withdrawal of foreign forces. When he talked with US Ambassador Kirk, Soviet Deputy Foreign Minister Gromyko suggested that the negotiation should be limited to military matters, thus avoiding "political or territorial" considerations, but the Chinese were not informed of this suggestion (Blair 1989:927–928). However, considering that Kennan only mentioned a "gradual" (not immediate) withdrawal of all foreign forces and that the UN side regarded the "withdrawal of foreign forces" as a matter of the related governments instead of a jurisdiction of the UN Command, the North replaced "the withdrawal of all foreign forces" with a much softer phrase: "recommendations to governments of countries concerned on both sides." The final agenda was agreed to on 27 July; it included the following (Chai and Zhao 1989:150–151):

1. Adoption of agenda.
2. Fixing of a military demarcation line between both sides to establish a demilitarized zone as a basic condition for the cessation of hostilities in Korea.
3. Concrete arrangement for the realization of cease-fire and armistice in Korea, including the composition, authority and functions of a supervisory organ for carrying out the terms of the cease-fire and armistice.

4. Arrangements relating to prisoners of war.
5. Recommendations to governments of countries concerned on both sides.

10.5.2 Negotiation 2: Demarcation line

There must be a demarcation line in any cease-fire agreement. One salient possibility was the original 38th parallel (on saliency, see Schelling 1960:110–118; Smoke 1977). However, the 38th parallel was not a natural defensive front, and its selection would imply that the CPV finished the task of restoring the peace at the status quo ante. China could use this result for propaganda purposes, and this was unacceptable to the US government.

As mentioned above, negotiating in Kaesong under the control of the enemy was uncomfortable for the UN team. Ridgway wanted Kaesong to be under UN command for four reasons:

1. Kaesong is the ancient capital of Korea, giving it symbolic significance, and its significance had been increased because of the war and the negotiations.
2. The UN had held Kaesong before the talks.
3. Kaesong is the gateway to Seoul.
4. Kaesong, located slightly below the 38th parallel, originally was under control of the ROK before the war.

To get Kaesong and open a truly neutral location, Ridgway first suggested moving the negotiations to a new neutral area, then offered a DMZ that included Kaesong, and finally planned to occupy Kaesong through military means if the enemy did not agree to move to a new place.

Being guided by these undeclared intentions, the UN exercised its military power together with a tough position at the negotiating table to seize Kaesong, but failed. This strategy, however, made the North give up its insistence on the 38th parallel as the demarcation line.

The UN delegates proposed a line that would give the UN side a territory of 12,000 square kilometers, including Kaesong, but only yield a tiny piece of indefensible hill to the North. In reply, the North rejected the UN's offer and insisted that the 38th parallel be the demarcation line as Kennan had suggested. The UN team made a "concession," in which it agreed that the width of the DMZ would be 20 kilometers rather than 20 miles, in exchange for which it hoped that the enemy would agree to its position on the truce line. This attempt failed. At the same time the North was also trying another line because the 38th parallel was not an ideal line for the North either. If the 38th parallel were agreed as the demarcation line, the CPV would have to withdraw from Kaesong because it was located south of the 38th parallel. China wanted this place to be under the control of the North as a sign of honor after the cease-fire. Therefore, the North side planned to suggest the contact line as the truce line. This offer was delayed by one incident.

On 9 August, a CPV security guard was killed by ROK soldiers in the neutral zone. In protesting the violence, the North boycotted the meeting. The UN side became angry about the bargaining because it thought the North side stopped the talks without any response to the concession. During July and August, a series of incidents occurred in the neutral zone, which brought up charges, protests, denials, investigations, and apologies one after another. The negotiations were frequently broken off by each side.

At the same time, to maintain unrelenting military pressure, the UN command launched "summer action" from 18 August to 18 September; and "fall action" from 24 September to 22 October. Both sides suffered heavy losses. In total, the UN forces incurred 60,000 casualties within this period, of which 22,000 were American. It was "the shocking number of American casualties incurred in the August and October fighting for the seemingly inconsequential ridges" that had "finally and conclusively turned most Americans against the war" (Blair 1989:950).

Being unable to gain Kaesong in the truce-line negotiation, even after the offensive, Ridgway became impatient and planned to capture Kaesong by war (FRUS VII 1951, pt. 1:811–882). Sadly enough, an unintentional UN air bombing in the Kaesong neutral zone on 10 September completely ruined his plan. Ridgway had to issue an apology, and consequently the JCS dismissed his operation of occupying Kaesong after the accident. CPV commander Peng and DPRK Commander Kim proposed resumption of talks after Ridgway's apology, but Ridgway refused to do so and reiterated his demand for a truly neutral site for negotiation. Ridgway believed that President Truman and JCS Chairman Bradley would agree with a hard-liner position in the truce-line bargaining, even if the negotiation dragged on indefinitely (FRUS VII 1951, pt. 1:1074). To the contrary, the JCS believed that keeping the negotiation going was most important and ordered him to be practical about the truce line.

After US Ambassador Kirk paid a visit on 5 October to Soviet Foreign Minister Vyshinsky to ask for help to facilitate the negotiations, Kim Il Sung and Peng Dehui agreed to open a neutral zone at Panmunjom. Both sides quickly worked out the memorandum on the regulations for the neutral zone, and the talks resumed on 25 October at the new site. But the UN team still demanded Kaesong (Chai and Zhao 1989:170–171). Rejecting the UN's offer again, on 6 November, the Chinese side suggested that the existing contact line could be the truce line, which almost matched the UN's position except at the point of Kaesong. The JCS intended to accept, but Ridgway was still reluctant. If the UN commander accepted this offer, cease-fire would come, and then the CPV and DPRK could be relaxed in their negotiations with the UN on other items of the agenda without military pressure from the UN forces (FRUS VII, pt. 1:1099).

On 8 November, in a UN General Assembly speech, Soviet Foreign Minister Vyshinsky again demanded that all military forces withdraw from the 38th parallel within 10 days after a cease-fire (FRUS VII 1951, pt. 1:1104). It seemed that the North was going to revert to the original position on the 38th parallel. The JCS pressed Ridgway to accept the offer of the contact line as the demarcation line. Under pressure, the UN team conditionally accepted the contact-line principle by putting a one-month deadline on it, valid only if agreements on all other items in the agenda would be reached by 27 December (FRUS VII 1951, pt. 1:1131). Eventually, Ridgway gave up Kaesong.

According to the contact-line principle, the area north of the 38th parallel occupied by UN forces was larger than the area to the south occupied by the Chinese and North Koreans. The UN could get a "territory-honorable" demarcation line, and China got a "place-honorable" demarcation line. However, the other two items became unexpectedly thorny.

10.5.3   Negotiation 3: Provision for enforcing armistice

The negotiations on the third item started immediately after parties agreed on the truce line. The UN side had two objectives. The first was to prevent the secret introduction of reinforcements into North Korea sufficient to overpower UN and ROK forces. Ridgway demanded severe restriction on CPV and DPRK troop rotation and free inspection to all North Korea. The second UN objective was to prevent rehabilitation of certain militarily useful facilities in North Korea, such as railroads and airfields (Blair 1989:961).

Knowing that the UN side would propose unrestricted inspections, the North side prepared a counterproposal according to which the inspections in the rear ports would be conducted by neutral countries and only the inspection in the DMZ would be performed by the joint team of the UN and the North (Chai and Zhao 1989:189). The North side focused on:

1. The procedure of withdrawal of foreign armed forces.
2. Severe restrictions on troop rotation and introduction of military equipment.
3. International inspections of these activities to ensure that no new troops and equipment be brought into Korea.

Facing the UN's hard-line position on rehabilitation of facilities, the North completely rejected the UN's proposal and insisted that reconstruction was a basic sovereign right of a nation that could not be violated. The UN team challenged the sovereignty argument by saying that the DPRK's national sovereignty had already been violated in the war and would be violated through the international inspections too, so why should the North side safeguard the right to construct airfields? The North replied that the UN's argument was the logic of US imperialism, against which the CPV and DPRK troops were fighting.

UN delegates rejected the rigid rotation restriction proposal from the North side, arguing that the UN troops would eventually disappear if no new troops could enter Korea because the US troops need frequent rotations. The Chinese side made a concession in which it was agreed that the maximum amount of rotation within one month should be 5,000.

The JCS also felt that the restriction on all civil infrastructure was too rigid and unreasonable, and ordered the UN negotiator to focus only on airfields capable of receiving jets fighters (Blair 1989:961). The restriction on jet-capable airfields was left unsettled until the end of January 1952.

10.5.4   Negotiation 4(A): Repatriation of prisoners of war

On 11 December 1951, the UN team suggested concurrent negotiation on exchange of POWs. It would have been an easy item if the US government had followed the rules established by the Geneva Convention concerning POWs. For propaganda purposes, President Truman made it more complicated by introducing the principle of voluntary repatriation.

The United States alone paid a price of 37,000 casualties to show off its ideological superiority.

Among the POWs under the custody of the UN commander, 20,500 were Chinese and 40,000 were South Koreans. The US negotiation team presented two arguments for voluntary repatriation. First, they claimed that some of the Chinese POWs, believed to be old KMT soldiers who had surrendered to the PLA during the Chinese Civil War, might be punished if repatriated, so they might be unwilling to return. The UN team argued that those Chinese POWs who were reluctant to return should be sent to Taiwan instead of to the mainland. Second, some of the DPRK soldiers were South Koreans, therefore they should be reclassified without repatriation because they had the right to stay on in their own homeland instead of going to North Korea again.

If some of the "volunteers" really refused to return to the control of Communists, then the United States would gain some credit in the propaganda game and would also achieve the purpose of humiliating the Chinese government. Repatriation of POWs became an issue of psychological warfare. Moreover, retaining the POWs was both a way for South Korea to expand its manpower in the armed forces and a way for the KMT government in Taiwan to get back part of its forces lost in the civil war.

The principle of humanitarian mediation sounded reasonable, but the voluntary repatriation was controversial. Ridgway strongly opposed voluntary repatriation by arguing that it was illegal to effectuate and would be unacceptable to the Communists. However, Truman insisted that the voluntary repatriation should be the essential condition for the armistice; "This is not a point for bargaining" (Blair 1989:961).

The UN delegates did not reveal their voluntary repatriation position when they discussed the POW item at the beginning. The UN delegates suggested an exchange of the lists of POWs and a visit by the International Red Cross to POW camps of both sides. On 18 December 1951, both sides presented their lists. The UN list had 132,474 names, of which 95,531 were DPRKs and 20,700 CPVs. The list of the North had 11,559 names, of which 7,142 were ROK and 4,417 non-ROK, including 3,198 Americans. The North side argued that the UN was withholding about 44,000 names, and the UN team argued that the North was withholding 88,000 names. Negotiations made no progress through the charges and counter-charges. The one-month deadline passed (27 December). Fortunately, both sides ignored it and continued their talks.

On 2 January 1952, the UN side added "fair and equal exchange" to "voluntary repatriation," whereby each side would exchange the same number of POWs. Because the UN was holding many more POWs than the Communist side, the UN side could get all their POWs back and still keep a large number of POWs. The Chinese delegates rejected it by charging it as "slave trade" and stated that POWs should be repatriated on the all-for-all principle laid down in the Geneva Convention (Chai and Zhao 1989:213).

To sell the offer of voluntary repatriation, the UN side softened its position on the jet-capable airfields and minimized the number (16,000) of POWs whom the UN would not repatriate. The North felt comfortable and implicitly agreed to a screening of POWs in UN custody. On 19 April the UN team reported that a total of about 70,000 POWs would not return to the North. The CPV and DPRK negotiators felt they had been cheated by the UN team, and walked out. The negotiations broke up indefinitely.

To charge the UN side with being inhumane in the war and lying in the POW screening, the governments of the PRC, the DPRK and the USSR launched a series of propaganda offensives against the UN command. First, after Soviet UN Delegate Malik on 2 February 1952 accused the United States of firing "toxic-gas" bullets, China and North Korea charged that US air and artillery forces had fired bacteria-infected insects into North Korea. Later 38 US pilots in Chinese captivity confessed that they had done that. These attacks, together with demonstrations all over the world, successfully damaged the image of the United States and won sympathy from neutral countries.

Second, to counteract the voluntary repatriation supported by the UN, the North persuaded some UN POWs to refuse repatriation. Third, the POWs under UN custody were organized together to resist screening. Riots occurred in camps on Koje Island. On 12 May, POWs captured the American POW camp commander, Brigadier General F.T. Dodd, tried him, and sentenced him to death. Dodd signed a document in which he agreed to cease torture and mass murder of POWs, to halt the illegal voluntary repatriation program, and to stop forcible screening of POWs. This event brought the voluntary repatriation principle into question.

Both sides firmly insisted on the positions they proposed in the negotiations; therefore, no concession was made. Fighting revived on 18 September when the CPV–DPRK started their offensive to exert military pressure against the UN command (Chai and Zhao 1989:241–243). On 8 October, the UN adjourned armistice negotiations indefinitely until the CPV–DPRK either accepted voluntary exchanges or made a suitable counteroffer, and a week later the UN attacked the CPV–DPRK positions. On 17 October, Kim Il Sung and Peng Dehui suggested the negotiation be reopened, but the UN refused. The Korean War Armistice Negotiations went into deadlock for six months.

10.5.5 Negotiation 5: Recommendation for political conference

Without reaching the agreement on POW repatriation, the negotiations on other items still made progress. The discussion of "recommendation for political conference" began on 6 February 1952. This was a post-armistice issue, and both sides put less effort in addressing it. For the United States, the real need was to stay in the Korean Peninsula to deter possible future attack from the North. Before the cease-fire, the UN negotiator insisted that the armistice was only a military cease-fire negotiation and had nothing to do with such political issues as withdrawal of foreign troops and unification of Korea. The US government had no interest in holding a political conference to discuss the unification of Korea. The UN side tried to substitute the term "political means" for "political conference" to avoid any obligation to hold a conference after the armistice.

For China, any political conference on the unification of Korea would offer a forum to urge withdrawal of United States forces; at least China could use the conference to show moral support to its neighbor and to keep lip-service pressure on the United States. On 16 February, the UN side backed down and agreed that "a political conference on a higher level of both sides be held by representatives appointed respectively to settle through negotiation the question of withdrawal of all foreign forces from Korea, the peaceful settlement of the Korean question, etc." (Article IV of the Armistice Agreement).

10.5.6 Negotiation 4(B): Repatriation of prisoners of war

After the armistice negotiations terminated and fighting revived, the UN General Assembly began to debate the Korean question in November 1952. USSR Foreign Minister Vyshinsky urged the General Assembly to create a special committee to settle the Korean question. The United States maintained its stance on voluntary repatriation of POWs. On 17 November, Indian delegate V.K. Menon introduced a compromise

truce plan that included a Repatriation Committee and a free POW decision, without constraint, on repatriation (*New York Times*, 18 November
1952:1). Both China and the United States were dissatisfied with the Indian proposal. However, knowing that China would definitely reject the
proposal, Acheson declared that the United States government would support the Indian resolution if it were revised. Menon revised the plan on 26
November; the amendments allowed that the UN had final jurisdiction on
POW repatriation. Ninety days after the armistice, a higher-level political conference would make the decision on repatriation for the remaining
POWs; 30 days later, all remaining POWs would be adopted by the UN.
On 2 December, the UN General Assembly passed this resolution. Zhou
En-Lai rejected it on 15 December.

At the end of 1952, President Truman was under heavy criticism for
being unable to win or to end the Korean War. By pledging "I shall go
to Korea," Dwight Eisenhower won the presidential election. Returning
from a three-day tour in Korea, President-elect Eisenhower believed that
there could be no positive and definite victory without enlarging the war.
On 2 February 1953, in his first State of the Union address, Eisenhower
ended "neutralization" of the Taiwan Strait, allowing the KMT forces on
Taiwan to attack the mainland of China if the KMT dared to.

Both the military pressure and the UN resolution made no progress
on the issue of POW repatriation. The Chinese negotiators reckoned that
the UN side probably would send out some message to resume the negotiation, but they did not know what the UN side would do (Chai and Zhao
1989:256).

On 22 February, the new UN commander, Gen. Mark Clark, suggested that sick and wounded POWs be repatriated first, with or without
an armistice agreement. The Chinese side interpreted this as a willingness to resume negotiation without saying so directly. The Chinese side
considered it was necessary to save the face of the superpower. Therefore,
the Chinese unambiguously suggested resumption of the negotiations and
prepared to make a fundamental concession on the POW repatriation issue. With Stalin's death on 14 March 1953, the Chinese response was
delayed for two weeks for the USSR, PRC, and DPRK government to
readjust their coordination. On 28 March, Peng and Kim accepted the
UN proposal to discuss the exchange of sick and wounded prisoners of
war and also suggested that the negotiation be resumed at Panmunjom.
On 30 March, Zhou En-Lai suggested that those POWs who wanted to
return be repatriated immediately after the cease-fire and the other POWs

be transferred to the custody of neutral nations. India, Poland, and the Soviet Union supported the initiative by the Chinese. On 18 April, the UN Assembly passed the Brazilian proposal that the wounded POWs be exchanged first and the negotiation be resumed at Panmunjom (*New York Times*, 19 April 1953:3).

The exchange of sick and wounded prisoners – "Operation Little Switch" – was conducted from 20 April to 3 May, and on 26 April negotiations resumed at Panmunjom. On 7 May, the Chinese and North Koreans accepted a UN proposal that prisoners unwilling to be repatriated be kept in neutral custody in Korea rather than removed to a neutral nation. China offered a counterproposal that a period of time was necessary to explain the measures before the voluntary repatriation, claiming that voluntary repatriation would be a coercive action for the UN to keep POWs in South Korea.

Because the UN was part of the negotiations, it could not be the supervisory organ. Four neutral countries had to be selected as the supervisory organ, which the United States and the UN could not totally control. The United States wanted this organization to be as weak as possible. At last, each side selected two countries, and agreed to Czechoslovakia, Poland, Sweden, and Switzerland as the members of the supervisory commission. As to the decision-making rule by majority (where each side has a veto) or by unanimity (where each side has a veto) – the former is an action-accomplishing rule, the latter a damage-limiting rule – the United States preferred unanimity, and the North agreed.

To continue military pressure, UN air forces launched a massive bombing campaign to destroy the earthen irrigation dams and flood the rice paddies (because there were no other objects worth bombing) when the UN team on 13 May proposed that all Korean POWs who were not repatriated after armistice be immediately released as civilians. The Chinese and North Korean team rejected it. On the same day, the CPV and DPRK launched a strong offensive along the entire contact line, the UN forces withdrew from several hilltops, and the CPV advanced their front to Kumsong. On 8 June, the UN side gave up the demand of releasing Korean POWs, and agreement was reached on the prisoner of war issue (Chai and Zhao 1989:262–265).

From the beginning of the talks, South Korean President Syngman Rhee had opposed the cease-fire. When the UN and the CPV–DPRK reached tentative agreement, the South Korean National Assembly unanimously rejected the truce terms on 9 June. On orders from President

Rhee, approximately 27,000 North Korean prisoners were freed on 18 June and returned to civilian life in South Korea. The Chinese and North Koreans accused the UN command of complicity in freeing of prisoners and suspended truce talks on 20 June. The US Assistant Secretary of State for the Far East, Walter Robertson, went to Seoul to persuade Rhee to accept the cease-fire. The US government promised to supply economic and military aid to South Korea, and in exchange, South Korea agreed to implement the armistice agreement. While the United States was offering benefits to Rhee, the Chinese and North Korean army launched its heaviest offensive against ROK troops in the eastern sector on 14 June and again on 13 July. Interestingly, the UN forces stood aside without protecting the ROK troops. President Rhee was brought into line by carrots from the United States and sticks from the CPV.

On 27 July, DPRK and CPV representative Nam Il and UN representative William W. Harrison signed the Korean War Armistice Agreement at Panmunjom. Later DPRK Commander Kim Il Sung, CPV Commander Peng Dehui, and UN Joint Force Commander Mark Clark signed the agreement in their respective headquarters. The Korean War ended at 11 p.m. on 27 July 1953. To this day, no formal peace treaty has been established by the parties.

10.6   Conclusion

Within the Korean War, there were four wars: a Korean civil war, a war to contain the expansion of Communism, a war to resist American imperialism, and a war for an honorable cease-fire. Although the United States and China confronted each other militarily in Korea, the war was not fought directly against one another: it was limited within Korea. Both sides had sufficient reasons to intervene. The United States went to the war to show off its prestige as the leader of the free world, the PRC went to safeguard its border security.

"During the three years of the Korean War, the total number of CPV forces deployed was more than 2–3 million troops, including 66% of the entire field army, 62% of all artillery divisions, 100% of all tank divisions, and 70% of the entire air force that the People's Republic of China had at that time. The total casualties of the CPV in the Korean War were 360,000, excluding 20,000 people captured by the United Nations force" (Hao and Zhao 1989:114).

Americans paid an equivalent price to the Korean War. The total American casualties were 157,530, of which 54,246 were dead and 103,284 wounded. "The cost of the last two years of the talking war, in order to fix the DMZ at line Kansas, to guarantee former enemies freedom of choice of repatriation, and to effect the release of 12,773 surviving UN POWs (including 3,597 Americans) was especially dear: 63,000 American causalities alone" (Blair 1989:976).

North Korea's successful attack on South Korea, which was a US ally, strongly undermined the US national interests in the dimensions of both self-pride and ideology-superiority, and it induced a strong reaction from the United States. The US actions of both crossing the 38th parallel and neutralizing the Taiwan Strait damaged China's national interest in the dimension of national security, and in turn induced China to intervene in the Korean War. Facing a potential Soviet threat in Europe, the United States perceived a high opportunity cost of engaging China in the Korean War, for the United States needed the resources to safeguard its security interest in Europe. Although the United States was a high-capability state, the high opportunity cost cooled its will to commit more resources into the Korean War. The US Joint Chief of Staffs, General Omar Bradley branded the war as "the wrong war, at the wrong place, at the wrong time, and with the wrong enemy" (Bradley 1983:640).[5] Although China was a low-capability state during the 1950s, the stake to safeguard the national security was so high that China possessed the strong will to commit more resources into the Korean War. These two opposing asymmetries made the two sides into a pair of symmetric high powers.

While power was matched in the stalemate and both parties' intentions for peace were clear, what was left for the parties to pursue was honor and justice. Facing the strongest army of the world, the PRC recaptured almost all the territory to North Korea (this was not the territory of China); therefore any agreement on a cease-fire near the 38th parallel was honorable to China. The United States successfully contained the expansion of communists; by beating DPRK back to the 38th parallel, occupying more territory, and building up a defensible demarcation line, the United States showed that it was the credible leader of the free world.

China successfully maintained a buffer zone by fighting against UN troops. The Korean War Armistice Agreement was the first equal agreement signed between China and the Western countries. Given that, during the wars in the century from the Opium War to the 1940s, all the treaties signed between China and the Western countries were unequal, the cease-fire brought glory to the Chinese people. China showed the whole world that the Chinese were able to stand up for their own fate and had a voice in international affairs. Already gaining these honors, the Chinese side gave up almost all the proposed principles in the armistice negotiations, but the American side still needed relatively favorable terms to compensate for the prestige lost in the war. Therefore, the UN side stuck to its principles throughout the negotiations. These stubborn decisions for political honor caused the Korean War to last longer than expected.

Notes

[1] The 38th parallel as the demarcation line in General Order 1 was approved on 15 August 1945 by US President Harry Truman and later cleared with the British and Soviet governments (Appleman 1961:3).

[2] The PRC government believed that the US military action both on Taiwan Island and Taiwan Strait was a direct intervention in the Chinese Civil War, an aggression to Chinese territory.

[3] The United States and China had no formal diplomatic relations; China could only deliver messages through a third party or through public announcements.

[4] UN Security Resolution 7 October 1950.

[5] General Bradley, speaking for the Joint Chiefs in his famous "wrong war" statement, pointed out:

> ... From a global viewpoint ... our military mission is to support a policy of preventing Communism from gaining the manpower, the resources, the raw materials, and the industrial capacity essential to world domination. ...
>
> Korea must be looked upon with proper perspective. It is just one engagement, just one phase. ... As long as we keep the conflict within its present scope we are holding to a minimum the forces we must commit and tie down. The strategic alternative, enlargement of the war in Korea to include Red China, would probably delight the Kremlin more than anything else we could do. It would necessarily tie down additional forces, especially our sea power and our air power, while the Soviet Union would not be obliged to put a single man into the conflict. ...
>
> Red China is not the powerful nation seeking to dominate the world. Frankly, in the opinion of the Joint Chiefs of Staff, this strategy would involve us in the wrong war, at the wrong place, at the wrong time, and with the wrong enemy. [Bradley 1983:640]

Bibliography

Acheson, D., 1971, *The Korean War*, W.W. Norton, New York.

Ambekar, G.V., and Divekar, V.D., 1964, *Documents on China's Relations with South and Southeast Asia (1949–1962)*, Allied Publishers Private Ltd., New Delhi, India.

Appleman, R.E., 1961, *The US Army in the Korean War*, Office of Military History, United States Army, Washington, DC.

Blair, C., 1989, *The Forgotten War*, Doubleday, New York.

Bradley, O.N., 1983, *A General's Life*, Simon and Schuster, New York.

Chai, C., and Zhao, Y., 1989, *Panmunjom Negotiations*, PLA Press, Beijing, People's Republic of China.

Clark, M., 1954, *From the Danube to the Yalu*, Harper, New York.

Council on Foreign Relations, *The United States in World Affairs 1950, 1951, 1952, 1953*, Council on Foreign Relations, New York.

Cummings, B., ed., 1983, *Child of Conflict: The Korean–American Relationship, 1943–1953*, University of Washington Press, Seattle, WA.

Foot, R., 1988, *The Wrong War*, Cornell University Press, Ithaca, NY.

FRUS (Foreign Relations of the United States) VII, 1951, Part I.

Gardner, R., 1972, *The Korean War*, Quadrangle, New York.

Goodman, A, 1978, *Negotiating While Fighting*, Hoover, Stanford, CA.

Goodrich, L., 1956, *Korea: A Study of U.S. Policy in the United Nations*, Council on Foreign Relations Inc., New York.

Hao, Y., and Zhai, Z., 1990, China's decision to enter the Korean War: History revisited, *China Quarterly*, **121**(March).

Hermes, W.G., 1988, *The United States Army in the Korean War: Truce Tent and Fighting Front*, Office of Military History, United States Army, Washington, DC.

Joy, C.T., 1955, *How Communists Negotiate*, Macmillan, New York.

Leckie, R., 1962, *The Korean War*, Barrie and Rockliff with Pall Mall Press, London.

MacArthur, D., 1950, Special Communiqué, Military Situation in the Far East: Hearing before the Committee on Armed Services and the Committee on Foreign Relations, U.S. Senate, 82nd Congress, 1st Session.

MacDonald, C.A., 1986, *Korea: The War Before Vietnam*, The Free Press, New York.

Morgenthau, H., 1954, *Politics Among Nations*, Knopf, New York.

Nan Xiang [Xiao Shizhong], 1997, *The Modern China's Famous Campaigns and Battles*, Volume 11, Book 5 of the Series for Future Military Scientists, Yellow River Press, Jinan, Shandong Province, People's Republic of China.

New York Times, 1950, 1 December.

New York Times, 1952, 18 November, 1:2.

New York Times, 1953, 19 April, 3:1,3.

New York Times, 1992, 26 February, Mao's telegram to Zhou En-Lai.

Paschall, R., 1995, *Witness to War in Korea*, Berkeley Publishing Group, New York.

Pillar, P., 1988, *Negotiating Peace*, Princeton University Press, Princeton, NJ.

Ridgway, M.B., 1967, *The Korean War*, Doubleday, Garden City, NY.

Schelling, T., 1960, *The Strategy of Conflict*, Harvard University Press, Cambridge, MA.

Smoke, R., 1977, *War*, Harvard University Press, Cambridge, MA.

Sneider, D., 1993, Archives revise Cold-War history, *The Christian Science Monitor*, 20 January.

United Nations, 1948, General Assembly Resolution 195(III), 12 December, New York.

United Nations, 1950a, Security Council, Official Records, Document S/1501, 473rd Meeting, 25 June, New York.

United Nations, 1950b, Security Council, Official Records, 474th Meeting, 27 June, New York.

United Nations, 1950c, UN Security Resolution, 7 October, New York.

United Nations, 1952, Special Report by the Unified Command to the United Nations, Document A/2228, 18 October, New York.

Vatcher, W., 1958, *Panmunjom*, Praeger, New York.

Whiting, A.S., 1960, *China Crosses the Yalu*, Stanford University Press, Stanford, CA.

Zartman, I.W., and Berman, M., 1982, *The Practical Negotiator*, Yale University Press, New Haven, CT.

Part IV

Power and International Negotiation

Chapter 11

Lessons for Practice

Jeswald W. Salacuse

Power is an intensely practical subject for all international negotiators, who by their very missions are intensely practical persons. Diplomats, business executives, international civil servants, and other practitioners of negotiation apply power in all phases of the negotiating process. Whereas scholars seek to understand the theoretical nature, sources, and uses of power, practitioners are concerned almost exclusively with using it to achieve desired results in the negotiations that they are conducting.

For practitioners, as for scholars, negotiating power means the ability to move the decisions of the other side in a desired way. Diplomats and executives devise their strategies and tactics with this end in mind, but they hardly ever spend time searching for a theory of power. Indeed, practical negotiators are as unlikely to speculate on the nature of power as the active lawyer is to ponder the jurisprudential nature of law or the busy surgeon to contemplate the essence of human life. This neglect by practitioners of such an important element in any negotiation may limit their potential as effective practitioners of their art. Perhaps negotiators, in their training and in their preparation for specific negotiations, should spend more time explicitly considering the nature, sources, and implications of power. Perhaps an articulated theory of power would enable them not only to obtain what they want in a negotiation, but also to reach the kinds of agreements that are the most advantageous for both sides of the negotiating table. The case studies in this volume provide an opportunity for practical negotiators to deepen their understanding about the uses of power and to learn more about how best to develop and apply power in a negotiation.

Outcomes are no guide. How should one measure the respective power of the two sides in a negotiation? For example, was the United States really much more powerful than Canada during the Free Trade Agreement negotiations? In the case of the Korean War armistice negotiations, both parties had "high power" in the war; however, a comparison of the relative power of the two sides just prior to the outbreak of the conflict would have found the United States – and the United Nations – immensely more powerful than China. What is clear in most cases is that at the outset of the negotiation, one side was *perceived* to be more powerful than the other because of the disparity in resources that each possessed. Thus, the United States was certainly more powerful than Canada when one compared the vastly different sizes of the American and Canadian economies; India had much more power than Nepal when one weighed the relative sizes of their populations, land areas, and armed forces; and the US economy and military gave the United States power far in excess of what China appeared to possess. But as the case studies show, the party that appeared weaker at the outset of each case was able to augment its power in the actual negotiations.

Generally, the party most preoccupied with power in a negotiation is the side that perceives itself to be weaker – an evaluation that is usually made by comparing the two sides' aggregate resources, rather than their individual power with respect to particular issues under discussion. Like the rich who take their wealth for granted, the stronger side in a negotiation often does not think much about power because power is something it already has. On the other hand, the failure of the stronger side to examine its power in a rational and systematic way may make it less wise in the use of the resources that it has. For example, through its words and actions, it may communicate in provocative and arrogant ways – ways that antagonize the other side, make the other side defensive, and in the end impede the negotiation and reduce its ability to move the other party. Thus, Indonesia's perception of the United States as a powerful adversary,

Nepal's offense at India's domineering ways, and China's and the United States' sensitivities to each other's overbearing manner inhibited negotiations over the embargoes, dams, and cease-fires, respectively. The strong powers would have done better by being more gentle in their strength.

Reading the cases in this collection is an exercise in optimism. For the most part, they renew one's faith in the ability of the underdog to deal with a powerful adversary. Although the cases offer many lessons, perhaps they teach one fundamental lesson above all others: A less powerful party in an international negotiation is not necessarily at the mercy of a more powerful party. Often the less powerful party is able to gain more from the stronger side than one assumes is probable at the outset of the negotiation. The cases teach us that the weaker side is generally more powerful than it appears at first glance and that the more powerful side is often weaker than it first assumes. In addition, they demonstrate consistently that the aggregate resources of each side are not a good predictor of the results in a particular negotiation. More important than aggregate power in predicting outcomes are the resources that a particular side can bring to bear on the issues in a given negotiation (issue power) and the skill and will with which a party applies its resources to the negotiating process. Thus, behavior or bargaining power is indeed the action by which one party seeks to move the other.

The weaker party in an international negotiation can augment its power through skillful tactics, resource mobilization, third parties, and a variety of other devices. Consequently, when less powerful parties are confronted by the seemingly vast resources on the other side of the bargaining table, they must remember that their own negotiating resources include their own skill and will, and that in most cases competent negotiators can find tactics and strategies to improve results. The strong also have much to learn from this examination of power. The case studies in this volume thus offer practical lessons for both the weak and the strong.

11.1 Lessons for the Weak

How were the parties that appeared to be weak at the outset of negotiation able to achieve a more balanced result? In explaining this phenomenon, the cases provide some important lessons for the weak.

Lesson 1: To increase your power, build relationships with appropriate third parties.

The case studies clearly show that one of the most effective ways for a weaker party to increase its power at the negotiating table is to build supportive relationships with strong third parties who are not at the table. In most cases, a strong third party means one who has influence over your adversary in the negotiation. Mali's strong relations with France, Senegal, and the Ivory Coast gave it power to achieve a favorable end to the conflict with Burkina Faso in a way that its army and economy alone could not. Similarly, the ability of Arabs and Israelis to achieve gains in their various negotiations has depended on the strength of their respective relationships with the United States. A pervading lesson is that in negotiation, as in other exercises in politics, your amount of power depends on who your friends are.

But who is an appropriate third party? The choice of a third party must be made carefully. In particular, the weaker side should ask, What interests does the third party have in becoming involved? How might those interests affect the weaker party's interests? How might the third party influence the decisions of the other side in the negotiation? As was pointed out in the EC–Andorra case, if a party is too weak, a desired independent state or organization may see no benefit from a relationship with it and will therefore avoid becoming involved. Even worse is to select a third party who has much to gain by intervening, as Lebanon learned to its sorrow when, during its civil war, the Maronite government invited Syria, who had long sought a role in Lebanese affairs, to intervene. The Syrians did so and have remained in Lebanon to pursue their own interests.

Yet no third party is an altruist. Third parties always pursue their own interests even when they claim only to work on behalf of the parties, and the pursuit of those interests may complicate and even obstruct the negotiation process. Having many friends involved in a negotiation may pressure an adversary; however, too many states in a negotiation may serve to preserve weaknesses and complicate the search for power. Thus, in the UNCED process the fact that the South comprised many states with such diverse interests inhibited its ability to augment power in its negotiations with the group of industrialized states from the North.

In choosing an appropriate third party with which to seek a relationship, the weaker side has basically three options: a friend of the other side, an adversary of the other side, or an independent (preferably strong) neutral. These cases demonstrate advantages and disadvantages of all three options.

Probably the option with the greatest risk is the selection of an ally who is an adversary of the other side. This choice may indeed sometimes wring concessions from the stronger side, but it may also provoke the stronger party's hostility and increase its determination to dominate the weaker side because it now faces what it considers to be a threat, not just an apparently small conflict that is easily handled. Whereas Mali used its relationships with strong allies to good advantage, Burkina Faso sought to augment its power through a relationship with Libya and with Nigeria. That was a poor choice because not only did Libya and Nigeria prove unhelpful, but the threat of their presence in French-speaking West Africa served to coalesce other African states into opposing Burkina Faso. On the other hand, raising the specter of a competitor, without actually involving it in the conflict, can be an effective form of influence as it was for Nepal in its relations with India and for Indonesia in its negotiations with the United States. For Nepal or Indonesia to have actually become allied with adversaries of parties on the other side of the bargaining table might have resulted in unpleasant consequences for both states.

A friend of the other side is the most appropriate third party, provided the friend does not merely seek to hand over the weaker party to the adversary. Getting the adversary's friend involved in the process harnesses the friend's interest in an agreement, which can then be used to extract concessions from the adversary as the price of the agreement. Sadat, in the classical example, borrowed Israel's friend, the United States, with the promise of an agreement and got it to help win concessions from the adversary. The United States even invoked the USSR's good offices on a few occasions to help move China and North Korea along toward agreement or at least to return to negotiations. This strategy is not without risks, however. Egypt made major concessions to get a US-mediated agreement. After all, the friend of the adversary is only as useful as its friendship can bear and as its interest in an agreement can support.

The third option, an independent neutral, can also be helpful as a friend of the weaker party if the latter feels that its cause can be furthered by impartiality and justice. Because power often serves as a "corrective" to justice, a neutral third party is often useful but its sense of justice, out of many possible interpretations, must fit the notions of the weaker party. The International Court of Justice's findings favored neither Mali nor Burkina Faso, and the United States, stronger or weaker, was wary of neutral determinations of POW destinations. Arbitration by a neutral is not negotiation, and weaker parties often enjoy the help of neutrals but like to use their own skills in negotiation.

And what is an appropriate relationship? A further lesson from the cases is that weak parties must not only choose their friends with care but also be cautious in determining the precise kind of relationship they will build with third parties. The problem with applying this lesson in practice is that the weak, by nature, usually have few potential friends to choose from. Andorra, for example, really had only two options: France or Spain. Any effort by Andorra to build a relationship with another significant power, such as the United Kingdom or Germany, would have been rebuffed and, perhaps, even ridiculed.

As the cases indicate, even though a negotiation appears to be bilateral, it always has the possibility of involving other parties, directly or indirectly. Weak parties in bilateral negotiations build their power by breaking the bilateral framework and seeking to build relationships with other parties. On the other hand, it is generally in the interest of the strong to maintain the bilateral framework to keep itself and its weaker adversary enclosed in a dyadic mold.

Lesson 2: The importance of power in negotiation may not be so much its reality as its perception.

Because power for the practitioner is the ability to move the other side's decisions in a desired direction, it is important to understand how the other side perceives and evaluates the events and actions relating to the negotiation. One must look to the perceptions both of the weaker side and of the stronger side, the perceptions of each of its own power and of the other side's power. For example, at the outset of the Korean War, the United States, and particularly General Douglas MacArthur, perceiving China through the lens of conventional military assessment, underestimated the power of that country and especially its will to defeat what it perceived as a threat to Chinese sovereignty. Indonesia, viewing the world through ardent nationalism, saw the United States as a potential threat to its recent, hard-won independence. Each party brings its own set of lenses – its prejudices, assumptions, and desires – to the negotiating table, and those lenses may prevent it from objectively evaluating the nature and extent of its own and the other's power.

Because culture always influences perceptions, differences in culture – a factor constantly present in international negotiations – can affect power. Culture affects how words and behavior are communicated and how messages are interpreted. One culture may interpret certain phenomena as indications of power, but another may not. For example, as was shown in the Mali–Burkina Faso case, age augments power in Africa. Houphouët-Boigny, the most senior African head of state, brought great influence to the negotiation because of his age, whereas Sankara's youth reduced his influence. One may compare this case to the American perception that a youthful president, such as John F. Kennedy, was a vigorous and therefore a powerful leader. Nikita Khrushchev, in his famous confrontation with Kennedy over Berlin in 1961, probably viewed the young American president through a Ukrainian cultural lens: a rich, spoiled, inexperienced, womanizing young man, who had been politically wounded by the Bay of Pigs fiasco. In short, Khrushchev saw Kennedy as weak and treated him accordingly.

Lesson 3: Aggregate power is not as important as issue-specific power in a given negotiation.

Nearly all the case studies indicate that the perceived weaker party often does better in the negotiation than one would expect at first glance. The reason for this initial erroneous assumption is that first judgments of relative power are made on the basis of each party's *aggregate power*. At the beginning of a negotiation, it is the relative total power of each side that attracts attention. Thus, the United States seemed far more powerful than either Egypt or Indonesia at the outset of their respective negotiations, and the United States was obviously more powerful than Canada when the Free Trade Agreement talks began. But a negotiation is about specific issues and interests, and the crucial power question for each side is, What resources and devices will influence the other side on the specific issues under discussion? In the Andorra–EC case, France, despite greater size and wealth, had relatively few resources that would compel little Andorra to introduce progressive social legislation. Negotiation, however, is a learning experience. As the negotiation progresses, the parties begin to learn what specific resources will influence the other side on a given issue – something that they might have tried to foresee at the outset of their discussions.

Lesson 4: Getting the stronger side's attention at the highest level is often a first step to increasing power.

As the case on the Canada–US Free Trade Agreement shows, it was important for Canada to gain the attention of US political leadership to increase Canadian power in the negotiation.

Lack of attention by the stronger party is often a statement that it does not consider the other side particularly powerful or significant. Such lack of attention may manifest itself in many ways, but it is almost always demonstrated by entrusting the negotiations to relatively low-level officials who have circumscribed authority and limited access to their country's political leadership. Both Canada and Andorra faced this problem in their respective negotiations.

The tactics of attention-getting may include stalling and walking out of the negotiations. In the Canada–US Free Trade Agreement talks, Canada walked out when they felt that the United States was not taking the negotiations seriously. This action provoked a diplomatic crisis between the two long-time allies and succeeded in getting US attention, which led to high-level American participation in the negotiations. Canada augmented its power by playing on the historically strong relationship between the two countries.

But walking out may not always bring that result. Indeed, it carries significant risks. Had a country of less importance to the United States than Canada walked out of negotiation, it is doubtful that such action would have had the same effect as it did in the Free Trade Agreement talks. Consequently, the particular power tactics used by a weaker party in a negotiation depend on the whole network of relationships that exists between it and its stronger counterpart.

In a similar vein, Andorra, dissatisfied with dealing with low-level French diplomats, got France's attention by trying to act as a state and by stirring anti-French feelings in the Andorran population. In the end, Andorra got the attention of the French president and no longer had to deal with the French bureaucracy exclusively. This tactic of going over the head of the other side's designated negotiators also has risks; if the tactic fails, the weaker side is then required to continue to deal with those same negotiators, who are now likely to be hostile because their authority and status have been challenged.

Lesson 5: The stronger side's size and complexity offers opportunities for increasing power in the negotiation.

The stronger side gains its power from the magnitude and diversity of its resources; however, its large size usually means that it has many interests and relationships to manage and many internal constituencies to hold together. The multiplicity of those interests, relationships, and constituencies can create opportunities for the weaker side to augment its power at the bargaining table. For example, divisions over policy within the stronger party's organization, as was the case between US Secretary of State John Foster Dulles and Secretary of the Treasury George M. Humphrey over aid to Indonesia, can be exploited by the weaker side to increase its leverage in the negotiations. Then too, the many obligations of the stronger side, as was the case with the American commitment to European defense during the Korean War, may limit the amount of resources it can devote to other negotiations and conflicts. On the other hand, the weaker side, often being smaller, with fewer external relationships and fewer internal constituencies to satisfy, is able to devote more attention and resources to the negotiation, a factor which is to its distinct advantage. In the Canada–US Free Trade Agreement talks, Canada increased its negotiating power by having a clear plan and by linking the negotiations directly with the highest levels of the Canadian government.

Lesson 6: Positions taken by the stronger party in other arenas can sometimes be used to increase power in a given negotiation.

In negotiations and in other general dealings, powerful states usually clothe their positions in a doctrine or rationale. Rarely do they justify their demands on the basis of naked power alone. Indeed, powerful actors generally try to give the impression that they have an obligation to be generous to those who have much less power than they. These doctrinal justifications and public postures can become self-imposed constraints on power when that doctrine is applied in other circumstances. It is therefore important for the weaker side to examine these doctrines and postures carefully to see how they may be used in its negotiations with the stronger party. For example, the US-declared policy of free trade and its determined stance on that question in the GATT Uruguay Round gave Canada a lever for obtaining the Free Trade Agreement with the United States.

More generally, great powers like to appear to have a sense of responsibility toward smaller states. That sense of responsibility can sometimes be exploited by small powers in individual negotiations as was done by Indonesia and Egypt in their negotiations with the United States over aid. Indeed, a small state's vulnerability can itself be a source of power for obtaining benefits from a powerful state, as Egypt demonstrated in its talks with a United States that feared that the collapse of a weak, but friendly, Egyptian government would harm US interests in the Middle East.

Lesson 7: The power value of a specific resource changes over time, so waiting for the appropriate moment to act can increase power.

With time, specific resources of the parties can either increase in value, such as Nepal's water, or decline, such as Egypt's or Indonesia's strategic role as a bastion against the spread of communism after the end of the Cold War. The passage of time creates new opportunities for the weak party since the value of resources change and coalitions disintegrate. So Egypt's strategic value to the United States was high during the Cold War, declined with the breakup of the Soviet Union, and then rose again with the Gulf War against Iraq. Egypt's influence with the United States in aid negotiations fluctuated accordingly.

The ability to respond at crucial turning points is therefore critical for the weaker party to take advantage of these changes in circumstances. Equally important, the weaker side, like a trader in commodities or securities, must be able to understand the "market," to gauge how and to what extent changes in circumstances over time will strengthen or weaken its ability to influence the decisions of the other side. Having determined that the value of its resources will increase in time, it then has the task of convincing the other side of that particular vision of the future.

Lesson 8: Power can be augmented by taking initiatives in negotiation.

By making proposals to which the other side has to respond, the weaker side can influence the course of the negotiations. Thus, Canada took the initiative from the very beginning of the Free Trade Agreement talks, and this approach contributed significantly to its success. The United States' previous hard line on international free trade at the GATT Uruguay Round buttressed Canada in making this initiative. The fact that the weaker side has fewer internal constituencies to manage and fewer external relationships to satisfy may facilitate formulating and advancing such definite initiatives. On the other hand, developing serious initiatives often requires a commitment of resources, particularly human resources, and it is in this area that weak states are often seriously deficient. Nepal suffered from this deficiency in its negotiation with India. It did not have enough sufficiently trained personnel to negotiate complex agreements skillfully and confidently with its Indian neighbor. Developing countries, with few trained negotiators, have the same sort of difficulty in their dealings with large states and multinational corporations. Consequently, rather than taking initiatives in negotiations, they are usually in the weaker position of having to respond to proposals put forward by more powerful states in the form of their "model treaties," "prototype agreements," and "standard form contracts."

Lesson 9: Power can be increased by understanding and exploiting the international context in which the negotiation is taking place.

The parties to an international negotiation are not totally independent entities; rather they are integral parts of the international system, a system that is in constant change. As the case study on Arab–Israeli negotiations rightly points out, all negotiations between two parties either involve or have the potential to involve other parties. In this sense, there are few strictly bilateral negotiations. The international context in which states must operate can influence decisions in individual negotiations. Consequently, it is important for weak states to understand that context and to seek to exploit it to their advantage. In virtually all of the cases, the weaker parties took this approach with varying degrees of success. Thus, Indonesia, China, and Egypt all sought to exploit the US–Soviet competition in their negotiations with the United States. In its trade talks with the American government, Canada took advantage of the US commitment to free trade and its concern over Japanese trade practices and the creation of the new single market by the European Community.

Lesson 10: Power can be increased to the extent that you can foster in the leadership of the stronger side an increased commitment to a negotiated settlement of the dispute.

Political leaders pursue their own interests as well as their nations' interests. To the extent that leaders of strong states in negotiations become convinced that a negotiated settlement of a dispute is important for their country, for their political future, or for their place in history, such increased commitment serves to enhance the power of the weaker side. When Canada walked out of the Free Trade Agreement negotiations and thereby placed US–Canada relations in a state of crisis, Secretary of State James Baker became actively concerned about placing those relations on a better foundation by reaching a settlement. The French president's commitment to reach an agreement over Andorra also strengthened the principality's position. The extent of commitment of the stronger side to a negotiated solution (as opposed to mere domination or doing nothing) can be a factor that strengthens the weaker side. As a result, it is important for the weaker party in a negotiation to determine how committed the leadership of the other side is to reaching an agreement and to find ways to heighten the intensity of that commitment.

11.2   Lessons for the Strong

The case studies in this volume on asymmetrical international negotiation also offer lessons for the stronger party on the uses of power. Many lessons, it is true, are simply the reverse of the lessons for the weak. For example, the stronger side should try to inhibit the weaker side from bringing third parties into the negotiation or should make sure that the third party works to achieve an agreement, not to extract concessions from the strong. The strong can gain an advantage by understanding the various strategies and tactics that the weak may employ in an effort to augment their power. But in addition, these case studies yield some lessons that are specifically tailored for the strong.

Lesson 1: Carefully analyze the nature and the sources of power in the negotiation.

Normally, it is the weaker side, confronted with what appears to be the stronger side's overwhelming resources, that analyzes the negotiation in terms of power. If the stronger side thinks about power at all, it is usually to assume that it is more powerful and therefore does not have to be concerned with the question of power in the negotiation in any depth. The information that emerges from the case studies is that the stronger side should not take its power for granted, but rather should analyze and study it carefully. In particular it should ask what its sources of power are in this particular negotiation or dispute, rather than merely calculate its total resources. Had the United States objectively examined this question at the outset of the conflict in Vietnam, which President Lyndon Johnson labeled a "piss-ant country," and had France asked the same question at the outset of the war in Algeria, which the French mistakenly considered a part of France, neither country might have wasted the lives and resources that it did in the two wars.

Power – or action to move the other side's decisions in a desired way – can emanate from a variety of sources. It can arise from the strength of a party's commitment to attain a particular result (as was the case with China, Canada, and Andorra), from the resources that it is prepared to commit (as was the case with China and Canada), from the allies or third parties it can bring into the negotiation (as was the case with Mali and Egypt), from a favorable international context (as was the case with Egypt, Andorra, Mali, and the United States in Korea), and from the experience and skill of a party's own negotiators (as was the case with Canada, India, the Ivory Cost, and UNCED negotiations). Such careful analysis may give the strong side a more realistic assessment of what it can hope to achieve in the negotiation and may encourage it to seek creative solutions that will give maximum benefit to both parties.

Lesson 2: The weaker party is generally stronger than first assumed.

If the cases teach nothing else, they demonstrate that the weaker party has devices and tactics at its command to augment its power and that the stronger party usually does not fully understand or appreciate them at the outset of the negotiation. The United States did not fully appreciate the potential strength of Canada at the beginning of the Free Trade Agreement talks or of the Chinese at the outset of the Korean War. Blinded by the disparity in the two sides' power, the stronger party often does not fully examine the other side's power potential with regard to the specific issues under negotiation, and it fails to grasp the degree of commitment and priority that the weaker side has placed on achieving a particular end. For example, it was only when Canada walked out of the negotiations that the United States fully understood the importance that the Free Trade Agreement had for Canada. And it was only when Andorra began to act like a state that France realized that the problem of achieving a solution would be more difficult than it had first assumed.

In evaluating the two sides' relative negotiating strength, the stronger party should ask, How important is the desired goal to the weaker side?

What is the strength of the weaker side's commitment to achieving that goal? To make that analysis, the stronger party must first put itself in the shoes of the weaker party. Had the United States seen its offensive on the Yalu River and its protection of the Taiwan Straits through the eyes of the Chinese, it might have avoided a Chinese counterattack. Perhaps, the EC–Andorran negotiations would have proceeded more smoothly if the French initially had looked at the problem from the Andorran perspective. India might well have obtained more dams if it had taken Nepalese interests into account in the previous agreements it negotiated. Unfortunately, throughout history, strong states have been notoriously unable or unwillingly to make this kind of analysis in a realistic and hardheaded fashion in their dealings with perceived weaker powers.

Lesson 3: Use power sparingly.

The stronger side seeking to achieve an advantageous agreement in an efficient and inoffensive way should use its power sparingly. In particular, it should avoid the temptation of trying to overpower the weaker side through domineering words or actions. Such an approach creates two types of risks for the stronger party. First, behaving exploitatively and flaunting power often leads the weaker side to become defensive and cautious, or indeed to avoid making any commitments until the last possible minute. Consequently, displays of power, instead of leading to quick agreement, may stall or slow the negotiations considerably. Indonesia was clearly defensive, cautious, and unyielding in its negotiations with the United States because of the latter's status as a superpower.

Second, demonstrating and using power may indeed result in an agreement with the weaker party, but that agreement may prove unstable in the long run. Inevitably, weak states that are parties to what they consider to be unfair, imposed agreements will seek ways to avoid implementing those agreements over time and to take advantage of changed circumstances to undo them in the future. The stronger party that wants to create a long-term relationship with the weaker side should not behave exploitatively during a negotiation. Rather, it should seek to create the appearance, if not the reality, of power equality to allow the negotiations to proceed smoothly and to arrive at an agreement that will endure. Moreover, as the Nepal–India case illustrates, a weak party that believes it has been exploited by a stronger party in past negotiations will be slow and reluctant to negotiate other agreements with that same party in the future.

The strong must remember that they are in a constant process of negotiation and interaction with the weak, and it is the long-term nature of that relationship that should be kept in mind. The cases have shown conclusively that relationships matter, and act as a restraint on responsible strong-party behavior. In any given negotiation, the strong must weigh the short-term advantage to be gained through overt application of power against the long-term benefits to be derived from a productive relationship brought about through wise restraint.

11.3 Conclusion: Lessons for Others

The chapters of this volume contain many lessons for both the weak and the strong in an international negotiation, but one also finds some implicit instruction for parties not directly involved in the negotiation. Each chapter demonstrates that in an international system every negotiation may become multilateral in substance if not in form and that there are no permanent bystanders to a state's international relations. In every conflict, the potential exists for nonparticipants to become involved in what is ostensibly a bilateral problem. They become involved in a whole array of capacities – as mediators, allies, facilitators, adversaries.

Although a nation may be tempted to exploit a bilateral negotiation between two other states for its own advantage, it should also recognize that once it has willingly or unwillingly become directly or indirectly involved in the negotiation it has permanently changed the power relationship between the two original parties and that it may not be able to withdraw from the arena as easily as it entered. Indeed, withdrawing may leave all parties – the weak, the strong, and the intervenor – in a worse situation than they were in before the intervention.

Further study is needed on how third states should approach conflicts and negotiations between two other states. For the time being, perhaps the best advice to other states is that they should recognize their potential to change the power relationship in any existing dispute and that they, like the strong, should use that potential wisely and with restraint, to foster a mutually satisfactory agreement.

Chapter 12

Symmetry and Asymmetry in Negotiation

I. William Zartman and Jeffrey Z. Rubin

This study has set out to examine the structural paradox – why and how it is that weak states negotiate with strong ones when by all counts they should lose, since common wisdom has it that the stronger side wins. In so doing, it has examined an opposing (and more scientific) principle – that equals or perceived equals negotiate more productively than unequals. Contrary to received knowledge and experimentation, it appears that this is not true: perceived asymmetry is the more productive condition for negotiation, whereas perceptions of equality actually interfere with efficient processes and satisfying results. These are important findings, and they lead immediately to the equally important, operative question: How then do unequals negotiate so well?

To arrive at a conclusion, it has been necessary to determine whether perceived power inequalities between parties produce inequalities in their negotiating behavior and whether these asymmetries produce unequal negotiated results. It has also been necessary to examine whether a party's perception of its power, the target's power, or the power relation between the two is the key to understanding its behavior. Finally, this study has used diplomatic reality to test a number of experimentally derived

271

propositions, including the view that perceived equality is the best condition for productive and efficient negotiations.

Addressing issues such as these has first required a sharpening of definitions and then a look at the record. Despite the fact that the number of cases is much smaller than experimental scientists typically require, controls are nearly absent, the amount of extraneous detail is confusingly rich, and the results are less clear than might be desired, the case studies point to several important lessons.

12.1   Lessons Learned

Lesson 1: Equal power (or perceptions thereof) does not lead to more effective negotiation than unequal power.

This, of course, is in direct contradiction to proposition 1 and by extension to proposition 3. In the admittedly small (but arguably representative) number of cases used, symmetrical negotiations were notoriously contentious, inefficient, and unsatisfactory in their outcomes. The US–Chinese experience shows that in cases of equality, and indeed because of that condition, other considerations, distractions, and ideologies get in the way, making the process more protracted than ever. In this, the negotiation findings are similar to results of studies of the balance of power, which indicate that equality (or near-equality) is the most unstable condition (Bremer 1992; Geller 1993; Gochman and Sabrowski 1990; Organski 1958:299–338). Equality is certainly not a sufficient condition for efficiency.

Symmetry produces deadlock because the behaviors associated with the particular power status obstruct rather than facilitate the effective process to satisfying results. High-power symmetry brings together two parties experienced in dominating behavior; it allows each party to hold the other in check; therefore it makes them primarily concerned with maintaining their status – locking in their side of the symmetry – rather than reaching an agreement. Low-power symmetry brings together two parties that act in the reverse way – symmetrically – to produce the same result. They deadlock because they do not have the power to make the other move, and this therefore makes them primarily concerned with defending whatever little status they have – locking in their side of the symmetry – rather than reaching an agreement. Symmetry in conflict situations tends to produce and reinforce hostility and prolong negotiations. As a result, it calls for a mediator, a role that symmetry favors (Cot 1968; Liska 1961,

1962; Young 1967:44) particularly among low-power parties but also between high-power opponents (Bercovitch and Rubin 1993; Touval and Zartman 1996). When symmetry is only approximate, the slightly or momentarily stronger party fights to achieve a decisive edge in results, which the slightly or momentarily weaker party fights to deny, "creating an escalation that often wrecked the negotiation" (Pruitt and Carnevale 1993:131).

Why, then, is there a difference in findings between the social scientist's laboratory and the field? The present analysis is based on a small number of cases (nine altogether), in contrast to the behavior of hundreds of participants in dozens of experimental studies. Since studies of reality are based on what is available rather than what can be constructed, the sources of historical data are limited. Nonetheless, there is a certain authoritativeness in reality that experiments cannot capture; the challenge is to identify the elements that cause the difference in the results.

The world is a messy place, fraught with intervening, confounding variables, making clear quantities of power and sharp distinctions between symmetry and asymmetry hard to find and difficult to test with the degree of control possible in the laboratory. It is simply insufficient to evaluate power equality/inequality in the absence of other pertinent considerations. In particular, as implied in propositions 5, 6, and 7, to understand the effects of power equality one must also understand the nature of motivational orientation (MO) and interpersonal orientation (IO). Proposition 7 predicts that negotiators will function least effectively when power is equal, when the negotiators are competitively oriented toward each other, and when they are highly attuned to information about their counterpart. The latter two conditions are almost always present in international conflict: that is, there is both an intensely competitive stance (competitive MO) and heightened sensitivity to information about the other side (high IO). When, in addition, there is perceived near-symmetry, the sense of proposition 7 asserts:

> The worst suspicions of each are likely to be confirmed, and an already costly and ineffective relationship is likely to deteriorate even further. The possession of comparable power, is ... likely to bring to the fore a plethora of intangible issues whose resolution may be close to impossible. [Rubin and Brown 1975:257]

When the negotiations take place under different circumstances characterized by friendly relations and cooperative MOs, these conditions predominate over any power structure and produce integrative results under symmetry or asymmetry (Elgström 1993; Nicolson 1949). In other words, the reason the laboratory-derived proposition based on power equality alone is not supported in the present study is that power equality in the presence of competitiveness and high interpersonal orientation makes conflict more difficult, rather than easier, to manage.

But probably the most important reason for the differences lies in the notion of perceived equality. As noted, in reality the fine line of equality is hard to draw; in many of the more formal studies of system stability, for example, symmetry is only approximated, with ranges as wide as 1.2:1 (Gochman and Sabrowski 1990) or even 3:1 (Geller 1993). In fact, even experimental studies (Hornstein 1965; Vitz and Kite 1970) that make a more careful distinction between equality and near-equality (mild power discrepancies) indicate that it is the latter that is conducive to escalating power struggles; equality is indeed stable and productive but impossible to find in the real world (Pruitt and Carnevale 1993:131–132).[1] Contrary to proposition 3, small or ambiguous power differentials can well lead parties to devote unusual amounts of attention to forestalling any attempt to increase the differential or make a decisive change. Both near-symmetrical cases illustrate the point. This distinction supports the results of the cases studied here, but it brings experimental research in line with them.

This finding is in line with the "liberalist" or "cooperationist" literature in international relations, which holds that power imbalances are conducive to cooperation (Milner 1992: esp. 471–472, 480, 484). Strong and weak – hegemonic and balancing or bandwagonning – states know their roles, as will be discussed further below, and seek absolute gains for themselves, whereas rival hegemons and even competing coalescers contest each other's roles and seek relative gains at the other's expense. It is also important to note that the findings in this study relate to states as parties, and one may well ask whether things would be different for other types of parties (such as those used in the social psychology experiments). For states are already equal, in the mythology of international law, as sovereign entities, an equality that in no way contradicts or invalidates the resource or power inequalities under discussion. Nonetheless, in this sense, even asymmetrical states are symmetrical, a fact that acts as a limitation on the findings (and a reinforcement of the importance of a sense of equality just noted).

Lesson 2: Parties do not function more effectively when there is a small, rather than larger, total amount of power in the system.

As the cases make clear, and in contrast to the findings of laboratory experiments (proposition 4), near-symmetric low-power negotiations (Mali–Burkina Faso) were no easier, and fared no better, than symmetric high-power negotiations (US–PRC). Even asymmetric negotiations with limitations imposed by rules or distance that kept the power intensity low, such as US–Canada or US–Egypt or US–Indonesia negotiations, were not by that fact rendered more effective or efficient. Nor were they so where the absolute level of power resources was lower than others. Thus the India–Nepal conflict proved no more tractable than the US–Indonesia case; even though India is less powerful than the United States, Nepal is less powerful than Indonesia, and the total amount of power in the system is thus less in the former than the latter case.

Again, social science experiments incorporate varied total power into a specific way, largely through manipulations of coercive ability: one side's ability to unilaterally impose costs on the other, to threaten, to prevent the other from reaching its objective, and so on (Rubin and Brown 1975; cf. Pruitt and Carnevale 1993:132). In contrast, the aggregate power represented in the case studies constitutes a broad range of moves and measures, some coercive in their implication (e.g., military might), others inducive (e.g., foreign aid), and still others of a more neutral or ambiguous sort (e.g., gross national product, international legitimacy), all used in defense of sovereignty and national interests.[2] When that quantity was low, states still had the same absolute values to defend and they became even more sensitive to small power differences in small power levels. There was less of a cushion; the raw nerve was exposed.

Lesson 3: Stronger parties typically attempt to dominate the exchange with their less powerful counterparts.

Perceived asymmetries – based on power resources such as gross national product, military strength, physical size, and other objective indices, but also on power as will and skill – do indeed produce different attitudes and strategies in the exercise of power by the strong.[3] Thus, the party perceived as the stronger on the basis of undeniable power possessions – the United States, the European Community, India, and the entire developed "North" – adopted forms of a take-it-or-leave-it strategy toward its negotiating partner located along a spectrum of weakness – Canada, Egypt,

Indonesia, Andorra, Nepal, and the G77 South. On first encounter (except in the UNCED case), this strategy dominated the negotiations. The weaker party was interested enough in a positive outcome to the negotiations not to want to "leave it" because its security point (position without an agreement) was uncomfortable; it felt obliged to take it. If the weaker party hesitated, the stronger added a second strategy of pressure: take-it-or-suffer, in effect, worsening the target's security point even further. The stronger parties regarded themselves as having more important things to do, since they were strong, and although they valued the bilateral relationship, they were often annoyed by their weak partners' lesser concerns and narrow interests (cf. Kritek 1994:317). No one showed special indulgence or generosity toward weak targets, as one set of writings shows might be a preferable alternative behavior (Rubin and Brown 1975). No particular positive power or inducement was exercised as an initiative; if any inducements were forthcoming toward the weak, they were responses to low-power pressure tactics.[4]

The six cases of asymmetry lend clear and unequivocal support to proposition 2, as advanced in the Introduction: The more powerful do indeed attempt to dominate in their exchanges with less powerful counterparts. The United States opened prenegotiations with Canada with antidumping and countervailing duties as pressure, and it imposed its notion of a free trade agreement to resolve a series of irritants rather than a set of fundamentally changed set of trading rules between the two countries. The United States brought significant pressures on Indonesia and on Egypt to impose its conditions as a formula of terms of trade for aid: on Indonesia's foreign trade policy with China and on Egypt's domestic economic practices. France and Spain turned their attention to Andorra's trade and labor practices with heavy-handed domineering. India continues to treat Nepal with dominance and disdain, as it did throughout the extended negotiations. Only in the UNCED negotiations did the North allow the South to set the agenda, in order to draw it into a process that the North considered important. It then dominated the remainder of that process as it produced agreement on items and terms the North considered important. It is important in this regard to note the difference between "setting the agenda" through the introduction of issues or the call for negotiations and "framing the issues" through the definition of issues of the identification of terms of trade. If the weaker party was able to do the former (Keohane and Nye 1989:198–202), it was the latter activity (framing the issues) that remained in the hands of the stronger.

It is unclear whether the stronger side behaved as it did because of its sense of its own strength or because of its perception of bilateral asymmetry, that is, whether it acted on the basis of absolute or relative power positions. The one case that would test the second hypothesis, the high-high case of negotiations between the United States and China, does suggest that the parties acted on their self-perception and that they locked themselves so obstinately into their impasse because both acted with a high self-perception of power toward the other. This incompatibility was couched and justified in Cold War terms but was caused by each party's sense of its "high-ness." But whether perceived high-power parties act in a domineering way over low-power parties because of their high-power notions of themselves or whether they achieve high-power status on the basis of their experience in dealing with low-power adversaries is a chicken-and-egg question that is impossible to answer.

Lesson 4: Weaker parties respond not by acting submissively, but by adopting appropriate counter-strategies of their own.

In no case did the weak or weaker states act submissively.[5] Ingratiatingly cooperative and knavishly evasive, sometimes even ideologically aggressive, they were anything but submissive. Rather than remain in their subordinate role, as the asymmetry (and buttressing data from laboratory experiments) would have predicted, the weaker parties pulled a number of tricks out of their bag. They blustered, dawdled, appealed, borrowed power, exercised their veto temporarily (by walking out) or longer (by at least threatening withdrawal), and generally made a nuisance of themselves over issues that mattered much more to them than to the distracted strong partner busy with other problems. In this way, they increased their (effective) power far more than initial asymmetry would have predicted. While the dominant parties were standing tall, the smaller parties were dodging between their legs. Often the big parties set the framework or the principles for the agreement, and the little parties gnawed away at the details.

The weaker parties' diverse efforts to level the playing field were ways of borrowing sources of power, enabling actions intended to move the stronger party in a desired direction and countering the actions of the stronger party (Aggarwal and Allan 1983; Andrew 1970; Deutsch 1973; Fox 1959; Rubin and Salacuse 1990; Singer 1972; Zartman 1973, 1987). Power, says Foucault (1984:311), "is a collection of action on possible actions ... an action on actions." For every action taken by the stronger in the case studies, the weaker develops an action of its own – an action on an action. And there were many such actions to be taken. The feisty Canadians, the ideological Indonesians, the bureaucratic Egyptians, the intriguing Andorrans, and the clever Nepalese all found their own ways to challenge, circumvent, upstage, or outmaneuver their supposedly stronger negotiating partners. Most if not all of these sources of power were available only to the perceived weaker party and not its target, for the very reason that it was weaker. These sources can be categorized as targets, context, process, and third parties.

1. Weaker parties try to borrow power from the stronger target, by seizing on aspects of the target's nature or position that can support their own demands or in other words can add value to their own positions, making them more attractive to the target itself. These aspects include common interests in a position, common interests in solving a problem, pairing of two positions, and common interest in the joint relationship.

    - *Appeals to common interests*: Both Canada's and Andorra's evocation of common interests with adversaries in features of a free trade arrangement.
    - *Solutions to common problems*: Egypt's indication of both parties' interest in overcoming the problem of its underdevelopment; Nepal's reminder of both parties' need to resolve the water problem.
    - *Pairing positions*: The South's agreement to support environment in exchange for the North's support for development; Canada's demand for a dispute-resolution procedure in exchange for an agreement that removed minor irritants for the United States.
    - *Appeals to relationships*: Nepal arguing that, as India's longstanding neighbor, it deserves special consideration; Canada's admonition to the United States to preserve the special North American relationship; Indonesia's insistence on the American position of world leadership and its own position of neutrality to create a delicate relationship.

2. Weaker parties try to borrow power from the context. Many contextual features are intentionally designed to level the playing field, or to give it the appearance of levelness. These sources of power do

not provide added value to position, but rather give equal access to proceedings. These features and elements include procedural rules, agents, norms and principles.

- *Use of rules*: Canada's effort to set up dispute settlement procedures as the price of its agreement; G77 insistence on using UN procedures that allowed it to comment on secretariat proposals.
- *Appeals to higher authority*: Mali's and Burkina Faso's efforts to draw in the OAU; Andorra's appeals to the EC over the heads of France and Spain.
- *Use of intermediaries*: The South's use of the secretariat and the conference chair to provide a procedural buffer in dealing with the North; Egypt's efforts to bring in the United States as a "biased mediator" to deliver an Israeli agreement.
- *Appeals to principle*: Egypt arguing with the United States for increases in annual economic assistance on the grounds that their counterpart, Israel, is receiving more aid than Egypt; the South arguing justice for the underdeveloped at UNCED.
- *Co-opting external forces through warning and predictions rather than making one's own threats and promises*: Canadian arguments to reinforce the value of a free trade agreement to the United States; Indonesian and Egyptian warnings of unavoidable internal reactions if the United States pushed reforms too far; G77 predictions that resources will be distributed in their favor in the future.

3. Weaker states gained sources for power by using the negotiation process and its evolution to make their moves at appropriate times. These times are at the beginning, in snagging the attention of the stronger party, and then further down the line, after the stronger party has played its dominant role in setting the agenda, leaving the details open to be shaped by the weaker party.

- *Efforts to seize opportune moments*: Canadian use of anti-GATT feeling to create bilateral trade agreements and fast-track procedures to give specific deadlines and a window of opportunity.
- *Attention to details*: Egypt's assertion that it is requesting a temporary increase in US economic aid – not an indefinite commitment; Canadian focus on dispute management procedures.

4. Finally, weaker parties try to borrow power from various third parties and sources, existing or created. These sources either directly provide added (including negatively, i.e., subtracted) value for positions or directly provide alternative sources of support that add to or subtract value from positions to make them more attractive or more costly. Such external sources include other parties to the issue, internal segments of the target, other opponents of the target, external sources of gratifications and deprivations, and public opinion.

- *Coalition with other parties*: Attempts to maintain G77 solidarity at UNCED; Indonesia's repeated attempts to rally neutralist support.[6]
- *Links to internal factions*: Andorra's effort in the EU to play off France against Spain; Southern use of Green and development lobbies in the United States and other Northern countries to weigh in on Northern government positions.[7]
- *Joining one's enemy's enemy*: Mali's efforts to ally with France (traditionally an adversary of Burkina Faso); Indonesia's act of cooperating with China.
- *Use of public opinion*: The South's use of the media in the press-covered and NGO-attended UNCED sessions; Syngman Rhee's attempt to take the prisoners issue to public opinion.
- *Resort to unconventional violence*: None of the cases studied but other instances (Kosovo, Sri Lanka, Euzkadi, etc.) show resort to insurgency and terrorism to force negotiations (Zartman 1995).

In what order will weaker states choose from this tactical menu? No order is imposed in the sense that one category must be exhausted before turning to another, and picking from the menu will to a large extent depend on the opportunities of the moment and the issue, determined in part by the openings provided by the behavior of the stronger party. Nonetheless, it can be noted that the fourth plate in the menu – borrow power from outside parties – is not likely to be chosen first and is likely to be held in reserve until other means are tried. This is because the entry of third parties indicates that the bilateral process has failed and therefore adds offense to weakness in dealing with the other party. It also complicates the agenda with third-party interests.

The weaker parties' diverse efforts to level the playing field can also be understood through categories of low-power influence tactics, involving the types of actions that weaker parties can take (Deutsch 1973; Rubin and Salacuse 1990; Zartman 1987). These actions can be initially divided – as suggested in the first chapter – into carrots and sticks: co-operative gratifications or promises and predictions ("if you concede, together we can make things better for you" or "the results will be better for you"); coercive deprivations or threats and warnings ("if you don't concede, I will make things worse for you" or "the results will be worse for you"); and neutral arguments ("if you concede, it will have no effect on your interest"), recognizing that in logic, if not in presentation, the first is only the reverse of the second. In addition, a fourth category of action is negative – delay or veto, a frequently noted power of the weak used by Egypt, Indonesia, Andorra, and Nepal, among others (Harper 1968:49; Scott 1985:32).

Cooperative Gratifications

- Promised tradeoffs and linkages: "Do what I want and I will do something that you want in return" (Egypt–US).
- Predicted relationship advantages: "Do what I want and our centuries-old cooperation will thrive" (Canada–US).
- Predicted ripe moments: "Now is the time for us to take advantage of a window of opportunity and solve the problem once and for all" (Andorra–EC).
- Predicted equalizing rules and procedures: "Let's set up impartial rules by which to judge your disputes with me as well as mine with you" (Canada–US).
- Predicted common interest: "Together let's try to solve this problem that threatens us both" (South–North).
- Predicted damage limitation: "Let's just make a short-term agreement on a few items that we can agree on, to get the problem off the agenda" (South–North).
- Appeals to separate principles: "Do what I want because it is fair [to me]" (Indonesia–US).
- Appeals to separate interests: "Allowing me to get what I want will in no way affect your own ability to address your interests" (Egypt–US).

Coercive Deprivations

- Threats to worsen the status quo: "If you don't give me what I request, I will have no choice but to boycott or strike" (Indonesia–US).
- Threats to form coalitions: "If you don't give me what I want, I will band together with others like me" (Indonesia–US).
- Threats to ally with a stronger enemy of your enemy: "If you don't give me what I want, upstream of you is someone I can appeal to for help" (Andorra–EC).
- Threats to go elsewhere: "If you don't give me what I want, I know someone else who will" (Indonesia–US).
- Threats to change the process: "If we can't reach a friendly agreement among ourselves, I will call for an outside mediator" (Andorra–EC).
- Threats to appeal to higher authority: "If you don't come to a friendly agreement, I will have to take the case to court."
- Threats to go public: "If you don't give me what I want, I will let the media know how unfairly you have treated me" (Arab–Israel).
- Warnings of internal dissension within the ranks of the stronger party: "If you don't give me what I want, you will be in trouble by the internal dissension in your own side" (Arab–Israel).
- Warnings of coercive deficiency: "If you don't give me what I want, I will fall prey to the very evils you fear most" (South–North).

Delays

- Stonewalling: "If you don't negotiate in good faith, I am going to walk out and leave you with the problem" (Canada–US).
- Passive resistance: "Unfortunately, poverty, weakness, ignorance, underdevelopment, or followers make it impossible for me to do what you want" (Egypt–US).

It is not clear, among the nearly two dozen possibilities, which actions were more effective, or which of the three or more subcategories were best suited to which sorts of cases. The small number of cases in comparison with the larger number of strategies and tactics does not allow for correlations and conclusions, but it does present an array of potential propositions to pursue.

As a result of this counterexercise of power, most of the weaker partners in the case studies – with the exception of the South at UNCED and the partial exception of Nepal – were able to work out results that were not to their disadvantage, and often in their favor. The initial asymmetry was not played out to the end but was righted in the course of the exercise. It is this righting action that overcomes the structural dilemma and allows perceived weaker parties to engage in negotiations to obtain a fair outcome. Rarely, if ever, does the weaker turn the tables totally and emerge the winner. Both parties' agreement must be bought by some part of the outcome.

Often it is the invocation of contextual benefits for the stronger that allows the weaker to make off with incidental benefits of its own. Such benefits may be found in the relationship itself, which the stronger wants to preserve (Keohane and Nye 1989; Stein and Pauly 1993). This relationship – a geographic imposition of neighborliness (US–Canada, EC–Andorra, India–Nepal) or a geopolitical imposition of dependency (US–Egypt, US–Indonesia, North–South) – is something precious enough to the stronger power that it does not want to lose it. It is an error to talk of one-sided dependencies in such cases (Bacharach and Lawler 1980), when in fact what is involved are interdependencies at different levels, serving as the basis for power in both direction (Elias 1970:93–94, 107–109). Power relations of interdependence at different levels, along with power exercise through different tactics, serve to equalize initial asymmetries in the exercise and the resource structure of power.

In coda, it should be noted that when these interdependencies are no longer available, the equilibrating structure falls apart. If the United States were no longer to care about maintaining good relations with Egypt or Indonesia, the latters' tactics or counterpower would likely be met with increasing impatience and decreasing effect. Thus, the blandishments of the South at UNCED, designed to press the North into giving equal attention to development as much as to environment, fell on the same deaf ears as did even sharper blandishments by the same weaker side two decades earlier in the negotiations on the New International Economic Order (Rothstein 1977; Zartman 1987); indeed, the softening of Southern tactics in the 1990s was a harbinger of the diminishing importance of the relationship between the First and the Third Worlds in the absence of the Second. The symmetrical cases reinforce this finding: China and the United States had no relationship to restrain them from acting, and Mali and Burkina Faso, despite their common membership in West African organizations of cooperation, cared more about their relationship with France than with each other.

Geographic impositions are less vulnerable: the United States and the European Community continued to care about maintaining good relations with their weaker neighbors, Canada and Andorra, respectively; although India sometimes did take its neighbor, Nepal, for granted, it knew that Nepal had its back against the mountain and was unlikely to borrow power from China on the other side.

It should also be clear that neither relationships nor the specific items under negotiation in these cases are public goods. Whereas small states may well be free riders on benefits provided by a great power in many situations, that fact does not explain their limited successes in specific negotiations. Their accomplishments are tactical and procedural, not simply situational; the relationships are used, not simply enjoyed.

Lesson 5: Negotiating parties are effective to the extent that they adjust their behavior to the relative power of the other side.

Combining lessons 3 and 4, targets that appeared less powerful than the agent occasioned exploitative behavior – whether from high-power or low-power agents – but responded rather creatively and effectively, in an effort to level the playing field; in the mutually beneficial cases, they wheedled the stronger away from its exploitative behavior and the stronger complied, enough to make an agreement. Targets that appeared to be comparable in power to the agent occasioned symmetrical negotiations that were painful and inefficient, but for identifiable reasons, and productive behaviors can be identified and recommended to produce negotiations appropriate to the situation. Each conclusion bears further examination.

In high-low negotiations, particularly within a relationship established over time, the parties know their roles and play them complementarily. High-power parties may try to dominate initially, but they are restrained by three factors. One is the clever tactics of weak parties who know how to handle their bigger partner, like mice and elephants, children and their parents, and workers and their employers. The second factor is that the powerful are distracted by many other issues, while the weak are able to face the issue with concentration and commitment. A third factor is the constraining effect of the relationship itself, which limits the crushing effects of high-sided dominance and gives the low side a threat, an appeal, and a chance. Asymmetry, the most common structural setting for international negotiation, brings better results more efficiently than we tend to think possible. Weaker parties do better than expected because they look for ways of empowering themselves. In asymmetrical negotiation strong and weak work together, organizing themselves around predictable moves and responses.

It must be noted, however, that in relations of perceived power, satisfaction too is a function of perceptions and expectations. The weaker party may well be more easily satisfied, even with an asymmetrical result, because its expectations are asymmetrical, and the stronger party may well also be satisfied because it has kept relative and made absolute gains, even if less than hoped. But, important as this observation is, it is merely a function of subjective and perceptional elements like power and satisfaction, which elude quantification or even positivistic grasp.

If asymmetry can be turned into effective negotiation, what about symmetry? One of the implications of the original notion of symmetry was that parties should try to convey to each other a sense of equality to facilitate effective negotiations. This implication still holds and is reinforced by the findings on near-symmetry negotiations. The lesson of the present cases is that precisely because parties in the symmetrical relation are more or less equal, they are afraid of losing that equality to any small edge of advantage that the other might produce. In this delicate situation, it would be useful for the parties to spend some energy – in fact, probably a lot, given the atmosphere of suspicion that reigned – to assure the other of its equality.

It should be remembered that asymmetric negotiations are not necessarily easy negotiations either, for much the same reason. Perceptions of inequality delayed negotiations, either by causing their breakdown as in the US–Canada case, or by inserting considerations of feeling, reputation, and status that required extra time to handle, as in the UNCED negotiations or the US negotiations with Indonesia and with Egypt, where status became one of the principal issues. Furthermore, equalizing actions, rather than simple status equality, were often required before the parties could get on with their business. The Canadian walkout, the Chinese and American meticulous (sometimes ridiculous) concerns for equal treatment, and various incidents in the Arab–Israeli negotiations are cases in point. In a dynamic rather than a static sense, the hypothesis about power symmetry finds support in the need for an enabling atmosphere of equality, even if that atmosphere or its detailed translation into action is not alone sufficient to ensure efficiency (Kritek 1994:108, 242, 317).

12.2 Concluding Observations on Power and Negotiation

Four broad conclusions of relevance for the practice of negotiation and the analysis of power emerge from this study.

12.2.1 Conclusion one

It is difficult to judge the impact of power asymmetry since the symmetry or asymmetry of outcomes is not beyond controversy; indeed, both the positive-sum nature and the ambiguity of negotiated results are necessary elements in the overall success of the negotiation process.

As noted from the outset, asymmetry itself is a slippery notion, not least because the concepts of power on which it is based are slippery concepts. As already noted, asymmetry (or symmetry) in the exercise of power is ambiguous. As an accumulation of past exercises, it enters into the reputational perceptions of the parties. As a present exercise, it is as much a corrective as a reinforcement of asymmetry, not necessarily determined by perceptions of the past. *Resource power asymmetries do not yield corresponding asymmetries in the exercise of power.*

The same mode of analysis needs to be adopted with regard to outcome, for more complex reasons. Successful negotiation is a positive-sum exercise, in which each party feels better off with the agreement than without one. It is necessarily so, or the parties would not make their agreement, and their agreement is evaluated against the parties' individual security points, the outcome that they could or would have obtained without negotiation. The total of these "better off" feelings produces a positive-sum outcome. Because the individual parts of the sum are subjective, it is as difficult to give them an objective measure as it is to measure power.

What is more important, the creation of a positive sum often depends on the ability of each side to claim that it did well in the negotiations, frequently in different terms than those used in the other party's claim. Differential values of the same items, or different items differently valued, are the keys to successful negotiations. As the Cuban Missile Crisis negotiations – along with many others – indicate, the difference between magnanimity and crowing can make the difference between agreement and continued conflict. The United States bought the withdrawal of Soviet missiles from Cuba with praise for the Soviet statesmanship, renunciation of plans for invasion that it never had and withdrawal of Turkish missiles that had already been decided upon (Kennedy 1969). The USSR bought the end of the blockade and the pledge of noninvasion with the withdrawal of its missiles (Krushchev 1962, 1970). Who bought more or paid less? Both parties felt that the agreement was better than its alternative – nonagreement and its consequences. The balance sheet is as ambiguous as the relative power of the parties going into it, and that ambiguity was the key to the agreement. It usually is. It is therefore necessarily inconclusive to attempt any correlation between symmetric- or asymmetric-feeling parties and the symmetry or asymmetry of their negotiated outcomes.

12.2.2 Conclusion two

The power of the weaker parties in the cases studied derived from their ability to draw on a broad array of resources. Perhaps the primary source of power – seen as a means of controlling outcomes – was the ability to bring in support from external actors. This calculation was not a constant element in the initial preparations for the negotiations, and even when it was it was a very subjective estimate. For the most part, parties engaged in negotiations on the basis of positive estimates of their capabilities and then, as the negotiations proceeded, worked to overcome their difficulties through the acquisition or materialization of external support. As noted, it is the last resort in the list of sources from which to borrow power.

It is interesting that this element of asymmetry, which proved critical in negotiations, is the one carryover from the elements identified in the study of asymmetry in the initiation of war (Paul 1994:31–33), and it relates directly to an established understanding of the process of escalation (Rubin et al. 1994). Parties run through their estimates of domestic sources of power, both material and intangible, making necessarily subjective evaluations. They enter into negotiations when they feel that they have a favorable edge in some relevant aspects of issue power, whatever the larger aggregate power position may be. In the military context, Paul (1994:35) writes:

> The weaker challenger can initiate war against the relatively stronger adversary if its key decision-makers believe that they can achieve their political and military objectives through the employment of a limited aims/*faits accomplis* strategy. ... Superior aggregate military and economic power of the defender need not deter a challenger. ... The support of a great power ally and the possession of short-term offensive capabilities can increase the probability of such war initiation.

Negotiation has no equivalent to short-term offensive capabilities, but differences can straighten out faulty perceptions of relative power. However, in negotiation, external involvement in negotiation is mediation, and the crucial conclusion about biased mediators is that they can be effective in assisting negotiations only if they deliver the party toward whom they are biased (Touval and Zartman 1996). *In negotiation, external intervention rides the diplomatic equivalent of a Trojan horse.*

Another source of power lies in the parties' interest – often to different degrees – in maintaining their relationships. Relationships imposed by geography or strategy add supplementary interests to the negotiated stakes, equalizing power, and limiting its asymmetrical exercise. They also restore a certain sense of equality or symmetry to the proceedings – what the Africans dealing with the Europeans, their manifest unequals in power, called the "spirit of equality" in the negotiations over the various Lomé accords between 1975 and 1990 (Ravenhill 1980, 1993) – and thus create a trap for future interactions. Weak as well as strong parties have an interest in preserving their relationship (until a significant breaking point occurs) and therefore system maintenance effects tend to outweigh the momentary calculations of power and interests.

12.2.3   Conclusion three

Most of the cases have demonstrated that things are not as they seem and that one's aggregate power position, using power as resources, is not an accurate indicator either of the relevant issue power of parties going into negotiations or their perception of their power relationship. The UNCED case is a useful reminder that power position and negotiating power may well coincide on occasion. However, coincidence is not automatic, and for aggregate power to be relevant to negotiating power, it must be translated into issue-specific terms (Habeeb 1988).

A number of cases indicate that two elements stand in the way of any direct coincidence or translation. One, previously noted, is the ability to borrow power from an external source, which is unproved until the event and which cannot, by definition, fall within the prior calculations of power as resources; this is true both inherently and because it too is subject to the same type of decision calculations and uncertainties on the part of the external power lender as are being analyzed on the part of the power borrower. The other is the attention (or mosquito) factor: bigger, stronger parties tend to have bigger, broader concerns, and weaker, smaller parties tend to have fewer, more focused concerns, enabling them to concentrate on the subject of the negotiations with a single-mindedness that strongly increases their ability to get what they want (power). It is the spear, after all, that kills the elephant, even though the elephant has far greater total strength than the spear. And it is the beggar who gets the alms from the rich, even though the beggar is weaker on all counts than the wealthier patron.

This study thus lends support to the broad proposition that, in any power position or perception, there are available and appropriate tactics that equalize power, defined as a move by one party intending to produce movement by another toward a mutually agreeable outcome. Rather than submit to the dominating effort of a stronger counterpart, the weaker does best to look for ways of framing the conflict to gain some sort of (even temporary) advantage. To truly counter efforts to dominate by a stronger counterpart, the weaker must also have access to resources other than its imagination. It must have something that the other side values, and which the other chooses not to take by force or stealth – but through the give-and-take of negotiation. Similarly, the other, who though stronger is presumably not strong enough to take what it wants by force or stealth, can do better by giving a sense of equality to the weaker, who will then be less impelled to seek compensating advantages in other, more disruptive and escalatory ways.

12.2.4   Final conclusion

This study has demonstrated that negotiation, like all other social activity but unlike the phenomena of natural science, is composed of observable regularities of interaction and of matters of free choice and imagination. Parties make up images of their situation in relation to their opponents', including in them some elements of accuracy and delusion, interest and inspiration. Even though one party may objectively be weaker or equal to the other party, it tends to create strategies and imaginations to overcome the difference; indeed, even when the cause is hopeless, it may find worldly or other-worldly justifications for finding heroism in standing in front of the locomotive, in the hope that it just might be persuaded to stop or, if not, that the world will celebrate true courage. But once it enters a bargaining encounter with equals, inferiors, or superiors (objectively measured), it tends to use both common and specific strategies that apply to any negotiation.

The very act of negotiation works to level the playing field. States that were heretofore ignored entirely or exploited mercilessly are now seen to perform acts that move the exploiters. In some sense the findings concerning the surprising effectiveness of weaker parties are not surprising at all. Once the game becomes the one known as negotiation, the rules change and everyone becomes empowered by this transformed reality.

Notes

[1] I am grateful to Dean G. Pruitt for pointing out this distinction. The effect is also noted in evolutionary game theory (Hammerstein and Parker 1982; Parker and Rubenstein 1981:649, 654).

[2] Compare the three sources of power in Hindu writings, discussed in Chapter 6 by Dipak Gyawali.

[3] The expectation that "the strongest side wins" is not the only expression of triumphant asymmetry in this world. The French instinctive analysis is that "the cleverest [*plus futé, plus habile*] side wins," a different way of conceptualizing power (will and skill). In either case, the problem of perceived power asymmetry remains. For similar use of recognized asymmetries in animal behavior, see John Maynard Smith (1982) and P. Hammerstein (1989).

[4] The same phenomenon is observed in asymmetrical trade wars (Conybeare 1987).

[5] Incidentally, Andorra and perhaps Nepal may be weak in any company, and act accordingly, but Canada, Egypt, and Indonesia are high-power parties compared with a number of their other usual partners. Egypt especially is a dominant power among Arab states and acts it, as Indonesia has been a leading power in Southeast Asia.

[6] Special coalition behavior, such as being the last to make up a minimum winning coalition, gives particular bargaining power to otherwise weak or small states (Brams et al. 1994).

[7] The mastery of a two-level game of internal and external negotiations is an example of a process by which weaker states can emerge with substantial concessions from the stronger (Evans et al. 1993; Lehman and McCoy 1992; Park 1998).

References

Aggarwal, V.K., and Allan, P., 1983, *Evolution in Bargaining Theories: Toward an Integrated Approach to Explain the Strategies of the Weak,* American Political Science Association, Chicago.

Andrew, A., 1970, *Defense by Other Means: Diplomacy for the Underdog,* Canadian Institute of International Affairs, Toronto, Canada.

Bacharach, S.B., and Lawler, E., 1980, *Power and Politics in Organizations*, Jossey-Bass, San Francisco, CA.

Bercovitch, J., and Rubin, J.Z., 1992, *Mediation in International Relations: Multiple Approaches to Conflict Management*, MacMillan, London.

Brams, S., Doherty, A., and Weidner, M., 1994, Game theory: Focusing on players, decisions and agreements, in I.W. Zartman, ed., *International Multilateral Negotiation*, Jossey-Bass, San Francisco, CA.

Bremer, S.A., 1992, Dangerous dyads: Conditions affecting the likelihood of interstate war, 1816–1965, *Journal of Conflict Resolution*, **36**(2):309–341.

Conybeare, J., 1987, *Trade Wars*, Columbia University Press, New York.

Cot, J.P., 1968, *La Conciliation Internationale*, Pédone, Paris.

Deutsch, M., 1973, *The Resolution of Conflict: Constructive and Destructive Processes*, Yale University Press, New Haven, CT.

Elgström, O., 1993, *Strong or Weak? Friends or Foes? Bargaining Relationships as a Determinant of International Bargaining Processes*, paper presented to the Acapulco meeting of the International Studies Association, 23 March.

Elias, N., 1970, Qu'est-ce que c'est la sociologie? Aix-en-Provence, Pandora, Des Sociétes, reprinted in F. Sawacki, ed., 1994, *Le Pouvoir: Science Politique, Sociologie, Histoire, 1*, Belin, Paris.

Evans, P., Jacobson, H., and Putnam, R., 1992, *Double-Edged Diplomacy*, University of California Press, Berkeley, CA.

Foucault, M., 1984, Michel Foucault, un parcours philosophique, in H.L. Dreyfus and P. Rabinow, eds., *Michel Foucault, Beyond Structuralism and Hermeneutics*, 2nd edition, University of Chicago Press, Chicago.

Fox, A.B., 1959, *The Power of Small States*, University of Chicago Press, Chicago.

Geller, D.S., 1993, Power differentials and war in rival dyads, *International Studies Quarterly*, **37**(2):173–193.

Gochman, C.S., and Sabrowski, A.N., eds., 1990, *Prisoners of War?* Lexington Books, New York.

Habeeb, W.M., 1988, *Power and Tactics in International Negotiations: How Weak Nations Bargain with Strong Nations*, Johns Hopkins University Press, Baltimore, MD.

Hammerstein, P., 1989, Biological games, *European Economic Review*, **33**:635–644.

Hammerstein, P., and Parker, G.A., 1982, The asymmetric war of attrition, *Journal of Theoretical Biology*, **96**(4):647–682.

Harper, E., 1968, Social consequences of unsuccessful low caste movement, in J. Silverberg, ed., *Social Mobility in the Caste System in India*, Mouton, The Hague, The Netherlands.

Hornstein, H.A., 1965, Effects of different magnitudes of threat upon interpersonal bargaining, *Journal of Experimental Psychology*, **1**(3):282–293.

Kennedy, R.F., 1969, *Thirteen Days: A Memoir of the Cuban Missile Crisis*, Norton, New York.

Keohane, R.O., and Nye, J.S., 1989, *Power and Interdependence*, 2nd edition, Scott Foresman, Boston, MA.

Khrushchev, N., 1962, Messages exchanged by President Kennedy and Chairman Khrushchev during the Cuban Missile Crisis 1962, *Department of State Bulletin*, 19 November.

Khrushchev, N., 1970, *Khrushchev Remembers*, Little Brown, Boston, MA.

Kritek, P.B., 1994, *Negotiating at an Uneven Table*, Jossey-Bass, San Francisco, CA.

Lehman, N., and McCoy, J., 1992, The dynamics of the two-level bargaining game, *World Politics*, **44**:600–644.

Liska, G., 1961, *The New Statecraft*, University of Chicago Press, Chicago.

Liska, G., 1962, *Nations in Alliance*, Johns Hopkins University Press, Baltimore, MD.

Maynard Smith, J., 1982, *Evolution and the Theory of Games*, Cambridge University Press, Cambridge, UK.

Milner, H., 1992, International theories of cooperation, *World Politics*, **44**:466–496.

Nicolson, H.G., 1949, *Diplomacy*, Oxford University Press, New York.

Organski, A.F.K., 1958, *World Politics*, Knopf, New York.

Park, C., 1998, Mastering the Two-Level Game, School of Advanced International Studies, Johns Hopkins University, Washington, DC.

Parker, G.A., and Rubenstein, D.I., 1981, Role assessment, reserve strategy, and acquisition of information in asymmetric animal conflicts, *Animal Behavior*, **29**:221–240.

Paul, T.V., 1994, *Asymmetric Conflicts: War Initiation by Weaker Powers*, Cambridge University Press, Cambridge, UK.

Pruitt, D.G., and Carnevale, P., 1993, *Negotiation in Social Conflict*, Brooks/Cole, Pacific Grove, CA.

Raiffa, H., 1982, *The Art and Science of Negotiation*, Harvard University Press, Cambridge, MA.

Ravenhill, J., 1980, *Collective Clientelism*, Columbia University Press, New York.

Ravenhill, J., 1993, When weakness is strength: The Lomé IV negotiations, in I. Zartman, ed., *Europe and Africa: The New Phase*, Lynne Rienner, Boulder, CO.

Rothstein, R., 1977, *The Weak in the World of the Strong*, Columbia University Press, New York.

Rubin, J.Z., and Brown, B., 1975, *The Social Psychology of Bargaining and Negotiation*, Academic Press, New York.

Rubin, J.Z., and Salacuse, J.W., 1990, The problem of power in international negotiations, *International Affairs*, 4:24–34.

Rubin, J.Z., Pruitt, D.G., and Kim, S.H., 1994, *Social Conflict: Escalation, Stalemate, and Settlement*, 2nd edition, McGraw-Hill, New York.

Scott, J., 1985, *Weapons of the Weak*, Yale University Press, New Haven, CT.

Singer, M., 1972, *Intercultural Communications: A Perceptual Approach*, Prentice-Hall, Englewood Cliffs, NJ.

Stein, J., and Pauly, L., 1993, *Choosing to Cooperate*, Johns Hopkins University Press, Baltimore, MD.

Touval, S., and Zartman, I.W., 1996, International mediation in the post-Cold War era, in C. Crocker, F.O. Hampson, and P. Hall, eds., *Managing Global Chaos*, US Institute of Peace, Washington, DC.

Vital, D., 1967, *The Inequality of States*, Oxford University Press, Oxford, UK.

Vitz, P.C., and Kite, W.R., 1970, Factors affecting conflict and negotiation within an alliance, *Journal of Experimental Social Psychology*, 5(3):233–247.

Young, O.R., 1967, *The Intermediaries*, Princeton University Press, Princeton, NJ.

Zartman, I.W., 1971, *The Politics of Trade Negotiations between Africa and the European Community: The Weak Confront the Strong*, Princeton University Press, Princeton, NJ.

Zartman, I.W., ed., 1987, *Positive Sum: Improving North–South Negotiations*, Transaction, New Brunswick, NJ.

Zartman, I.W., ed., 1995, *Elusive Peace: Negotiating an End to Civil War*, The Brookings Institution, Washington, DC.

Zartman, I.W., and Berman, M., 1982, *The Practical Negotiator*, Yale University Press, New Haven, CT.

Index